DATE DUE

LISTEN, HUMANITY

Other Works by Meher Baba

DISCOURSES

GOD SPEAKS

THE EVERYTHING AND THE NOTHING

LIFE AT ITS BEST

BEAMS FROM MEHER BABA
ON THE SPIRITUAL PANORAMA

LISTEN, HUMANITY

by Meher Baba

NARRATED AND EDITED BY

D. E. Stevens

A CROSSROAD BOOK
The Crossroad Publishing Company / New York

1998
The Crossroad Publishing Company
370 Lexington Avenue
New York, NY 10017

Listen, Humanity Copyright © 1957 by
Sufism Reoriented Inc.
Copyright © 1982 by
Avatar Meher Baba Perpetual Public Charitable Trust
Introduction to the Fifth Edition Copyright © 1998 by D.E.Stevens

First Edition published in 1957 by Dodd, Mead and Company
New York, N.Y.
Second printing January, 1967

Second Edition published in 1971 by Harper Colophon Books,
New York, N.Y.

Third Edition published in 1985 by In Company with Meher Baba,
Atlanta and Denver

Fourth Edition published in 1989 by Companion Books,
St. Helier, Jersey, Channel Islands

Printed in the U.S.A.

Library of Congress Cataloging-in-Publication Data

Meher Baba, 1894–1969.
    Listen, humanity / by Meher Baba ; narrated and edited by D.E.
Stevens. — [5th ed.]
        p. cm.
    Includes bibliographical references.
    ISBN 0-8245-1731-8-(hardcover). — ISBN 0-8245-1732-6 (pbk.)
    1. Spiritual life.   I. Stevens, Don E.   II. Title.
BP610.M4315   1998
299'.93—dc21   97-32417
                                                                    CIP

Acknowledgments

A work of this type is brought to completion only with the assistance of many persons. It is difficult to know just who should be gratefully acknowledged for their part in the collecting and editing of the original essays which were combined to form the body of Part II of this volume. Certainly Professor C. D. Deshmukh, best known for his editing of the *Discourses*, and Adi K. Irani, Meher Baba's tireless secretary and manager of Meher Publications, played an extremely important role.

In connection with certain other material included in Part II, grateful recognition is also given to Meher Publications, to Circle Publications and to *The Awakener* for the use of portions previously printed by them.

Part I, which describes the *sahvas* programs given by Meher Baba in India during November, 1955, makes copious use of material faithfully transcribed at that time by Faram and Kishan Singh, and later collated by Ramju Abdullah. Both Ramju Abdullah and Eruch Jessawalla have made frequent suggestions and assisted greatly with clarifications in the final text.

The sequence of events given in Part I is approximately that followed by Baba in the first week. However the various persons, incidents and statements made by Baba were woven together from the entire four weeks' program. The original on-the-spot translations of Baba's gestures made by Eruch have often been modified in the interest of continuity and greater ease of perusal.

There are also certain persons who have performed the invaluable service of offering suggestions from the viewpoint of the public. This especially difficult task has been faithfully performed by Meher Baba's sister, Manija S. Irani, by Murshida Ivy O. Duce, and by Ben and Shirley Courtright.

Finally, the entire contents of the volume have been approved by Meher Baba. It cannot be pretended that therefore everything is as Meher Baba would have described it himself, nor that Meher Baba necessarily agrees completely with certain expressions of opinion which have inevitably been the narrator's. However the reader can be assured that the major content of the volume is as given directly by Meher Baba, and that the remainder finds some point of acceptance or at least tolerance by him.

D. E. STEVENS

Red Bank, New Jersey
February, 1957

Introduction to *The Crossroad (Fifth) Edition*

In a manner of speaking, *Listen, Humanity* has become a historical recording of principal events in my own life. Now, after another quarter of a century, this narrative of some completely typical events in Meher Baba's life with those drawn to him is going through a further edition. It has been forty years since Meher Baba asked if I would care to record the occasion I had witnessed in 1955 in his presence in India. The book has taken on a life of its own, and by now I have found that it has entered in a fascinating manner into the lives of a very great many people, often acting as the initial step into deep relationship with Meher Baba and his description of the meaning of human life.

In the Introduction to the Harper edition of *Listen, Humanity* written in 1970, I described the events surrounding the death of Meher Baba in early 1969. I included as well my own conjectures about his promise to break his silence, and the push to Creation to which he frequently referred. Where has all that gone, now, and what other unexpected events have occurred during these following years?

Basically, the physical plant has continued much as it was. The Avatar Meher Baba Trust as set up by Meher Baba himself goes on flourishing under the guidance of those close ones who still remain. Meherabad and Meherazad are much as they were during Baba's lifetime, with the addition at the former of a beautifully designed and executed Pilgrim Center. And Mehera's garden at the latter seems to expect the appearance of both Baba and Mehera at any moment, although it is now without its mistress in physical form. The centers established in Baba's time to receive him in Myrtle Beach, South Carolina and near Brisbane in Australia are almost as he last saw them, with those warming changes of detail that are much like the spiritual fragrance that often accompanies age in people drawing closer each day to the One. Groups continue to meet regularly in almost all of the locales established in the past, plus new ones in old countries and new ones in new countries that Baba has touched with his grace.

What about people? First of all about myself, as I see Don every day. I have no illusions now concerning my own importance in the manner in which God runs His Creation, but I can certainly see myself as a typical component of a highly complex and vastly intriguing medium in which consciousness is developed, and then very laboriously brought to perfection. I have watched myself and others put a great deal of time and energy into projects, hopefully based on some understanding of Meher Baba's descriptions of the meaning of Creation. I have often been stupefied by the love, care and discernment that have accompanied those activities. And now, after so many hours and years of investment of the best of one's labor, I am struck by how completely different are the results one observes and the manner in which they come about. There are the results, but it is as if they happen by coming around the corner, rather than as the direct product of invested effort. And from all that, and most exciting of all, I think I now see a relatively new manner of feeling into the path of Truth coming into being.

It is not a mass movement that one observes, with great crowds and high enthusiasm. The groups I know are usually in the eight-to twelve-persons range, and there are few stirring addresses given from public podiums. Rarely does one old-timer give a rousing description of events lived with the Great Master which moves the listeners to an inspired dedication of themselves to a new ideal. Oddly enough, it is a modest feeling out, often through such indirect channels that the very motion seems completely improbable. And yet, at the end of the day, there they are – the devoted ones – and through their individuality, they find deep and sincere links to others similarly drawn.

It is almost as if Meher Baba and the Spiritual Hierarchy have been drawing the threads together for a new type of spiritual commitment. Part of it, and indeed a very central and vital part, is love and great respect for the Master. Then there is a deep commitment to the process of daily living, and the clear understanding that this is a key means whereby each of us is brought constantly into the working laboratory in which we gradually perceive the Truth of living. It is as if a principal means for one's ongoing is in the school of daily life. And a third common factor frequently to be noted is the importance of inner commitment to the companions around one, who are deeply involved in the same convictions, in the companionship which opens so many doors of oneness, and in the devotion to the one who is the helper and the supporter at every turn on the way.

I like what I see. And I trust it. It has the smell of great simplicity and strength.

D.E.Stevens
Cagnes-sur-Mer
23 March, 1997

Introduction to the Colophon Edition

Fifteen years have passed since the occurrence of the events described in the first part of this volume. During that time the word of Meher Baba has raced around the world as he had predicted it would. Tens of thousands of devotees, as well as the interested and the curious, have made pilgrimages to the centers most closely associated with him near Ahmednagar in India, and near Myrtle Beach in South Carolina. Again, all this is as he had said it would be.

Meher Baba "dropped the body" during this time, in January 1969, and was entombed in Meherabad in the small building erected and decorated at his order years before. At the time of his entombment, and again during April-June of 1969,* he gave his *darshan* at Guruprasad in Poona, and at Meherabad and Meherazad, to his lovers who flocked to "his side" from all over the world in obedience to his invitation. Many, perhaps all, had wondered how arrangements for this great *darshan*, which were made while he was in the flesh, could be carried out with anything more than sorrowful obedience after he had left the body. Perhaps its accomplishment was "the great event, never witnessed before, and never to happen again," that he had predicted the year before. And if it was not, and that occurrence is yet to happen, the projection of his presence was, nevertheless, so real and so forceful that he seemed to fill all of the space as well as all of the hearts at Guruprasad, Meherazad and Meherabad. They had come expecting sorrow, and left filled with a lightness and joy most had never known.

But these recitations of the fulfillment of things to come leaves one

---

*Meher Baba had made detailed plans for a great *darshan* (literally a bestowing of spiritual blessing by the Master) for the many thousands of new and old devotees, to be held in Poona in April-June 1969. His close disciples or *mandali* carried out those plans, with results that will form part of the great lore of Baba through the centuries.

important blank. What about the breaking of the silence, which Baba commenced in 1925 and which he repeatedly linked to his manifestation? He had not audibly done so when his body lay lifeless on January 31.

Was this a great omission? Or had the entire forty-four years of his silence been a master stroke of technique to shake people and help them start to focus on the great Reality?

To the first question: certainly not. To the second: most probably yes; but a being as sublime as Meher Baba appears never to act within the restrictions of one sole aim. It takes little time in his presence to sense that he is everywhere at once, and his actions have a concentrated impact at many levels and points. When the entire story is in and one looks at the available facts, I feel one must draw the conclusion that Meher Baba did break his silence and manifested during his lifetime. Others whom I deeply respect feel differently. In any event, there will be hundreds of learned treatises on this subject in the future. It is not my purpose in this brief introduction to present one of the earliest of these analyses, but I do wish to record a few keys to this enigma, certain of which depend upon observations in the present.

Meher Baba often said that when he broke his silence he would say the only meaningful word, and that this would shortly be followed by his manifestation. Tradition, arising from thousands of years of profound spiritual activity, gives us certain keys to help understand the enigma of his words. Many sources describe the origin of Creation by saying, "First there was the Word" (or something similar).

How curious, that Meher Baba would say that when he broke his silence, he would say the only meaningful word.

Tradition also tells us that it is part of the job description of the Messenger of God that he shall renew the Word when *dharma* has decayed. Baba has said many times that this was his responsibility in his lifetime.

Clearly, then, a more basic meaning of "word," and the "breaking of the silence" to give the "only real word" has to do with the fundamental thrust of Creation, at all levels. But still another intriguing clue: Baba describes the origin of Creation as the whim of God stirring Him to know His divinity consciously, and compares it to a wave surging across the stillness of infinite, unconscious God.

A wave does not leave absolute calmness in its wake, but a succession of diminishing waves behind it. What is all of Creation, but a vast variety of different species of wave disturbances? What is sound, but a wave disturbance? And finally, the key, what is a Word, but a wave disturbance?

The train of association moves on inescapably. What more apt way to describe the origin of God's Creation than to say, "First there was the Word"? And if one is the Avatar, the Messenger of the age, whose role it is to renew and revivify God's Word, what more profound way can there be to break a silence than to give renewed impetus to the original "sound," which was the origin of all Creation? An audible word is dwarfed into meaninglessness in relation to a function so fundamental.

All this is fascinating theory, but the honest inner workman of the present and the future will ask, "What evidence was there in Baba's lifetime for a renewed vitality in Creation?"

A fair question. My specialty is people and what goes on inside them. If I could say anything meaningful in relation to the question, it would have to be based on observation within my specialty.

In the 1930s and 1940s, when I first became deeply involved in man's inner being and how it progresses, it seemed to me that internally aware individuals were either rare or not very evident, and that, in any case, internal motion was extremely slow at best. In the 1950s, this began to change. There were obviously more people searching, and they tended to be more vigorous in their search. By the mid-1960s, there were thousands, and their rate of motion was astonishing. It was evident that Meher Baba's "New Humanity" was literally at hand.

From then on there was no question in my mind that Meher Baba's true manifestation was already in flood tide. It only remained to trip across a few clues to the "word" and the "breaking of the silence" contained in the Bible and, among others, in Guru Nanak's utterances* to round out the picture. Then all of Baba's cryptic, intriguing, almost abrasive statements on his silence appeared to fall into place.

---

*Nanak, the inspiration for the Sikh movement, stated in a variety of ways that as Creation arises from the Word of God, so it is also possible for the individual soul to return to God through the Word. The Word is both an outward motion and a returning motion.

We are living in the flood tide age, when God's whim to know His own divinity consciously has been given another great push within Creation. Things are happening to man's inner being at a rate that could not be conceived of twenty years ago. Ours is the responsibility to look to this Being who has given us once again this great forward push, and by the reality of our devotion within his love, to make the most of this new springtime of humanity.

Not only is it a springtime because of the release of new vigor within creation and because of the freshness of the example of the Christ figure itself, but because it is also the end of a cycle of "destruction and suffering on a colossal scale." It is not only Meher Baba, but it is he most clearly of all, who tells us that all of Creation is now moving on under the Avataric touch into an age when not only the deserving but the undeserving as well will have their chance at divine grace. All one must do, in the shower of spiritual rain that is now descending, is to be alert to the opportunity that is about one.° How magnificent it is to sense the slowly thinning pall of gloom and destruction, and to sniff the moist fresh air that already gives hint of the rainbow in the heavens.

D. E. STEVENS

London
September 1970

° "Message of Cheer and Hope to the Suffering Humanity," from *Messages,* by Meher Baba, Ahmednagar, 1945.

Introduction

An introduction usually discusses the background of the contents of the volume or of its author. In the present instance it seems desirable to upset this precedent and discuss the reader instead.

This work is directed towards that very large group of people who want answers to their living problems. Perhaps it may seem odd to go to India for such answers. Actually it is not. The East has labored for thousands of years to find the keys to life so that daily living could be patterned in consonance with them.

The East has perhaps not yet found perfection, nor its people the perfect way. However they do provide a background of sincere effort and insight which is almost unique in the world. From that background one could expect great individuals to emerge who would be especially fitted to teach us how to live.

Meher Baba is clearly one of those invaluable persons. One has only to be in his presence for a short time to sense the mighty forces at work in him. One has only to be for a few days with his close disciples to know that his greatness flows readily into other persons. One has only to be in India for a short time, and to look and listen with sympathetic eyes and ears, to know that the spiritual greatness of India springs from roots which lie deep in the hearts of its people.

The rub for the occidental lies in the method of applying these living insights. This is where the present reader must be discussed. When he thinks of India, he thinks perhaps of a poor people, often illiterate, given to complicated superstitions. When he thinks of India's religious life, he sees ancient temples populated by many gods. Or if he plumbs a smaller area of knowledge, he recalls odd yogis and mystics given to strange practices.

This is the screen of partial or incorrect understanding through which one must pierce to draw on India for insight into western man's problems. The task seems almost too great, for ingrained notions yield only grudgingly. Yet India does have, buried in the great mass of extrania, a profound knowledge of man's purpose, and this the West needs desperately.

An astoundingly small proportion of persons in the western world know why they are here. And not knowing why they are here, few know how to starch their lives with a sense of vigorous, dependable purpose. Instead, life becomes a matter of energetic effort to solve today's needs. If tomorrow comes to mind, it can only be looked upon as an extension of today's problems.

It is no wonder that nervousness and irritability are produced. It is also no wonder that thinking, feeling people are dissatisfied, and ask in their hearts what it is all about. But where can they find the answers? Apparently not in a wild, negative bout with life. That was tried in the 1920's, and the results were so unsatisfactory that the next generation turned its back and began again to look for a positive answer.

Apparently the answers can't be found in ritual, form or ceremony. This is a matter of the spirit, and to tend to the needs of spirit requires men of spirit. But there are not too many of these. Where can they be found, and how can their answers be turned into answers for us? This is the great dilemma of a war-weary, soul-weary age.

If India has clues which could be of help, how can they be used? Certainly it is not in harmony with western traditions to build temples with many-armed gods and goddesses. Nor is it in the western tradition to engage in strange practices of breath or posture so that one may do impossible physical feats. Rather than attracting the occidental, such habits are apt to repel him.

If the East is to be of any help, it must be able to give western man something which can be welded into his practical, daily life. It cannot divorce him from his family and turn him into a lone whirling dervish, nor can it give him odd notions which will not allow him to earn a living in conventional business.

This is the real problem in trying to translate any eastern answers into western words.

It has often been said that the great world religions are furthest apart in their formal parts, and closest together in their true spirit. This seems true, and provides a clue by which the West may draw on the heritage of the East. It is the spirit which is needed, and form becomes only a meaningless husk to be discarded.

It is not necessary for the occidental to take up breathing exercises, postures, diets or the murmuring of sacred phrases. It is true that an unbiased analysis of such practices usually leads to the conclusion that they do produce astonishing results. However, in large part they are aside from the matter of spirit, which is the nub of the issue.

The first part of this volume describes how the great contemporary spiritual leader, Meher Baba, transferred something of this spirit to a picked group of his close followers in India. The western reader will be struck by the fact that there was almost nothing of ritual, dogma or strange practices involved. Yet the sessions produced results—often remarkable results. The narrator for instance, who has perhaps been a rather crusty person over the years, was told by many friends upon his return how much more enjoyable he had "suddenly" become. Such comments were made both by persons who knew of the nature of his stay in India as well as those who did not.

Apparently, then, there is a way of transferring some shade of spiritual greatness without use of the elaborate form and ritual which would be repugnant to much of western civilization. Further, there are apparently such resources presently available in the world which can be drawn upon. This is an important fact to each person who searches for a more certain meaning to life.

The first contribution to a searching reader can then be the reassurance that such wholesome answers exist. The second contribution, given in Part II, is a description of the nature of life and death, sleep and waking, love and obedience.

The third contribution is a very intriguing one, which is first suggested early in the *sahvas* program described in Part I. Meher Baba makes no bones about referring to himself as the Avatar or Christ of his age. Nothing could be more surely calculated to arouse the argumentative instincts of the occidental.

In the first place, many doubt that there ever was such a person as Jesus Christ, or at least that He had anything of the stature attributed to Him. Second, the time for such events always seems to be in the past. To have someone jolt the present with such a rude claim seems a deliberate challenge to a sense of modern rationality.

A third attitude often encountered is that Jesus Christ was the one and only Son of God, and there will not be another. Finally, there is a deeply ingrained conviction that if Christ should come again, good breeding would cause Him to avoid claiming that He was the Christ.

For all of these reasons it is upsetting to find a man of undoubted stature state with candor that he is the Christ. It is always easier to deal with such claims in the past. To have them occur today presents a challenge of frightening dimensions.

There is hardly a person reared in Christendom who has not jeered in his heart at the Pharisees for not having recognized Christ's stature, or at least for not having treated Him fairly. By implication, if one condemns a person who may turn out to be the modern Christ, then one becomes a modern counterpart of the biblical Pharisee. On the other hand, if one mistakenly accepts a man to be Christ then one has committed a major blunder which may have far-reaching consequences in one's personal life.

This peculiar dilemma in which the individual is placed, explains largely the violent explosivity of the issue. The greater the obvious caliber of the man, the greater the explosivity. And Meher Baba is certainly no mean man.

Section I is liberally sprinkled with Meher Baba's references to his divine stature. It is suggested that the reader deliberately put this question "on file" as he reads Part I, and allow the personality and the heart of the man to speak for themselves. Part II will provide much additional material to estimate Meher Baba's qualities. Part III in turn is an attempt on the part of the narrator to describe his own estimation of this extremely important and knotty subject.

The age of jet transport and atomic power does not render the question of Christhood obsolete, but brings it more insistently to the forefront. Mankind will need such a superhuman force in the world to dispense the clarity and balance needed to equate against the superhuman questions it now faces.

If God did not provide a means for answering the questions He allows man to raise, it would be an unreasonable world in which He forces us to live. But there is reason to believe that those answers do exist in the great nation which specializes in the inner springs of man's nature: India. Stripped of the refuse which the centuries produce, pared of inessentials which serve only to separate man from man, and reduced to the hard core of spirit, the answer can emerge from the wisdom of that land. The answer would not be a new one, but it would be a vital infusion into the lifeless stalks which once bore up in man the ripe knowledge of his own purpose and dignity.

D. E. STEVENS

The Theme

There is no creature which is not destined for the supreme goal, as there is no river which is not winding its way towards the sea. But only in the human form is consciousness so developed that it is capable of expressing the perfection of its own true self, which is the Self of all.

However, even in the human form the soul is prevented from realizing its birthright of joy and fulfillment because of the burden of *sanskaras* which it has accumulated as a by-product of its arduous development of consciousness. Like the dust that accumulates on the shoes of a traveler on foot, these *sanskaras* are gathered by the pilgrim as he treads the evolutionary path.

In the human form, which is the crowning product of evolution, the divine life is enmeshed in the *sanskaric* deposits of the mind. The expression of the divine life is therefore curtailed and distorted by the distractions of the *sanskaras*, which weld consciousness instead to the fascinations of the false-phenomenal.

One by one the many-colored attachments to the false must be relinquished. Bit by bit the *sanskaric* tinder feeding the deceptive flames of the separative ego must be replaced by the imperative evidence of the unquenchable flame of truth. Only in this manner can man ascend to the height of divine attainment: the endless beginning of life eternal.

The life in eternity knows no bondage, decay or sorrow. It is the everlasting and ever renewing self-affirmation of conscious, illimitable divinity. My mission is to help you inherit this hidden treasure of the Self.

MEHER BABA

Contents

CONTENTS

PART III

Avatarhood

PART I

The Sahvas Programs

CHAPTER 1

Meherabad

Old men, young men, middle-aged men greeted the silent master in the characteristic embrace reserved in the East for close friends. First the new arrival would hang his head over the right shoulder of the great man, to be patted or occasionally warmly thumped on the back. Then shoulders would be switched and the procedure repeated.

Some leaned their cheeks on the great man's shoulder and held him gently in the small of the back with lightly pressed hands, as a child reaches and clings to its mother. Others were "left-shoulder-oriented" rather than "right-shoulder-oriented", and for a brief moment confusion would ensue as greeter and greeted parried directions. But apparently Heaven is not particularly partial to the right-handed over the left-handed, for the master made no attempt to correct the situation and thumped just as heartily in the reverse order.

Occasionally some overflowing of feeling would cause one of the greeters to overstay, and imperceptibly the warm-hearted thumping on the back would change to a good-humored prod in the ribs. The smile of bliss would change equally imperceptibly to a brief grin of embarrassment and the shy guest would back away, with covert glances to the side to see if he had been detected in his small indiscretion.

The hall in which the greetings were taking place was one of a collection of buildings called "Meherabad". They lay on the edge of Arangaon, a small farming village several miles from Ahmednagar, which in turn had been an old fort post of the British army in bygone days of eastern empire. Ahmednagar lay in the Deccan, perhaps two hundred miles by meandering, human-packed roads from Bombay.

The present occasion was an event uncommon even in a land re-

3

nowned for Avatars (Christs) and saints and mystics. Here was a great master—perhaps more than that—greeting a picked group of his followers who were to spend one week of rare grace by living in close company with him as he discoursed, played, joked, exercised and rested, a true *sahvas*.* This was not a common practice, and the Indian mind regarded it as a treasure to be dreamed of, but achieved only once in many lifetimes.

These were the first early arrivals of a first group of two hundred. At the end of a week spent in the close company of the master, a second group of two hundred was to arrive, and so on until the four major language groups of Gujerati, Telugu, Hindi and Marathi had been successively received for a week each.

But even this early in the proceedings Pendu, who supervised the physical arrangements for the *sahvas* proceedings, was muttering because Meher Baba seemed unable to say "no" to a flood of entreating letters begging that the writers also be allowed to come. Already the first group was swelling beyond two hundred souls, and it seemed that the matter could not possibly be gotten under control until three hundred at least had been allowed to come.

Pendu's worries over the job of providing more steel sheets for shelter and more pulse for food and more matting for beds did not concern the rapt hundred already present. They showed only the widest of delighted smiles as each person moved with unconscious grace and simple dignity in a line formed down the center of the room.

Although the group had been selected for its common-language background, their dress defied all semblance of similarity. Some wore white cloth draped deep around one leg and high on the other. Others wore white pants so full and sheer that they seemed to form a solid floor-length skirt, while a few wore real full-length skirts. European trousers were much in evidence, and accenting the whole were the occasional robes of the priest and the wanderer.

Many carried garlands of fresh flowers which they hung about Meher Baba's neck. Others carried homemade candies or oranges or cocoanuts, or even portraits of Baba. All of these gifts Baba smilingly accepted and passed on to one of the close disciples (*mandali*)

* Literally, living in close companionship with the spiritual master.

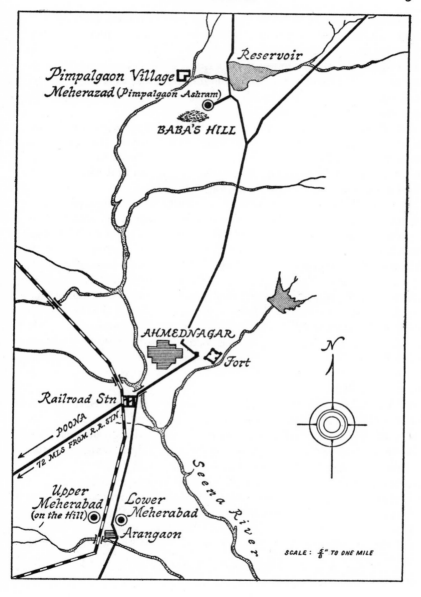

at his side.

Sometimes an exclamation would break out by way of abrupt gesture as Baba spied an especially cherished friend. Often there would be a brief interlude of quick questioning as he inquired about health or welfare of some family member.

Despite the apparent handicap of substituting fluid gesticulation for speech, Meher Baba's silence of thirty years' standing slowed the rate of his repartee not one whit. With only minor hesitations, Baba's gestures were caught and translated with uncanny ease by Eruch, one of the devoted *mandali.**

When no more than half the receiving line had been pared away Baba became wearied with standing. Abruptly he turned and walked back to a large chair set against the wall at one end of the room. Like a mobile centipede, the sinuous line of greeters followed immediately upon its prey and at once resumed its function of splitting off one segment after another in the ritual of salutation.

Without warning the even flow of feeling was interrupted at one point, and all in the room focused their attention on the frowning Baba and the apprehensive, uneasily shifting individual before him.

"Do you have a cold?" Eruch translated Baba's gestures.

"Only a very small one," was the low-pitched reply.

"Do you have a sore throat?" Baba queried further.

"A little."

"And your nose runs?"

"Also a little."

"And while you are like this you would embrace Baba and give him a cold too?" Baba persisted.†

"Oh, no, Baba!" came the horrified reply, and hesitantly, with jerky movements born of torn emotions, the individual backed away from his favored position at the head of the line.

Suddenly Baba's features softened and he gestured again.

"Perhaps tomorrow your cold will have improved and you can greet me with the remaining people who are yet to come."

---

* *Mandali* are close disciples who follow the instructions of the master implicitly.

† See Appendix II for discussion of the susceptibility to disease of saints, sages and the God-realized.

Once more the line began to move, and soon the sense of running rivulets of feeling was everywhere again. The room filled with soft humming overtones, the muted cellos and the lowly vibrating basses of deep human emotion. From front to back and back to front the rhythm changed and the key modulated by the moment in the 'fast-moving drama of human feeling.

"Have you all read the instructions at the back of the room?" Baba asked when the last member had been greeted.*

A majority nodded their heads in assent, but a few shook them in negation.

"Anyone who has not read the instructions should do so," Baba pursued. "I want everyone to be sure to read them before I come tomorrow morning. Now I will leave you and I will be here tomorrow morning at eight-thirty. If you find something which is not to your liking be sure to let Baba know. I want you all to be happy. Do not worry about your families, or your business. If you think of them, then you are with them, and you are not with Baba. While you are here, enjoy yourself, enjoy Baba, forget your cares."

He rose from his chair and strode out of the hall, a hurrying stream of hangers-on trying to keep pace with him as he walked rapidly to the waiting blue car. A few smiles and waves from the window and he was gone, Eruch and several of the other *mandali* in the back seat. They would spend the night at Meherazad, some miles on the north of Ahmednagar.

On the long narrow verandas on either side of the hall, small knots of old and new friends exchanged pleasantries. In the hall itself, opposite Baba's ponderous armchair, a smaller cluster carried out the injunction to read the instruction sheets for the *sahvas* programs. One man droned on in oddly accented English to his patient companion, "I want you to read carefully and absorb these instructions. . . ."

The sun sank below the far line of low hills, and the cowherd children from Arangaon hard by began to drive their charges back across the poor open pasture and down along the railroad tracks towards the tiny, poverty-ridden village. The combed clouds in the east took on soft oranges, and then reds, and shifted to violets and

* See Appendix I.

blues as the intense color of sunset ruby shifted to the mid-heavens. Slowly the color concentrated in the far horizon, and at last day withdrew its cloak from the landscape of India, showing only the faintest glimpse of the red lining as it trailed across the far mountains. The land slept.

CHAPTER 2

The First Day

At least half an hour before the appointed time on the following morning the honk of the blue car could be heard approaching from the direction of Ahmednagar. Caught unawares, the *sahvasis* rushed to perform last minute duties and to collect sundry garlands, presents, spectacle cases and other valuables. A frenzy of activity could be heard through the long line of doors of the outhouses. In a moment these were bursting open like exploding popcorn and their occupants racing across the back lot to be at hand for the first sight of Baba.

With a flourish, Meherji's red-fezzed driver brought the car to a halt before the great hall and a dozen eager hands reached out to open the front door of the car. Smiling broadly, Baba stepped out, clad in spotless white from head to toe, while the back seat unloosed its content of attentive *mandali*. Holding someone's face momentarily between his hands here, banging his hand warmly on a shoulder there, occasionally rearing back in surprise and grasping the arm of someone hand-to-elbow, Baba made his way slowly through the excited throng to the hall door.

With a rapid scuffling and scraping the motley group slid out of sandals and shoes and trod barefoot onto the closely carpeted stone floor of the hall. As if by instinct they formed a line again before Baba's armchair and the process of greeting the remainder of the group went on in high good humor. Close to Baba and on his left, at times almost crushed by the excited crowd, stood the indefatigable Eruch. He was immaculately turned out in blue-grey cotton suiting which was buttoned high to his chin. A black Gandhi cap perched easily on his head, and a fleck of grey in his clipped black mustache accented his quick smile and rapid translation of Baba's gestures.

Further towards the corner at Baba's left and already taking down hurried notes on the proceedings, were two *mandali* of long stand-

9

ing and faithful service. In the opposite corner was Baba's secretary and manager of publications, while leaning against the wall and smiling in merry delight was still another close disciple who had also preserved silence now for many years.

In the general babble and confusion Dr. Deshmukh, distinguished professor and editor of Meher Baba's *Discourses,* slipped into the line of greeters. The action was curious, as he had been among the first to be greeted the previous afternoon. Hard on his heels was Bal Natu, also apparently bent on a second try.

When Deshmukh had come to be the head of the line Baba eyed him quizzically.

"Deshmukh, I already embraced you warmly yesterday."

"Yes, Baba, but I thought perhaps you would have forgotten and would greet me again today," was the unabashed reply.

Eruch almost exploded with laughter as he translated Baba's reluctant reply, "All right, I will greet you this once more since it pains you so greatly to be any distance from me."

Therewith Baba drew Deshmukh over his right shoulder, and then his left. As he fumbled with the elated scholar, Baba deftly swiped Deshmukh's prized fountain pen from his coat pocket. Waving it first to the side for all to see, he hid it in his own coat as he poked Deshmukh in the ribs as a warning that the second share of greetings was at an end. Both men drew back smiling in high good humor, each equally satisfied that he had outplayed the other.

But it was now Bal Natu's turn to try his hand at this astute game of poker. He knew before he had put one foot in front of the other that he was already topped. "No, Bal Natu, not you too. That way I will have to embrace one and all again."

As the crowd began to subside it became clear that some of those still standing shyly in the background had never yet met Baba. One disciple of long standing came forward to handle the social amenities.

"Baba, these are faces which are new to you, but their devotion to you is not," he began, but Baba broke him off with a short gesture.

"How is it that your own voice sounds new today?" he inquired.

For a moment the able man was overcome with confusion, unprepared as he was for the sudden switch in subject matter. Then a light of comprehension broke across his face and he smiled in recognition.

"Yes, Baba, since I saw you last I have had some new dentures which make me sound new also. But I am your old friend, so I will introduce my dentures to you." Thereupon he smiled broadly and turned slowly about so that Baba and all might see these new friends.

A medical practitioner from Hamirpur drew close; Baba greeted him by holding out his wrist. "Feel my pulse and tell me how you find my health," he said.

After carefully reading the pulse, the physician said, "Baba, you are quite all right. In fact you look wonderfully well."

Several greetings later Baba confronted a newcomer by drawing back in his seat and asking, "How do you think Baba looks today?"

"I must say, Baba, my friends and I were just remarking how terribly tired you look. You must not do so much; you must rest more," was the frank reply.

"I get ill in five minutes and become all right within the next five minutes," Baba replied for all to hear. "In five minutes I grow old and in five minutes I am young again. What sort of a disposition do I have?"

None ventured to answer the question.

One of the men, a young fellow with long, black hair, full glossy beard and a slender figure belying the ferocity of the framing of his face, stepped forward to introduce a friend.

"Baba, this is one of my friends who has asked to come. He is not especially religious, but he wanted to come," he explained.

"I am not religious either, but that is because I am the only One in the whole of creation," was Baba's reply.*

So the greeting went, and so it finally ended. Then Baba leaned back in his seat and looked thoughtful for a few moments. The audience cleared throats, settled into comfortable crosslegged positions, exchanged hurried last minute greetings with neighbors, and did all

---

* Similar statements are often made by Baba. The meaning is clear only if one will assume that it is possible for the individual soul to achieve union with God. In such case the individual soul and God are one, and therefore the God-realized being inevitably experiences himself as all of creation.

the unaccountable small noisy things which must precede a public address.

"I hope you have all now read the instructions for the *sahvas* program which are posted in five languages at the rear of the room," Baba stated. "If you have not, then later this morning be sure to read them. If you are unable to read them, have someone read them to you."

Again there was a moment's pause while Baba shifted in his seat, blinked his eyes as if they were smarting, and wiggled the fingers of his right hand in momentary abstraction. Another small flurry of coughs, sneezes and whispers broke out from the audience.

"I have not asked you to come here for long discourses on philosophical subjects," Baba resumed his gestures as Eruch translated. "A proper *sahvas* means physical proximity, as well as mingling together, as do the members of one family. But my staying with you and your staying with me do not mean the same thing. For ages and ages I have been with you, nearer to you than you feel yourself to be. Now you have an opportunity to be with me for a week and also to come nearer and nearer to me for all time.

"During these seven days I want you all to live with me as freely and intimately as the resident *mandali* have done for years—*together*. On my part, I will be equally free and frank with you in all respects. But do not anticipate hearing only pleasant things from me. As the elder in the family I may find fault with you and scold you.

"During this precious week, try at least to forget everything else so that your hearts will remain clean and open for me to step in. Do not notice either your failings, weaknesses and shortcomings, or your prestige, position, learning and so-called knowledge of spiritual things. Try to forget what you think you already know.

"Let the atmosphere you have left behind remain there. You are now here physically. Try to remain here mentally as well. Follow me wherever I may be. Otherwise, though present here physically, you will remain mentally in your same old atmosphere.

"To have a passing thought, and to keep thinking of it, are two different things. If you fold your hands mechanically before me but go on thinking of your problems at home, you will be folding your hands to them and not to me.

"Do not worry about thoughts. *Never try to force your mind to* *check your thoughts.* Thoughts may and will come. Do not try either to invite them or to drive them away. Let the thoughts come and go unasked. By observing the most minute details about me and what I do and say, you will take little notice of your thoughts, good or bad.*

"Be careful of your health and keep fit. The moment you feel indisposed, do not hesitate to consult Doctors Nilu and Kanakdandi. Those who are used to homeopathic treatment should go to Padri. But for those who are suffering from the malady of love, I remain their doctor.

"At the first sign of a cold, get immediate treatment. Otherwise all of you will catch cold and start a chorus of sneezing."

With such powerful thought suggestion at work the audience broke out into a chorus of self-conscious coughs and clearing of throats. Baba looked carefully and critically at his flock.

"The most important things," he resumed, "which you have to forget for the time being are the troubles in your day-to-day life at home, such as health, money, social matters and other petty worries. Do not think that by coming here your day-to-day difficulties will necessarily be solved, and do not expect my blessings for health or wealth.

"I hold no key to such problems. I am not a yogi, *wali* or saint, who can and does perform miracles. If you count upon such things from me in return for your *sahvas* with me, you may lose even what you now possess.

"I have not come amongst you for you to bow down to me, to perform my *arti* (song in praise), to worship me. These things are good for the saints, *walis* and yogis. I expect much more from you. I have come to receive your love from you, and to bestow my love on you. I have descended to your level † for the one purpose of bestowing my love on you so that you may love God and become God. The rest

---

* To the student of eastern thought such instructions represent a necessary technique of removing the focus of attention from the self. Needless to say the results produced are in direct relation to the caliber of the teacher and the honest wholeheartedness of the student who employs the technique.

† Not specifically directed towards this particular audience, but in the sense of God descending into human form for the benefit of all mankind. The very thorny subject of Baba's Christhood (Avatarhood) is treated at length in Part III.

is all illusion. Do not expect anything from me except my love for you.

"Let us not hurry. Let us go slowly. You have fully five days here.*
Whether a point sounds small or big, be equally attentive. I may
crack jokes, I may be serious. Listening to me will never be in vain.
If you cannot grasp what I say, listen carefully regardless. Today, or
tomorrow, you will grasp everything that I say.

"Age after age I have the one same thing to tell, but each time I
say it in a different manner and from a different viewpoint. Do not
worry when you cannot follow what I say. Merely listening may possibly help someone to love me.

"Those who feel drowsy and are inclined to take a nap should
move back towards the walls. Only those who feel alert should sit
near me."

And then thoughtfully, almost with a trace of sadness, "People
generally remain indifferent when I am present among them. They
understand and appreciate me more after I drop my body. That is
the way whenever I come."

Whether moved by Baba's statement or by the need to relax mus-
cles held too long in unused positions, several older men in front
began to shift their positions with a self-conscious, apologetic air.
Baba noted this at once.

"Those who feel like straightening their legs should do so without
any hesitation. We are here in each other's company. Remain at ease
and do not become unnecessarily cramped through formality. Now
we will have a game of seven tiles," he announced unexpectedly, and
with a loud shout of enthusiasm everyone poured out of the back
door of the hall and onto the veranda. Baba quickly designated two
teams of seven men each, a small heap of tiles was stacked in the
middle of the floor, and the two sides ranged at either end of the
veranda with the spectators standing off on the ground at the side.

In playing seven tiles, the "in" team pitches at the tiles, perhaps
fifteen feet away, with a tennis ball. The "out" team tries to catch
the ball before it has touched the floor for a second time. To tumble

---

* Each language group was officially assigned a week, but allowing
time for arriving and settling down, and packing and leaving at the end
of the sessions, plus a day for the workers to clean between groups, the
actual time with Baba amounted to about five days for each group.

the tiles is a score for the in team, to catch the ball before a second bound puts the pitcher out of the running. But when the out man returns the ball to the pitcher, if he fails to make the ball bounce before it is caught, all of the caught-out pitchers are in the game again.

This last point is the real sauce of the game, for there is an almost insuperable instinct among ball players to lob a ball direct to the waiting catchers rather than to bounce it to them.

One of the teams had several frisky members from the universities in Poona and Bombay. One of these students, with dark hair and a small black mustache and the devil in his eye, had an uncanny ability to catch the opposing team's pitched balls before the second bounce. On the other hand, another member of this team, with great craggy features and the build of a football tackle, could pitch with a sizzle that almost defied catching. Between the two of them, and with not inconsiderable support from their teammates, they were licking the tar out of the opposition.

The underdog team was up, with two pitchers left and still without a hit in the entire game. One of their two remaining pitchers looked warily at the tiles and his grinning opposition, wound up and let fly. He was caught cleanly and easily out by the devilish one. As the latter lazily tossed the ball back a snowy arm reached out from nowhere and snatched it in mid-air. With a casual swing Baba tossed the ball on to the startled pitcher and with a wild cheer from the audience all of the caught-out pitchers rejoined the fray.

The precedent having been established and mob response having sanctioned it, three times the arm reached out from a jabbering knot of spectators and saved the weaker team on the verge of catastrophe. But finally Baba would save them no longer. It was Deshmukh's turn to pitch, and his ball was wide and slow. He was out.

"Deshmukh, for you we halve the distance," Baba gestured, and moved Deshmukh halfway to the pile of tiles.

Deshmukh smiled in nervous embarrassment, pitched and missed by a wider margin than before. Again Baba moved him a foot or two closer. Again the tense Deshmukh pitched, and it seemed that certainly the tiles must have skipped out of the way, for again they escaped at point-blank range.

A final time Baba moved Deshmukh closer, until he seemed more a bombardier sighting vertically on his target. Incredible! He missed again. Baba threw up his arms, walking off in sign that the game was done.

As the group came back into the hall, a few late arrivals were waiting to greet Baba. One smiling *sahvasi* came forward with a garland so large that he had difficulty unsorting himself from it. Baba chuckled as he saw the mass of confusion approaching him.

"What price did you pay for that great bulk of flowers?" he asked.

"Ten rupees," was the prompt reply, at which a shout of laughter went up.

Another approaching supplicant needed an entire basket to carry his tribute of flowers. As he struggled up to the chair Baba remarked on his sallow complexion. "You seem to be pulled down. Perhaps it is your love for me that makes your face look wan and withered."

Then one who had traveled several times with Baba on his strenuous journeys contacting the *masts* or spiritually intoxicated,* approached to pay his respects.

"Are you happy?" Baba asked. "You look just the same as when I saw you last."

The old friend nodded smilingly to acknowledge his health, the greeting and his appreciation of Baba's concern. Then he turned to go away.

"Wait. Did you garland me?" Baba asked as if there were some real doubt in his mind.

"No, Baba, I did not."

"You must also garland me," Baba signified by gestures as he removed one of the many strands of flowers from his neck and handed it to the waiting man.

As the crowd settled on their haunches on the mat-covered floor Baba sat back in his seat momentarily. Then he focused his attention on the group and began to gesture as Eruch translated.

"To garland me, to bow down to me and to sing my praises are comparatively the three most unimportant things. The three most important things on the path to God-realization are love, obedience and surrender. There is no possibility of compromise about these three.

---

* See *The Wayfarers*, William Donkin.

"Love is a gift from God to man, obedience is a gift from master to man, and surrender is a gift from man to master. The one who loves, desires to do the will of the beloved, and seeks union with the beloved. Obedience performs the will of the beloved and seeks the pleasure of the beloved. Surrender resigns to the will of the beloved and seeks nothing.

"One who loves, is the lover of the beloved. One who obeys is the beloved of the beloved. One who surrenders all—body, mind and all else—has no existence other than that of the beloved, who alone exists in him. Therefore greater than love is obedience, and greater than obedience is surrender. And yet, as words, all three can be summed up in one phrase—love-divine.

"One can find volumes and volumes of prose and poetry about love, but there are very, very few persons who have found love and experienced it. No amount of reading, listening and learning can ever tell you what love is. Regardless of how much I explain love to you, you will understand it less and less if you think you can grasp it through the intellect or imagination.

"Hafiz describes the bare truth about love when he says:

" 'Janab-e ishqra dargah basi bala tar-azaq'l ast;
Kasi in astan busad kay jan der astin darad.'

" 'The majesty of love lies far beyond the reach
of intellect; only one who has his life up his
sleeve dares kiss the threshold of love.'

"The difference between love and intellect is something like that between night and day: they exist in relation to one another and yet as two different things. Love is real intelligence capable of realizing truth; intellect is best suited to know all about duality, which is born of ignorance and *is* entirely ignorance. When the sun rises, night is transformed into day. Just so, when love manifests, not-knowing (ignorance) is turned into conscious-knowing (knowledge).

"In spite of the difference between a keenly intelligent person and a very unintelligent person, each is equally capable of experiencing love. The quality which determines one's capacity for love is not one's wit or wisdom, but one's readiness to lay down life itself for the beloved, and yet remain alive. One must, so to speak, slough off body, energy, mind and all else, and become dust under the feet of the beloved. This dust of a lover who cannot remain alive without God—just as an ordinary man cannot live without breath—is then transformed into the beloved. Thus man becomes God."

At this, Baba stopped briefly and looked around at the intently listening audience. Then he plunged ahead more pointedly.

"Listen to love without philosophizing about it. None present here loves me as I ought to be loved. If all of you had such love, none of you would be left before me. You would all have realized God and we would all have become the *One* which we all are in reality and in eternity.

"You accept me as being simultaneously God and man, the highest of the high and the lowest of the low; but by *accepting* me to be THAT, you do not *know* me to be THAT. To know me as I am you must become conscious of my *real state*, and for that you must love me as I love you.

"The *mandali* who have been with me through thick and thin all these years are fully prepared for love of me to lay down their very lives at such a sign from me. Yet even they do not love me as I love them. If they did, then they would have become one with my oneness, which in reality is the oneness of us all.

"It is love alone which can lift the veil between a lover and the beloved. Believe me, you and I remain divided by nothing but the veil of you, yourself.

"What does 'you yourself' mean? When you feel hungry, you say, 'I am hungry'. If unwell, you say, 'I am not well'. When you say, 'Baba, I slept well', 'I am happy', 'My son died', 'They abused me', 'I feel miserable', 'Those things are mine', it is this 'I', 'me' and 'mine' which is the veil.

"It is only because of the veil of the false ego lying between us that you find yourselves involved in so many difficulties, troubles and worries, all of which disappear automatically when touched by the reality of love. When the curtain of your limited 'I' is lifted—and it can only disappear through love, and love alone—you realize unity and find me as your real self, *i.e.* God. I say so because it is only I, everywhere. There is really nothing like you.

"It requires cycles and cycles for one to be enlightened with real knowledge of self, or God. Therefore millions upon millions of so-called births and deaths on your part are not sufficient in themselves to lift the veil of your limited 'I'. It can be removed through love though in infinitely less than a split second.

"All those who are true ascetics, yogis, *walis, pirs* and saints are not necessarily God-realized. Only real lovers of God, irrespective of sex, are the true *mardan-e-Khuda* (men of God). Even from among a hundred thousand such men of God, though, perhaps only one will become God-realized after many cycles.

"Both Hakim Sanai and Moulana Rumi say the same thing in different words: 'Daor ha bayad ke ta yak mard Sahib-dil shawad', and 'Salha mardaan burdand intezer, ta yakira barshud az sad hazar'. That is:

" 'It needs many cycles for just one advanced soul to be realized.'

" 'When for many years man has longed for God-realization, one out of a hundred thousand such men of God, achieves it.'

"No amount of rites, rituals, ceremonies, worship, meditation, penance and remembrance can produce love in themselves. None of these are necessarily a sign of love. On the contrary, those who sigh loudly and weep and wail have yet to experience love. Love sets on fire the one who finds it. At the same time it seals his lips so that no smoke comes out.

"Love is meant to be experienced and not disclosed. What is displayed is not love. Love is a secret which is meant to remain a secret save for the one who receives it and keeps it.

"To love Baba in hopes of achieving health, wealth, betterment of family and friends, etc., is to love all these and not Baba. Such love cannot be compared with that of Adi and his wife Roda Dubash, and Nariman and Navrozji Dadachanji and their family members. They can be justly proud of their love for me which remained unshaken in the face of tragic accidents which cost the lives of their dear ones among my dear ones. As a matter of fact Nozher (Dadachanji) has come to me, as all those do who remember me while breathing their last.*

---

* Baba tells the story of Nozher later in the week.

"Love God and become God. I have come to receive your love and to give you mine, as I have already said. If you love me you will find me. Unless you love me, you can never find me. Do not think that you can never love me or that you can find no time to love me. I often say that I want your love. I mean it, because that is *all* that I want from you. Therefore I always tell you to love me more and more.

"I have also said that you cannot love me as I ought to be loved. To do that you must first receive the gift of my love, and that gift depends upon absolute pleasure on my part in giving you just a glimpse of the reality of my self. No one can possess love by any means other than as a gift. But I give love to self and accept it myself. The giving of love knows no law save love, which by itself is the law which governs all other laws of nature.

"It is always infinitely easy for me to give—but it is not always equally easy for you to receive—the gift of my love."

Baba paused once again and his eyes moved over the faces turned patiently, quietly, even sadly towards him. Not one visage in the room indicated that the thinking, feeling, aspiring man behind it interpreted the master's words in any manner other than he intended them: that the great goal of each human being is the realization of his own oneness with God, and that there can be no greater, no more necessary boon in achieving this goal than the love and the grace of a Perfect Being who is already one with God.

"Sometimes it is also infinitely impossible for one to receive that love," Eruch interpreted Baba's wide, sweeping gestures as he continued his intense preoccupation with the subject. "That is why Kabir says that some ask for it and do not get it, some get it unasked, and yet there are those who are unable to receive it even when it is offered to them.

"I am ever prepared to give the gift, but you must also prepare yourself to receive it. That requires real daring.

"Even in ordinary animal and human love there are upper reaches in which a mother is sometimes negligent of her own life for the sake of her offspring. Or a man can remain without sleep or food or thoughts of lust for days due to his restlessness, born of true love for a woman.

"Divine love is the fire which not only eliminates all kinds of cold, but also all sorts of imagined heat. For example, amongst the very, very few who possess such love is the *mast* * known as Dhondiba at Kolahpur. Though exposed to the rigours of heat, cold and rain through all the seasons, his body remains healthy, well-fleshed and strong. The fire is burning within him unknown even to those in his surroundings. His mind has no link with his body. Love pervades him from head to foot.

"Although love is beyond intellect, there are innumerable points about it which can still be explained by reason and brought within its grasp. But in finality, I remain; everything else is zero, and I am the only reality.† That reality cannot be reached in illusion through illusions, and there can be no hide-and-seek about love. When God becomes man (Avatar, Buddha, Christ, Rasool), He can bestow both love and obedience upon and accept the surrenderance of any and all individuals.

"I say all this as much to those who have been living with or for me all these years, as to those who are only with me now for this *sahvas*. I tell you honestly that if you obey me honestly you will become me—your own real self.

"This is not the first time I have said this. For ages past I have been telling all to leave everything and to follow me. That means to obey me so that you may have conscious experience of me. Now is the time when those who obey me will realize me.

"Obedience which is greater than love is the one hundred per cent obedience described by Hafiz:

" 'Mazan ze chuno-chara dum kay banda-e-muqbil,
Be-jan qubul kunad, her sukhan kay Sultan guft.'

"Broadly translated, this means 'Carry out every command of the master without question, as is becoming to a lucky slave.'

"About thirty years ago, before I started observing my silence, and when Meherabad was a colony of hundreds of seekers, servers

---

* *Mast:* a spiritually preoccupied and divinely intoxicated person.

† Not in the sense of Meher Baba as a person, but as one who is one with God. Baba's constant theme is that all men are really one with God, and therefore inevitably one with all God-realized beings, and with each other as well if they only knew it.

and sufferers who lived in the *ashrams* (abodes), asylums (shelters), schools, dispensaries and the hospital here at that time, a visitor came to surrender to me. He could not help weeping when I told him that what he intended was very, very difficult since surrenderance means obedience, and obedience has but one meaning, and that is to obey.

"He said he knew that, and was prepared to obey me implicitly. When I inquired if he would cut his own child to pieces if I asked him to do so, he even agreed to that. But when I asked him to remove his clothes and walk about naked in the streets of Ahmednagar he began to protest and ultimately went his way.

"I am not going to ask you to do that," Baba hastened to tell the audience. "I never expect anyone to do the impossible."

Chuckles of understanding greeted this comment. A reshuffling of cramped limbs took place as a small buzz of background conversation vented the feeling of a number of individuals to their neighbors that there was not much purpose in seeking a great master if the aspirant could not face even such a first test as this.

Baba's smile faded and he began to look serious again.

"Now that you are in my *sahvas* you should know all about my habits and about my behavior to the *mandali* who live with me. I love Kaikobad (one of the resident *mandali*) and often bow down to him. Whenever I go out on *mast* tours or for other congregations I ask Kaikobad to lay his hand on my head and bless me. Recently at Satara he wept and protested, but I told him to continue to obey me to the point of kicking me should I ask him to do so.

"Kaikobad has been with me for twelve years. He has his family. They are staying on Meherabad hill.* He has dedicated everything to me and I have accepted him. He belongs to the Parsi (Zoroastrian) priest class, and hence he is also called Dastoor, which means 'a priest'. And he is a real priest. He sees Baba as Baba is to be seen, and he takes Baba's blessing as blessings are to be taken.

---

* A separate group of buildings about one-half mile from the collection in which the *sahvas* programs were being held. During this time they were occupied, in addition to the staff, by Francis Brabazon, the distinguished Australian poet, and the narrator, who were the only occidentals present at the *sahvas* programs.

"He has also been silently repeating Baba's name one hundred thousand times every twenty-four hours all these years. He had the first glimpse of Divinity at Meherabad in 1946. Again on August 31, 1953 he experienced at Dehra Dun such bliss that he was on the point of dropping his body. Now he says he can see glimpses of my reality whenever he wishes.

"At such moments he sees even a dark room lit up with such brilliance that compared with it the brilliance of the sun is nothing. Then in that light he sees me. That is no miracle performed by me. I cannot do that myself. I know only one thing, that I am everywhere and in everything.

"Despite all that, Kaikobad has yet to realize God. He is on the path, and he has to go on and on. He often tells me that he is enjoying my grace, and I always tell him—and I mean it—that it is his love for me that gives him the wonderful experiences of the path. Even though glimpses, his experiences give him deep bliss and the unshakeable conviction that I am his master. Therefore he will carry out any of my orders promptly and cheerfully.

"Kaikobad," Baba gestured as he looked towards the back of the audience, "stand up."

A slim, gentle-faced man stood up about two-thirds of the way back in the hall.

"Is not what I have said true?" Baba queried.

"Yes, Baba, everything you have said is exactly true," Kaikobad replied, and looking for a moment at Baba to see if anything further was demanded of him, he sat down again.

"Whatever I say," Baba resumed, "I say it in all sincerity. Unquestioning obedience to me, without consciously knowing me, will bring you nearest to me. But it is impossible to obey me literally and spontaneously. If I were in your place, I myself would not be able to do that.

"The best thing for you would be to obey me cheerfully. In any case, though, to obey me now when you have not yet consciously experienced my greatness is in itself a great thing. Much of the value of obedience is lost once conviction is transformed into actual, conscious knowledge of my reality. That is the purpose for which you have been called.

"Obedience is greater than all the spiritual experiences, but obedience for show is worse than no obedience.

"Even if one among you succeeds in loving me and obeying me, the purpose of the *sahvas* will be amply, even fully served. Otherwise, instead of my *sahvas*, you will have enjoyed a week's picnic.

"Now it is time for you all to have your midday meal. Eat well, rest after lunch, and all be here at two o'clock." Baba rose from his chair and strode at once from the hall and out into a small separate hut which had been fitted up with a small couch and a few toilet articles for his use.

The busily chattering throng remaining in the hall swirled into small knots, large knots, dreamily-moving individuals intent on not talking, and a few who instantly set off about their business. Soon the hall began to empty as nature added its reminder to Baba's injunction to eat. At last only the muffled clatter and laughter of scores of light-hearted persons eating and joking could be heard.

Even in late fall and winter—for this was Friday, November 4, 1955—a brief rest in the heat of the day feels good in this part of India, although its greater altitude and scant rainfall lessen the discomfort experienced in the lower coastal areas. The excitement of being with Baba was not enough to keep more than a handful of the *sahvasis* from relaxing and taking a brief nap after lunch.

Long before the designated time, however, the majority were back on their feet and awaiting Baba's return. Soon the nature of the afternoon's agenda became apparent. A large tent had been erected some days previously at the front and to the right of the great hall. It was open on two sides and closed to the rear towards Arangaon and to the west. Its dirt floor was well covered with carpets and liberally sprinkled with cushions. At the enclosed end had been built a low platform, and on this was placed more carpeting and a chaise longue.

In and around this tent began to accumulate a motley collection of villagers from Arangaon. Here Baba was to receive the families of the small army of workers required to staff Meherabad for the *sahvas* programs. Most of these people had grown up in Baba's aura, as the four decades of his work had often centered at Meherabad.

To these villagers he was more than a great religious figure, for that would have commanded only veneration and a shyness born of awe. Each time Baba's car paused briefly at the railroad tracks when driving between the *sahvas* headquarters and Meherabad-on-the-hill, or slowed to negotiate a hairpin turn on the dirt road near the village, scores of delighted children and mothers clasping the inevitable infant to their shoulders reached out with shouts to touch the car or even the man himself. This was a person they loved.

Now, many of them were to have the rare privilege of passing singly in front of him, to be smiled at by him, possibly even touched by him. The almost ecstatic veneration of the Indian for his religious master is something foreign to the western mind. Inevitably it involves a sacrifice of part, even all, of the self. To the occidental this appears dangerous, and in the East where it is often practiced it is still not without its dangers. Regardless, the Indian feels instinctively the necessity for spiritual progress, and to accomplish it he works out a relationship to the teacher which has no exact counterpart in the occident.

These people of Arangaon, simple, poor, sometimes uncouth, often tattered, collected in the tent in anticipation of a high point in their daily life. Many of the small children were clothed only to their navel, and gaping holes in clothing often rendered questionable any real contribution either towards protection or modesty. But they were in their very best, and their cleanest, and they had scrubbed their bodies and faces.

The tent filled tighter and tighter; people began to spill up along the sides and over onto the front veranda of the hall and even into the sun beyond the shadow of the tent. Each worker at Meherabad must have discovered that day that he had close relatives whose ties of blood he had never suspected before.

A small chorus of male adults and boys began to sing to the accompaniment of bells. The air grew tense in anticipation. At the extreme far corner of the tent a magnificent appearing Hindu woman appeared with several young girls who were apparently in her care. This was Godavari Mai, beautiful, gentle, shy, the chosen disciple of the late great Hindu Perfect Master, Upasni Maharaj, now administering his *ashram* at Sakori.

As the singing voices wove in and out of the complex tonal system of Indian music and the bells jingled even more insistently, Baba

appeared at one end of the tent and made his way with characteristic speed to the platform. Hands were stretched up to him as he
passed. A swirl of villagers threatened to draw him in like an under-
tow, and would have absorbed him but for the firm action of his
mandali.

Eruch bawled out orders in the local vernacular (Marathi), and
a long line of women and very young children formed to Baba's left
along one side of the tent. This was the receiving line, and no king
receiving his court ever had more excited attention. Before the line
started to pass in front of him, however, Baba invited Godavari Mai
to sit with him on the platform, and her girls to stand at her side to
the rear.

As Godavari Mai took her place at Baba's side a sense of magnificent spirit passed between these two people and swept out and over
the rapt audience. No words can record the air of peace, beauty, devotion and regard which thundered in complete silence between
these two. Why try? Words break their backs in trying to carry the
slightest part of the load describing what occurred that warm afternoon under the tent near Ahmednagar.

Black faces, dark faces, light faces, everywhere the great round
brown eyes of the Indian woman, so startling in their size and their
framing of long black lashes and thin pencilled eyebrows. Fat-
stomached, lean-stomached, fully-clothed, half-clothed children
clutched to a shoulder or carefully led along the edge of the low
platform. Anything to show one's devotion—a garland, a bouquet, a
small wilted flower, a ripe fruit.

The closer to horizontal, the closer to expression of one's feeling
of veneration. But this could not be, for Baba had long ago declared
that greetings should be given upright—a function of the heart, of
feeling—not horizontal. This was the one point of true confusion in
a vast mass of physical confusion, with straining *mandali* trying
mightily to keep the pressing, eager crowd in line.

Before each villager was to greet Baba, she was reminded that she
was not to bow down nor prostrate herself, nor try to touch her forehead to his feet, those age-old symbols of veneration for the royalty
of heaven. Yet, as each woman found herself actually in the presence
of this deeply loved man, she became unstrung and instinct took

over. Finally the *mandali* gave up trying to keep the women upright and contented themselves with preserving order in the excited line.

At last the women and girls and small children had passed, and it was the turn of the old men, and then of the stripling boys, and finally of the workers themselves. And then it was done and the villagers returned to their homes and Godavari Mai and the girls left for Sakori and Baba drove off to Meherazad near Pimpalgaon. There was a beautiful sunset that night; the loosely scattered clouds scattered back to earth the pinks and the scarlets and the purples for more than two hours in a colored symphonic postlude.

The night crept on, the lights winked on at the *sahvas* quarters, and the lamplighter lit the gas mantle lamps at Meherabad-on-the-hill. Pandu, the attendant, trotted whistling up the stairs to turn down the covers on the two guest beds, and the night-watchman took up his seat at the front gate and began the periodic dry cough with which he accented the night.

"Well, did you enjoy the day, Don?"

"I've never known anything like it—the morning of discourses and sporadic horseplay, the afternoon of a kind and depth of human devotion I've never seen before. It's very difficult for me to comprehend it all, to be a part of it and not feel that it's happening a million miles away and I'm looking at it through a giant telescope."

"Yes, one has that feeling a bit at first, but it wears away and then you wonder how it is possible to live any other way."

"I can't help but think back to Baba's discussion of obedience, Francis. It goes so far beyond anything I've ever worked out or even speculated about that I get lost."

"It is rather hard for a westerner. Our trouble is that we have absolutely no idea of the use of obedience as a spiritual tool, at least the kind of obedience that is really important.

"It makes me think of a story I once read of a great king, Mahmud of Ghazni, who was also a spiritual aspirant. He had one slave, Ayaz, whom he appeared to prefer above all his great courtiers. This created some jealousy in his court, so he decided one day to demonstrate to his nobles just why he preferred this slave to all others.

"Mahmud had two heavy stones placed before his throne, and

on one was laid the finest jewel in his possession. He asked one of his great nobles to come before him, and then told him to pick up the second stone and smash it down on the jewel.

"The courtier was thunderstruck, and when he had recovered his speech he began diplomatically to try to argue the king out of his decision. Finally Mahmud told him to go away, and called for a second great noble who was in the court.

"Again the same command was given, with the same results. Once more the king ordered the reluctant noble away and called his slave. This time, on Mahmud's order, Ayaz promptly picked up the second stone and brought it instantly smashing down on the first. The precious jewel was shattered to dust.

"To test Ayaz still further, Mahmud berated him soundly before the court for having destroyed the magnificent gem. Finally, after Mahmud had run out of breath, Ayaz, who had stood quietly all the time, bowed his head and said, 'The fault is mine, my lord.' "

CHAPTER 3

The Toe of the Master

As Baba came into the hall that second morning of the first week—or was it the second week, or the third or the fourth?—there were more garlands, and insistent chorused shouts of "Avatar Meher Baba —ki-jai." First one cohesive knot would give the cheer, and one or two more garlands would be placed about Baba's neck. Then another group in another section of the hall would chorus out like a cheering section at a football game, and more garlands would be hung.

After this had continued for some minutes, and several slight diplomatic pressures on Baba's part had not served to quiet the enthusiasm, it became apparent that he had made up his mind to firm action. He raised both arms high in the air and at once the hubbub subsided.

"Compared with the essentials for the path, the three most unimportant things are to garland me, to bow down to me and to sing in my praise or perform an *arti*. These are not necessarily the signs of love for God.

"I know well that you garland me with love. This is a good idea when we first meet. But why do it every day? I have only two coats of the color (pink) I like most, and one is already spoiled by repeated garlanding.

"Do not waste any more time in garlanding me tomorrow. Let us not waste money, and let me not be burdened with garlands.

"Don't shout 'Avatar Meher Baba—ki-jai' every time I come in and go out of the hall. What is the use of that? Keep shouting, but do so within your hearts so that only you and not others may hear."

Like abashed schoolboys the group sat looking straight ahead, unwilling to catch a glance from the corner of a neighbor's eye.

Momentarily the air hung tense with the light reprimand, while Baba looked keenly over the hunched heads and forward-leaning shoulders.

"Did you sleep well last night?" he asked.

"Yes, Baba," was the general reply.

"Who did not sleep last night?"

Slowly one man stood up near the door, heavy brown scarf wrapped tightly about throat and head, eyes inflamed, nose running. His diagnosis was promptly read by almost three hundred pairs of eyes.

Another, and then another, then several, rose to their feet.

"Why didn't you sleep last night?"

"Because I was so happy to be near you again, Baba."

"And why didn't you sleep?"

"My stomach was upset, Baba. I think I ate too much dinner because I was so glad to see all of my old friends again."

"And you?"

"Some of the Parsis were playing cards and I couldn't sleep. I do not think they should play cards when they are here to learn of God from you."

Baba was prompt with his reply.

"What has playing cards to do with one's love and longing for God? Playing with cards is better than playing with the whole of life. Shams Tabrezi and his famous disciple Moulana Rumi were both very fond of playing chess. Shams' greatest work was done at the end of a game of chess with Rumi.

"When Rumi lost the game he could not help crying out to Shams, 'I have lost'.

"Then and there, with the words, 'No, you have won', Shams gave Rumi instant God-realization.

"But come now," Baba continued as he again looked searchingly at the audience, "many of you look sleepy this morning. Once more, quite honestly, who all did not sleep last night?"

Under such persistent prodding, several others rose, among them a slender boy dressed in white shirt and white shorts and with an American style crew-cut.

"Why did you not sleep?"

There was a struggle for emotional control in the handsome face of the youngster, but finally he placed his hand over his eyes and wept. "I could not, Baba, because all night I could not help remembering the happy times in the past when you used to stay at Dehra Dun," he choked out between his quiet sobs.

Baba looked gently at him for a moment, and then turned his attention to another heavy-set, intelligent-looking fellow of middle age.

"And you, what kept you awake?"

"I did not sleep because I was remembering you all the time," was the simple reply.

Staring abstractedly over their heads, Baba seemed to be thinking momentarily about the various answers given to him. Then recollecting himself he motioned to them to sit down and without a moment's hesitation looked straight at a very thin fellow, perhaps in his early twenties, who sat just in front and to the right.

"Why do you look so pale and tired this morning?" Eruch translated.

"I admit that I do not feel well and I did not get a good sleep," the pale one replied as he rose reluctantly to his feet.

"Why did you not rise to your feet when the others did?"

"I am a young man, Baba, and I did not want to complain like an old one."

Baba shook his head. "It is natural for all those who have bodies to develop ailments. Both young and old alike can catch colds. Youth in itself is no protection against disease. In exceptional cases, such as the one who becomes God-conscious and does not return to normal consciousness, such a one remains naturally immune to contagion. But having come down to your level, even I can catch cold and become ill as naturally as you can. You must take proper treatment." *

Thereupon the subject was dropped for that morning. Throughout the *sahvas* weeks, however, the most enduring daily theme was the meticulous questioning of the groups and of individuals about how they felt and how they had slept. At first one attributed this to the extraordinary attention of an extraordinary man, but soon it became clear that Baba was concerned that careful attention be paid to health at all times.

Part of the reason for this became apparent when Baba himself

---

* For more detailed discussion, see *God Speaks*, Meher Baba, Dodd, Mead, pp. 228–229. Also Appendix II of the present work.

began to develop mild cold symptoms after having been in close contact for days with hundreds of coughing, sneezing men. Frequently he would take advantage of a slight pause to clear his throat with a faint rasping noise, the only physical sound which he was heard to make. Even his hearty laughter was silent.

How did this silence affect those about him? After a first jolt, the fact was lost under a towering mass of thought and feeling. Many have remarked on the extraordinary fact that after a few brief moments of surprise one never misses speech with Baba.

But he seemed to have an impish problem on his mind. He brightened, a flickering smile playing about his mouth, and looked towards the two doors of the hall, trying to find someone. At last he gave up the search and began to gesture.

"In the basic spirit of my *sahvas* with you, what I now tell you I tell as to members of one family. This morning I had a tussle with Pendu in my room before I came to the hall. Pendu has been bearing the brunt of planning, executing and maintaining the various arrangements necessary for the *sahvas* program. Originally it was decided to invite only one hundred and fifty participants each week at a total estimated cost of twenty thousand rupees * and to spend an additional ten thousand rupees for the poor.

"I had agreed with Pendu not to allow any changes to be made in the original plan. But letters and telegrams soon began to pour in and the number of participants began to swell as the appeals were irresistible. My lovers in Andhra have proved themselves real workers in my cause. My name has become a household word in many parts there. The same is true of those who love me and work for me in the Hamirpur area where men, women and children go about singing songs of love for me during their daily lives, whether in the fields or at home or going to school.

"When the number one hundred and fifty was initially increased to two hundred, there was a preliminary tussle between Pendu and me. At that time he reduced the money to be spent on the four poor programs during the *sahvas* month from ten thousand to only five thousand rupees. Now the number of participants in each of the three remaining *sahvas* groups is likely to exceed two hundred and

---

* About $4,500.

fifty. In one case the total may reach a figure of three hundred. Due to the increase, Pendu must, among other things, have the dormitory extended and obtain more cots.

"Pendu now refuses to be responsible for sparing more than one thousand rupees for the poor. But see how things adjust themselves somehow. Nozher, who died and has come to me, has left one thousand for the poor. I have also accepted one thousand for the poor from the balance of funds which the Andhra Reception Committee had left from the mass *darshan* * programs there. This brings the total to three thousand. Let us try to knock a thousand more out of Pendu in order to complete four thousand rupees for the four poor programs. Have someone fetch Pendu from the office so that we can put this matter convincingly before him."

A swarm of chatter arose from the audience as a messenger departed posthaste from the hall and raced to the open office door at the end of the veranda. Almost immediately Pendu appeared, a handkerchief muffled over his nose to prevent spreading of the heavy cold he had contracted just as the *sahvas* programs were starting.

"You sent for me, Baba?" he asked.

"Yes, Pendu, we have been discussing the money which is to be used for the four poor programs during the *sahvas* month. I have endeavored to explain your difficulty in trying to keep aside enough for these poor programs while every day more letters and telegrams pour in asking that the senders be allowed to come," Baba explained. Then he outlined further the amounts received from Nozher and the Andhra committee, pointing out that the sum for the four weeks' poor programs now totaled three thousand rupees. Even in the misery of his cold, with Baba's intent look of urgency and scores of soft brown Indian eyes upon him, Pendu knew he hadn't a chance to resist the strategic nutcracker in which he was caught.

"Pendu, do you think that you could spare just one thousand rupees more from your funds so we may then have four thousand rupees for the four weeks, and that will be enough?" Baba looked his persuasive best.

"It will be difficult as you know, Baba, but if no additional persons are allowed to come, I will do it for you somehow," Pendu acquiesced,

---

* A spiritual blessing given by a glance or touch.

feeling that by this further sacrifice he had at least won public recognition of the fact that the size of the groups couldn't be allowed to grow any more.

"Thank you, Pendu," Baba smiled. "The Marathi group is the last to come. If need be I will give them such interesting discourses that they will feel well satisfied with the cheapest food for the week. I know the trick of it." Then he turned his gaze back from Pendu to the audience.

"When I tell you things like this, do not forget, as I often tell you, that under all circumstances I always remain what I really am. Since for all practical purposes I am amongst you, I also remain practical about everything and take care of the most minute details. I have asked Pendu and Adi to send to all participants in my *sahvas* a copy of the complete accounting of expenses taken from the thirty thousand some odd (rupees) contributed towards the *sahvas* weeks."

With this, Baba rose and signaled that it was time for the mid-morning break. No game of seven tiles was proposed this time, however, and in a few moments the major part of the group had left the hall while Baba disappeared through a distant doorway.

The day was already warm, and scarfs and sweaters began to be peeled off and the more usual light Indian dress came into display. Some of the sharp air of excitement had disappeared and conversation was more normal, even slightly lethargic, as the participants rested in the assurance of three and one-half days yet to come.

A light drone of voices rose from the cluster of white stuccoed buildings, occasionally bejeweled by small metallic clanks ringing from the kitchens or the dormitories, or even from the belled oxen and water buffalo in the surrounding country. Like waves on a seashore on a quiet, sunny day, the peace of India lapped up on the white sand of men's souls and ran back again into the mother sea, abrading softly, polishing slowly, sometimes rising, sometimes receding, occasionally thundering in stormy insistence.

Through all of the undertone of nature working in harmony with the ancient heritage of a land of spiritual values there ran another theme of greater urgency. This was the personality of Meher Baba, which quickened the vital current and lent to it a sense that something of great importance was happening *today*. Come and look quickly, and feel, and open up your hearts, and then think of what you have seen and felt, for like the flash of lightning in the heavens it may be gone in the next instant.

An eddy formed in the peaceful buzz which could not be lost. There was motion somewhere, significant motion, and the shimmering pool of sound began to ripple and move back and forth between its shores to find the source of disturbance. As if drawn inevitably to its center, the viscous mass of *sahvasis* began to flow back to the hall. As they stared in through the doorways they saw the reason for their unconscious disturbance. Meher Baba was pacing back and forth with rapid, determined stride at one end of the hall.

It was an interesting performance. It drew the curious onlookers like a loadstone, and yet made them self-conscious with the feeling that perhaps they were watching some private function to which they had no right. A few of the bravest slipped out of their sandals and slid in through the door, quiet and attentive, as if watching a ceremony of deepest significance. The others contented themselves with watching through the doorways, uncertain of the proprieties of the situation.

At last Baba finished. He loosened his light white coat and handed it to a waiting pair of hands. Clad now only in his loose white *sadra* and his full white trousers, his face and skin glowed with a soft pinkness, having come just to the point of a light sweat. He sank down in his large armchair and relaxed.

"Some of you may be thinking that while engrossed externally in walking, Baba was engaged internally in his works on the spiritual planes. Actually I was merely exercising to help my digestion and feel fresh." The great mystery was solved.

As if by magic the message seemed to be intuited everywhere that Baba was again in his seat, and the doors were filled with the returning throng. One fine looking student from the University of Poona went over to Baba's side and began a low, earnest discussion with him. It seemed that one of his university friends, a great admirer of Baba but not one of those formally invited for the programs, had just arrived in his car and had asked for permission to remain over the week end.

Baba looked serious, no doubt caught in his own web of an earlier weaving. Looking carefully around first to see if Pendu might be a witness to his iniquity, Baba finally raised his hands in resignation and nodded his acquiescence. The student slipped through the door and in a moment returned with a tall, lanky companion with camera and light meter hung around his neck. The two blended inconspicuously among those sitting back to the rear. Baba cleared his throat lightly, the audience quieted and the gestures started.

"Rest assured, I definitely know from my living experience that God is the one and only reality, and that all else is illusion. All that you see and hear at this moment—this hall, our being in each other's presence, these explanations which I give and you hear, and even my incarnation as the Avatar—all this is a dream. Every night you go to sleep and have different kinds of dreams, yet every morning you wake up to experience anew the same old dream that you have been dreaming since your birth into your present life in illusion.

"You will say, 'Baba, we are wide awake; we actually see you sitting before us; we can and do follow what you are explaining to us.' But you will admit that you would say the same thing to me if, in a dream, you found that you were near me and heard me telling you that all you felt, saw and heard was a dream.

"As long as you do not wake up from a dream, you are dream-bound to feel it to be stark reality. A dream becomes a dream only when you wake up; only then do you tell others that the life you lived in the dream was just a dream. Good or bad, happy or unhappy, in reality the dream is then recognized as having been absolutely nothing.

"Therefore I repeat that, although you are now sitting before me and hearing me, you are not really awake. You are actually sleeping and dreaming. I say this because I am simultaneously awake in the real sense * and yet dreaming—with one and all—the dreams which all dream.

"All your pleasures and difficulties, your feelings of happiness and misery, your presence here and your listening to these explanations, all are nothing but a vacant dream on your part and mine. There is this one difference: I also consciously know the dream to be a dream, while you feel that you are awake.

---

* *I.e.* one with God.

"When you really wake up you will know at once that what you felt to be wakefulness was just dreaming. Then you will realize that you and I are and always have been one in reality. All else will then disappear, just as your ordinary dreams disappear on waking. Then they not only cease to exist, but they are found never to have really existed.

"From birth to death you keep on growing. First you are young; then you grow old and die without knowing or caring from whence you came or whither you go. From 'Who am I?' to 'I am God' is just one long, long dream covering ages and ages in time. But this too is found never to have existed in the eternity and infinitude of your own existence, at the moment you realize your real self, or God.

"Every individual here and elsewhere is the same one, ever-indivisible God. I say this because I am responsible for the whole creation.* If I am not here, then not only will you not be here but the whole of creation with all its gross, subtle and mental spheres will not be here. In short, everything exists because I exist.

"In your case also the whole of creation exists because you exist. When you sleep soundly, then for you everything—body, mind, world and the universe—vanishes and is absorbed in your sound-sleep state, the most-original, beyond-beyond state of God. Then your consciousness, tired of focusing on the illusion of duality, is at rest within you.

"After being refreshed in the most-original, beyond-beyond state of God, your consciousness plunges you first into the dreams-in-sleep, and then you wake up once again within the dream of creation. This dream of creation emanates again and again from you and for you.

"This process of repetitive sleeping-dreaming-awakening is a result of your inability to wake up in your sound-sleep state (*i.e.* conscious union with God). Therefore alternately you remain asleep or keep

---

* It must be born constantly in mind that, once one grants the reality of God-realization or union with God, it follows immediately that such a God-realized individual would be speaking the simple truth when he said that all of creation flowed from him, that he was responsible for the whole of creation, and that all creation was one in him. This holds equally for the Avatar, despite the presumably different mechanics lying back of His oneness with God. The ensuing statement therefore is a simple development of the logic of this essential fact of oneness.

dreaming either the dreams-in-sleep or the dreams of creation.

"It is only when you wake up in the true sense (God-realization) that you find that you alone (God) exist and that all else is nothing. Only after cycles and cycles of time can one attain one's own conscious state of God and find that one's infinite consciousness is eternally free of all illusion of duality.

"The whole of creation is a play of thoughts: the outcome of the mind. It is your own mind which binds you, and it is also the mind which is the means of your freedom. You are eternally free. You are not bound at all.

"But you cannot realize your freedom by merely hearing this from me, because your mind contrives to entangle you in the illusion of duality. Therefore you only understand what I am telling you, and mere understanding cannot make you experience the truth which I tell you.

"For that truth, you must let your mind be halted and finally rooted out. Then, as soon as you see me as I really am, everything else will disappear and you will find yourself to be your own eternal and infinite self."

With this Baba signified that it was time to halt for lunch. He instructed everyone to relax after the midday meal so that they might be refreshed for the afternoon.

As he left the hall, Baba passed close to a thin, middle-aged man dressed in the loose, ochre-colored robe worn by ascetics, and known as a *kafni*. The unusual color caught his eye, and he seemed to think momentarily to penetrate through the robe to the man.

"What is this? Why do you wear the *kafni?*" he asked.

"I have put it on only for the occasion of the *sahvas* program, Baba," was the reply. Baba speculated a moment, weighing the answer thoughtfully.

"We have to give the shape and color of detachment to our hearts and not merely to the clothes we wear," he suggested gently and strode on through the door.

Lunch had hardly been eaten before a few stray persons returned to the hall. Among them was a young Parsi who sang and played the small harmonium. Soon the strains of devotional music floated out on the tepid midday air. Interest slowly agglomerated in the peaceful atmosphere, and by ones and twos and threes the *sahvasis* drifted into the hall. Occasionally all raised their voices in common acknowledgement of the greatness of God; more often the melody and words were original to the player, or even extemporized.

A thin, graying individual with deep-set eyes slipped in between the singer and the wall and picked up two small skin drums. Squatting, he placed one in front of his crossed legs and the other to his right. After a moment of flicking the surfaces to catch their tone, and gentle tapping of the wooden pegs on the sides which held the tension thongs, he too joined the tribute to the mystery of creation.

Often the drumming would grow wild and insistent, caught in the double intensity of the complex rhythm and the rapidly moving emotion of the inner man flowing through the channel of his art. Then, instantly, the crashing wave of feeling would be damped and the listener was caught in the antiphony of soft gentleness and quiet devotion.

Imperceptibly the sound of bells, like those on a winter sleigh, began to blend with the voice of the singer and the reedy tones of the hand harmonium and the complex beat of the drums. A very old man with long white hair and beard, peering behind his great heavy-lensed spectacles at nothing, had placed himself to the right of the sitting singer and was shaking a small set of bells bolted to a thin bar of steel. Even before the bells had been integrated, a fourth man joined the group. By common consent he began a long devotional song on the greatness of the master, while the absorbed audience clapped.

The performers were deeply engrossed in the moving strains and the alternately swelling and dying harmonies when Baba strode quietly into the room. At once the singer looked up, breaking the flow of his song of praise. With a short gesture Baba indicated that he should continue, and the melody began again while Baba clapped his hands in appreciative rhythm. Occasionally Baba would raise his head and shake it slightly, breathing heavily as he did so, as if from the immensity of the feeling.

When the hymn was over the quartette took up an extemporization on Baba's toe. Even this small part of the master's body was too much for the singer to encompass. It seemed that words, notes and rhythmic beat must explode in the effort to translate the feeling of the soul. On and on it went, the drum and bells stopping periodically as the harmonium alone strove to accompany the singer in his paean; at times the harmonium too was deserted as the voice soared on unaccompanied.

When it seemed that there was no way to drink in even one fraction of the infinite ocean of feeling inspired by the smallest toe of the master, Baba called the song to a halt.

"Kohiyar," he beckoned, "recite in your melodious voice the 'Banam-e-Yazdan' (In the Name of God Almighty)."

As Kohiyar's sonorous voice floated through the hall Baba rose from his seat and, folding his hands in front of him and with eyes almost closed, swayed slightly with the rhythm of the powerful prayer.

When it was ended, Baba remained standing and then began to gesture.

"For ages past I have been telling people to leave all and come to me. That alone is the way to liberation from all illusion. We always live in the present. From childhood to old age, we always live in the present. We forget the past because it is not there at all. There is always the eternal present.

"Even the great ones often fail to get a grip on eternity. At Hyderabad there is a well-known saint. His following runs into thousands, but even he has yet to find out truth. *Jisay pata laga hai uska pata kisiko nahin lagta* (NONE CAN KNOW THE ONE WHO HAS FOUND GOD)."

Then Baba sat down. For a few moments he preserved the characteristic pose of abstraction which usually served as a punctuation mark as he transferred from one subject to another. Then he began to gesture again while Eruch continued the task of clothing the graceful motions with a garment of words.

"Hearing is not equal to understanding. Understanding is not equal to conception. Conception is not equal to perception. Perception is not equal to experience. Experience is not equal to becoming God-realized. To realize God is to *become* God. This means consciously experiencing that you are God, for you are eternally God, but you do not know it. When God *becomes* man (Avatar) He understands completely why you do not know that you are God, and He knows how you can become THAT.

"There can be nothing like a rigid set of rules to outline the means by which you may be led to the one and only path to God-realization. This path lies through the subtle and mental spheres, which are independent of and 'above' * the gross sphere with its innumerable stars, suns, moons and worlds, including the earth.

"Whatever brings you nearer to the path and suits you best, is best for you, provided you are able to put it into practice whole-heartedly and in harmony with the natural bent of your mind. A good runner who remains indifferent to racing cannot make good progress, but a lame man who keeps on limping vigorously may soon arrive at the path. If it is not used properly the best car is virtually useless to the traveler, however concerned he may be to arrive at his destination.

"I have already told you that love for God and obedience to a master are beyond the reach of man on his own, and that complete surrender is almost impossible for him. The next best thing then is for man to purify his heart. This is also very difficult because every action, whether trivial or important, good or bad, has left its impression on his mind.

"Thus every human mind is a gigantic storehouse of accumulated and fast-changing impressions. How can one gain an adequate idea of these impressions left by innumerable actions—and particularly those born of anger, lust and greed—during the lengthy course of the evolution of man's consciousness through the progressive stages of the mineral, vegetable and animal kingdoms of life?

"The obvious remedies for this situation are to use no remedies. For example, if one engages in a secluded life of mere physical renunciation, one is more likely to drive underground than eliminate the dirt of impressions from one's mind. Under a false sense of external security born of the secluded life, the mind is apt to become weakened and so stop struggling. Then, instead of achieving freedom from the bindings of impressions, the mind is likely to succumb eventually to its impressions and thus develop greater bindings.

"By becoming physically free of the bindings created by the impressions in your mind, you have not rooted them out of your mind.

---

* In reality there is no "above" and no "below".

Although your *body* may be temporarily freed, as it is in the sound-sleep state, yet your *mind* remains bound by the impressions. Even when the body itself is dropped you do not become free, for your mind remains bound by the impressions which the mind has created.

"Even as the mind cannot be freed of bindings by mere physical renunciation, so the heart cannot be purified by mere mechanical following of the external forms and fads of religion. One must act on principles and not by rituals.

"For example, the essence of Zoroaster's teachings lies in the principles of good thoughts, good words and good deeds, and not in the multitude of rituals and ceremonies. These latter serve more as an escape from, rather than as an incentive to, the task of purifying the heart.

"In achieving good thoughts, good words and good deeds, one finds that good is not just something better than bad, nor merely the opposite of bad; and not-bad is not necessarily good. 'Good' and 'bad' are terms that reinforce illusory duality more than they remind one of divine unity. From the point of view of truth, thoughts, words and deeds are 'good' only when they are born of the longing for, or the love of, God, the one and only truth.

"Although born a Zoroastrian, all religions are the same to me insofar as they help men to come nearer and nearer to God, who is ever most near to man.

"It is better not to worship if your heart is not in it. Any prayer made mechanically in a spirit of show or ceremony is all a farce. It results in greater bindings through one's pretence to purity. Similarly, a self-imposed fast, if not observed through a sense of obedience or through love of truth, may make a clock the object of your fast through watching to see when it is time to stop. Such actions tighten more than they loosen the bindings of impressions.

"By not eating, you gather the impressions of 'not eating'. Doing or not doing anything—whether sleeping, staying awake or even breathing—creates impressions on your mind. Therefore you may fast indefinitely, hang yourself upside down or knock out your brains on a slab of stone, and yet not free your mind of its impressions.

"Why then should you necessarily give up eating, drinking, doing your duty to your wife and children and looking after the welfare of others? Such duties do not obstruct your way to the path at all. What *do* come in your way are the bindings which you create unnecessarily for yourself through attachment to the objects connected with those duties. You can own the world without being attached to it, so long as you do not allow yourself to be owned by any part of it.

"Suppose, for instance, that a man, in spite of doing his best, loses his family and is unable to obtain enough to eat for himself. If he remains unconcerned, this amounts to his having really given up both his family and eating.*

"A real fast for the mind is to have no thoughts at all, but ordinarily this is impossible. Knowingly or unknowingly, like breathing, thoughts keep coming and going, whether you are dreaming the dream of your life or the dreams in your sleep. You become completely free of thoughts only when you are in the state of sound sleep—the most-original beyond-beyond state of God. But in sound sleep you also lose consciousness. Your mind is then temporarily at rest, but not freed of its impressions.

"Let us soon finish these discussions, lest some of you slip right into the most-original state!

"The best way to cleanse the heart and prepare for the stilling of the mind is to lead a normal, worldly life. Living in the midst of your day-to-day duties, responsibilities, likes, dislikes, etc., will help you. All these become the very means for the purification of your heart. This natural, normal method depends for its success upon a clear idea of the force behind your thoughts, and the facts underlying your actions.

"The force behind your thoughts is the force of the impressions in your mind. The impressions are there due to your own previous actions. Actions are the cause of impressions and thoughts are but the expression of the impressions. This being true, the more you try to check your thoughts, the more you interfere with the natural process

---

* The thought of being unconcerned at the loss of one's family is repugnant to many western minds. However this must be framed in the context of a viewpoint which is convinced that the soul does not die, that it only moves along to its next phase of learning, that it is hindered rather than helped by sorrow on the part of the living, and that activity within a detached frame of mind is one of the greatest achievements to which one can aspire.

of their expression. Sooner or later, with the added force produced by suppression, the impressions are bound to express themselves completely.

"The truth of action is that every action, significant or insignificant, voluntary or involuntary, is at once impressed in turn upon your mind. Like a non-greasy stain, a light impression can be easily wiped out, but impressions caused by actions conceived in anger, lust or greed are hard to remove. In short, actions produce impressions, and impressions produce thoughts. Thoughts in turn tend to precipitate further action.

"For the purification of your heart, leave your thoughts alone, but maintain a constant vigil over your actions. When you have thoughts of anger, lust or greed, do not worry about them, and do not try to check them. Let all such thoughts come and go without putting them into action. Try to think counter-thoughts in order to discern, to discriminate, to learn, and above all to unlearn the actions which are prompted by your own impressions.

"It is better to feel angry sometimes than merely to suppress anger. You then have an opportunity to think about anger, its causes and its consequences. Although your mind may be angry, do not let your heart know it. Remain unaffected.

"If you never feel angry you will be like stone, in which form the mind is least developed. Similarly, if you never have lusty thoughts you cannot achieve the merit of having avoided lustful actions.

"Let the thoughts of anger, lust and greed come and go freely and unasked without putting them into words and deeds. Then the related impressions in your mind begin to wear out and become less and less harmful. But when you put such thoughts into action—whether overtly or secretly—you develop new impressions worse than those which are spent in the act. These new impressions root even more firmly in your mind.

"The fire of divine love alone can destroy all impressions once and for all. However, remembering me can keep down the impurities in the impressions in your mind, as alum catches hold of (flocculates) dirt in a vessel of turbid water. Therefore, when you feel angry or have lustful thoughts, remember Baba at once. Let my name serve as a net around you so that your thoughts, like mosquitoes, may keep buzzing around you and yet not sting you. In that manner you can prevent unwanted thoughts from turning into unwanted actions, and thus eventually bring your heart to the purification required for me to manifest therein.

"But it is not child's play to remember me constantly during your moments of excitement. If, in spite of being very angry, you refrain from expressing anger, it is indeed a great achievement. It means that when your mind becomes angry your heart does not know it, just as when your heart loves me your mind need not know it. In fact, your mind does not know that your heart loves when, prepared to give up life itself, you lead a life of day-to-day obedience and duty.

"You can also entrust your mind to me by remembering me or repeating my name in your heart as often as you can. Remember me so often that your mind is at a loss to find other thoughts to feed on.

"Although I am 'taking' my own name continuously, I have come to hear it repeated by my lovers, and even though I were deaf, I would hear it if you repeated it only once with all your heart in it. If you cannot remember me constantly, then always take (repeat, think of) my name before going to sleep and on waking up.

"At least remember to remember me when you breathe your last, and you will still come to me. But how will you remember at the last moment, unless you start to remember me right now?

"Kammu Baba, whom many revere as a saint in Bombay, recently sent me word asking to be relieved of his duties and to return unto me. I advised him also to take my name when breathing his last.

"In his last moments, Nozher took my name. So did my brother Jamshed and many others who have come to me. But it is only the heroes who come to me in their physical form. To these, death itself surrenders ultimately."

With these words Baba left off his gesticulations and gazed thoughtfully at the clock at the end of the hall. It was only four-thirty, but it had been a long, full day, with few interruptions in the flow of thought. Several times, in asides from the subject under discussion, he had given evidence of his impatience to be done with philosophizing. One sensed that his spirit raced behind the barrier of words, anxious to break through them and out into the untrammeled world of feeling.

"You have listened patiently today. I am eager to have done with these words and to finish what we must say during this week of *sahvas*. Then perhaps we can play games of marbles and listen to devotional music and do other things which are not as dreary as all this talking. So I have been anxious to finish these subjects which I have said (in the sheet of instructions) we might discuss during this week.

"Now you are tired from all this discoursing, and so I will leave you at five o'clock today."

Spontaneously a loud shout of "No" burst from the group.

"Very well," Baba smiled, "I will respect your wishes. I will not go at five o'clock but will depart from you now, at four-thirty."

Despite their concern, the audience howled with laughter at Baba's chicanery. "No, Baba, that's not what we meant," and "You *can't* do that, Baba," rose on every side.

In the general merriment Baba smiled and argued by gesture with several of the lead spokesmen. Finally a good-humored compromise was worked out. Five-thirty it was to be.

Baba motioned to the four musicians, and at once the audience hushed as devotional music filled the hall. Once again the rhythmic clapping of the audience kept time with the music and the men swayed to the surges of feeling in the song. There was an air of high good humor after the meaty discourse, punctuated by the recent sharp burst of humor.

By five o'clock Baba was on his feet and off on a brief inspection of the kitchens and the sleeping quarters. Here and there he would reach out for a brief scuffle with someone, much as a boy in his teens. A favorite trick was to raise his right arm high in a long, slow arc, then bring his hand crashing down into the grip of some grinning, tensed devotee. If the sting had not thrown the man completely off guard, a brief pushing and pulling ensued in which both parties tried to throw the other off balance.

Promptly at five-thirty Baba climbed into the blue car with the complement of *mandali* and they left for Meherazad to spend the night.

CHAPTER 4

Washing the Feet of the Poor

Penta shivered in the chill morning air as he served the grapefruit, cereal and eggs. Pandu scurried about in the background cleaning up after the morning showers, a scarf thrown about his neck and shoulders. There was suppressed excitement among the household staff to get the two *sahibs* off in good time for the full day ahead. Baba was to wash the feet of two hundred and fifty poor that morning, one for each member of the *sahvas*. Then moving pictures would be taken to show over television in the United States, demonstrating how *God Speaks* had been dictated on an alphabet board.

Finally, in the afternoon, the ashes of an American devotee were to be buried in a brief ceremony here at Meherabad-on-the-hill, followed by an inspection of Baba's tomb and the other buildings. Pandu's wife, who ground the herbs and washed the pots in the kitchen, peeked at the two *sahibs* around a corner of the shrubbery, completely overcome with curiosity after having spent four days hidden in the kitchen.

The sound of occasional shouts and laughter drifted up from the *sahvas* buildings below. Already the *sahvasis* had finished their breakfast and were awaiting the colorful ceremonies.

At last, after what seemed endless, unnecessary dawdling to the edgy servants, the two men rose from the table. Penta had rushed all during breakfast to take the plates from under their noses just as soon as they had finished each dish. Then he had placed the next course with equal speed to try to convey the urgent sense that they must not risk being late. But even this early in the morning the busy one with the quick cackling laugh had been telling a story and the quiet one had been too interested to hurry the matter on. Penta wondered what these people found to talk about so endlessly. They stayed on and on at the table after meals. It was really difficult sometimes to know whether to take the last things off while they were still

47

sitting there chattering away an hour after they had eaten.

But they must be fine men or Baba would not have invited them to come. So it was best to let them sit, and perhaps take away the last things when they were so deep in talk that they would not know it anyway. The slight disturbance of clearing the table seemed to bring the two back to earth. They got up and went to the outhouse.

Once more the two seemed to forget the passage of time, and as Penta felt he could bear the strain no longer the younger emerged from one door of the outhouse and called to the older. In a moment the busy one came out with his usual cheery call, and with a flourish of their hats and a good-by they were off through the gate and down the roadway.

None too soon. The honk of Baba's car could already be heard approaching from Ahmednagar. He would certainly be there before those two slow ones had even reached the railroad tracks.

But not so. As Baba drove up, the two dawdlers raced in from the opposite side of the drive and joined the group of bobbing, shifting heads, all anxious to catch a glimpse of the new man the night had wrought. With brief smiles and light touches of the hand here and there Baba strode with rapid steps into the hall. At once the *sahvasis* slipped out of their sandals and shoes and squatted with a minimum of chatter to listen to the matter which was clearly on Baba's mind.

"Today we will have a 'poor' program. While I wash their feet and bow down to them, all of you should repeat continuously and audibly enough to be heard by yourselves, any one of God's names. Pick the one which you are used to, and keep up the repetitions as long as the program lasts.

"Do this so sincerely that I will hear it. God is deaf, and only the sincerity of the devotee makes Him hear. So repeat the name of God from your hearts, and while repeating His name, think of God also.

"Now let us return to the matter of washing the feet of the poor and my bowing down to them. When I bow down, it is neither for show nor as an expression of humility. I do it out of my love for humanity.

"Today I bow down to these poor from Arangaon. They are very poor but they have great love for me. When I first came here, most of these people were children. I have sent them word to obey me today and to let me serve and worship them in my own way.

"When you see me washing their feet and wiping them dry, and when I put my forehead to their feet and give them four rupees each as *prasad*,* I am actually the poorest of the poor. It is of no use then to repeat my name. When you see me behave as an ordinary man, I am an ordinary man. When you find me angry I am angry. When I express ignorance I am ignorant. I am whatever I say I am, and I am also whatever you see and feel I am.

"There is no need for me to act or keep up appearances. When I come to this plane I become everything in the entire material universe. Just as you see me as a man, so an ant simultaneously sees me as an ant. Just so, I am the poor of Arangaon, too.

"Since I am actually the poorest of the poor when you see me serving and worshiping the poor, that is why I tell you not to repeat my name at that time, but to take the name of God which suits you best. After the program is over you may repeat my name. It is always best for you to repeat my name under all circumstances except when you see me wash the feet of the poor and bow down to them.†

"When you realize your own self you will find that nothing such as the 'poor' program has taken place. Nothing has ever happened or will happen. There is no such thing as time. The present moment *is*, from the beginningless beginning. And everything that IS, IS at this moment. There is no past or future.

"God has always existed. HE IS. Truth is truth. It cannot be changed. In order to appreciate truth, approach it through itself without any game of hide and seek.

"Yesterday, when the families of the workers here at Meherabad came before me to receive my *darshan,* I was worthy of giving *darshan.* Today, when you see me washing the feet of the poor, I will be the poor. It is not one and the same thing when sometimes I worship others and when sometimes I let others worship me. But if, when I am worshiped, I myself worship simultaneously, as sometimes I do,

---

* A gift from a spiritual master which is regarded as carrying a spiritual blessing.

† One not in Baba's presence at such a time has no reason to avoid repeating Baba's name.

then in that case both the act of worshiping and the fact of being worshiped amount to the same thing.

"Among the villagers yesterday were those seeking my blessings for the fulfillment of their worldly desires. I have not come for that. I have come for a few elect, though I have to see to the whole world, too.

"True worship is an expression of devotion, not just saying prayers and making supplications. For you to worship me truly, it is necessary for you to have my grace. What is grace? No bargaining whatsoever is possible in the receiving of grace, and there is absolutely no specific condition * for its bestowal. It may be given freely to anyone, whether saint or sinner, intellectual or illiterate, man or woman. Grace is just grace, nothing more and nothing less.

"Although it is next to impossible, yet it is conceivable that one might become one hundred per cent prepared by one's own efforts, and thereupon realize God. In such an improbable event, God-realization is not through grace.

"But if the worst sinner stood before me and I had the whim (*lahar*), I could make him realize God in less than the flash of a second. That would be grace. At the very instant my grace descends upon you, you also become me and we remain one.

"It is easier for me to come as an Avatar than for you to receive my grace. The problem is that once you have been conditioned by duality there is no end to the conditions which restrict your ability to receive my grace. Therefore it is difficult for my grace to flow from me to you.

"That is why it is not as easy as it sounds for me to get the whim to cause you to receive my grace. As a matter of fact it is flowing sufficiently all the time to fill one and all receptacles everywhere.

"There is rarely a vessel which is not filled with other things. A vessel must first be emptied before it can be filled by the flow of my grace. It is also my grace which helps a vessel to become completely emptied in the first place.

---

* *I.e.* there is absolutely no trait or achievement which guarantees the aspirant that he will receive grace. However there is no end to the characteristics or impressions in the aspirant which restrict his ability to receive grace.

"The sun is now shining brilliantly outside this hall, but the sunlight does not reach you here under the roof. The sun is doing its duty of giving light. You have also to do your duty in removing whatever comes between you and the sun.

"Unless you break open the roof, how can you ask the sun to pour its light upon you? You have raised this roof of 'ignorance' over your own self. Demolish it and you will find that you yourself are the light and you yourself are the sun.

"Through my grace, a sudden crack in the roof can let the sunlight in on you immediately, but one in a million roofs might thus attract my grace. I am an ocean of grace, but I am also hard as flint when you try to draw that grace from me. The flow of my grace to you depends upon the intensity of your love, for it is love which attracts my grace to you.

"Generally it is rightly said that the right time must arrive for grace to descend. Yet in a particular sense this is absurd. The contradiction arises because words are never enough to express spiritual truths accurately as they exist in the higher spheres, far above intellect and understanding.

"Suppose I happen to have the whim to make you realize God—simply because you happen to be near me physically at that moment —and you do realize God. That is grace, and it is also the right moment for you. In short, as long as you do not receive grace, the right moment has not come for you. And when you do receive grace, the right moment has come for you.

"The greatest difficulty lies in the easiest matter. It is most difficult for you to become (knowingly) God because it is easiest for you to be what you have (unknowingly) been all the time, and what (unknowingly) you will always be until it is the right moment for grace to descend upon you.

" 'Impossible' and 'possible' are opposites in the realm of duality, but truth lies beyond all duality. If on a bright sunlit morning I tell you that it is night, you will be lying if you agree with me that this is so. But if you do not agree, that will mean I lied to you.

"Such an impossible situation would not exist if, when I say it is night, you actually find that it is pitch dark in broad daylight. For this you need grace.

"You can find more or less all of what I am telling you in books of various kinds, but all of those, and all of this, pale in comparison with the spiritual realities which lead to the one divine reality—God.

"The time is rapidly approaching when a tidal wave will rise in the ocean of grace. Then the usual process by which the water in the rivers flows into the ocean will be reversed and the ocean water will rush through the river beds. Be prepared to receive this overflow of grace."

Although the *sahvasis* had sat with strained eagerness to take in every one of Baba's words, it was clear that many were floundering with the imponderables of his declamation on darkness in the light of day. Even for these people, though used to dealing with questions of devotion and implicit obedience to the master, the rapidly shifting innuendos of Baba's brief discourse were almost too much to comprehend.

Baba sensed this frustrated eagerness and, unwilling to stretch out the skein of tension beyond its present limit, switched abruptly to a different theme.

"Most of you know that, as I promised at our last meeting at Meherabad in September, 1954, I gave up the use of my alphabet board on October 7 of that year. For over twelve months now I have relied only upon ordinary gestures to express what I have to say. Sometimes, when it is absolutely necessary to express a particular word, I have one of you repeat the alphabet and stop you at the proper letters until the word is spelled.

"Now, however, I have promised Don to let him take a few moving pictures to show the American television audiences how I dictated *God Speaks* on the alphabet board. People there find it difficult to imagine such a work having been dictated on an alphabet board. That means I will have to take the board in hand and demonstrate. This morning after the 'poor' program I will dictate on it before the cameras for a few moments.

"It occurs to me however that the Americans are very clever people and some of them will be watching what I spell out on the board. I will write this on the board: 'I have given up the use of the alphabet board since October, 1954 and I will not use it again.'

"Although I can never forget that I am free forever of one and all

bindings, I have had the habit for ages of giving promises and forgetting promises. Yet not a single promise have I ever broken. You
cannot quite fathom my words. That is what Hafiz means when he
says:

> " 'Chu bishnavi sukhan-e Ehl-e-dil magoo
> ke khata'st;
> Sukhan shanaas na-ee dilbara khata
> eenja'st.'

"Freely translated, this means, 'Because you cannot grasp them
yourself, do not tell lies about truths you hear from a master.'

"None of you should do things just because you see me doing them.
Only do what I tell you to do. Never break a promise. First think
twice before you give a promise, but once you make it, keep that
promise at any price.

"I am also thinking of making a special journey to give my *sahvas*
to women and children who are eager for it in the north and the
south of the country. I may even pay a flying visit to those in the
western world who are also eager to see me. The time is drawing
nearer and nearer when I shall break my silence and manifest as I
truly am.

"But don't take any of these things as a promise from me. I am
always free from all promises."

Baba rose from his chair and went out from the room to the small
white building devoted to his personal use. The *sahvasis* scattered to
the four corners of the property.

Beyond Baba's small hut, there was an odd structure situated at
the edge of the road which rested on four low and entirely unen-
gineered stilts. These in turn rested on a well-constructed slab concrete floor. From this rose vertical posts on which an equally well-
constructed pitched tin roof rested. There were no walls. The effect
was one of an open-air meeting house in the middle of which someone had carelessly left a large chicken coop.

But India is a strange land, and strange things assume great value
to its people; and so after awhile the casual observer would think to
inquire whether the larger structure might have been built to preserve the insignificant box beneath it. This was the exact purpose,

for the crude box was one of the most sacred objects associated with Meher Baba. In this he had spent some months writing a great tome which he always referred to thereafter as his "bible."

In this work are said to be included many of the secrets of creation and man's relation to his Creator. But no one has ever been allowed to read it, and so it remains a matter of speculation, while the cramped coop in which it was composed has become an object of veneration.

On the edge of the concrete floor of this structure, a seat had been placed. Immediately in front of the seat and resting on the dirt, was a small platform with steps on either side. This was to be the scene of washing the feet of the poor. Already a large accumulation of tattered, unkempt men ranging in age from the late teens into the nondescript ranges of extreme age had gathered for the occasion.

Some used crutches, some seemed quite blind, still others had no apparent defect of body or clothing. All seemed in a highly electrical state of anticipation, and several unwound and rewound their turbans in a last minute effort at neatness.

Some of the younger *sahvasis* wandered out to take up their stands at various vantage points, carefully reading light meters and adjusting cameras. Several cowherd children from the town had wandered in to watch the proceedings, and hard on their heels came three dogs. Two were apparently inclined to tolerate one another, but the third had some distinctive feature which rendered him outcast. There was a constant rumble of growls in the background which finally erupted into the snarls and yelps of a dog fight. This went on for several raging minutes until two of the younger men stopped the scandalous proceedings with a few lusty cuffs.

Almost at the stroke of nine o'clock, several of the *mandali* came striding towards the shelter. With a few words and gestures they organized the lot of villagers into a coherent, slightly curving line. At once, members of the Meherabad household staff, clad in spotless white shirts and pants, arrived with large buckets of clear water. The scene was now ready for Baba's entrance.

A knot of *sahvasis* which had collected at the corner of Baba's white hut began to billow and threaten to break loose from its anchor post. Finally, with a great swirl, it swept into the dirt lane leading to the concrete-floored shelter, and from its heart strode Baba in his favorite pink coat.

With cameras grinding and clicking along the path, the group made its way to the simple platform and Baba sat down in the chair behind it. He drew his sheer white pants up to his knees, a heavy robe was placed over his legs, and off came the pink coat in preparation for the work.

The first old man in the line was led carefully up the stairs by one of the *mandali*. While another *sahvasi* supported him from in front of the platform, Baba poured the contents of a large tin cup over the ancient one's dusty black feet. The water leached a thin layer of brown off the arches and toes and rolled down into a shallow puddle on the metal surface of the platform.

The excess water was immediately scraped away from Baba and onto the ground by another of the *mandali*. Baba reached for a towel held in readiness for him, carefully wiped the thin, twisted feet and solemnly touched his forehead to them.

During this time the old man seemed about to collapse on the platform, perhaps out of extremity of age or excitement, perhaps from distress that this great one should be bowing to him rather than he falling flat on his face. Several times it seemed he must surely collapse, but always the *sahvasi* standing in front of the platform saved him by bracing him under the armpits.

Baba reached to the side with his right hand and four one-rupee notes were placed in it. These he handed to the old man, who was then led down in a state of great agitation from the platform.

As he reached the ground a second aged individual was brought forward. Again the large tin cup sloshed water over long, thin black feet, again the excess water was scraped away and the feet dried, Baba's forehead touched the feet, four rupees were placed in the old man's hands, and he too was led off.

The third person was a relatively young boy dressed in white. He needed no help, and held himself tall and proud as Baba repeated the routine. The thinness of his black legs was mirrored in the black gloss of the puddle of water at his feet, and then the image was destroyed by the deft motions which scraped the excess away.

Four, five, ten, twenty, a hundred souls were led up to the platform and then gently sent on their way. Some were so old and bent and diseased that they must be lifted up the steps, held carefully, and then lifted down. Large sores stood out on the calves or arms of some; others were so emaciated that there seemed little flesh left to clothe the skeleton.

At one point Baba stopped his routine and, pointing to the tall, rugged man who had just mounted the platform before him, began to gesture:

"This is Satya Mang. Once he was well known as a daring *dacoit* (bandit) who terrorized this part of the country. He is now going straight, but is practically starving. He was attracted to me more than thirty years ago and soon became devoted enough to promise to give up robbery.

"That promise caused him a great struggle. After some time, he could not help slipping back, and one night he set out to steal again. He succeeded with his plans, but just as he was about to take his plunder he saw me standing there before him. This reminded him of his promise and because of his love for me he was saved."

While Baba was gesturing and Eruch translating, Satya Mang shifted his weight first onto one foot, then to the other, unmindful of the attention being paid him. As the telling came to an end, it seemed as if Baba stroked the feet even more gently with the towel and bent his forehead to the gaunt feet even more tenderly. The craggy, graying man took the four rupees with a look of embarrassed devotion and walked stiffly down the steps and through the crowd.

As the morning sun rose higher its rays began to shine directly on Baba, the shade of the nearby tree which had originally protected him having slowly retreated. Soon Baba began to show signs of discomfort; he frowned from time to time as he waited momentarily for the next pair of dusty feet to lave.

At first the photographers, always sensitive to the possibility that they were fracturing the peace, concluded that they were the cause of Baba's apparent displeasure. As if by prearranged signal they stopped their grinding and clicking and drew off to a respectable distance. Their consciences had been guilty anyway, as it was a matter of recent history for Baba to allow relative freedom in the taking of pictures.

The discreet withdrawal of the photographers had no effect on the increasing frown which Baba wore. Finally he turned to the ready Eruch with an urgent message. Eruch hastily passed the information on to key workers, and with faultless timing the proceedings were halted and transferred to the great tent at the side of the meeting hall.

As Baba walked the scant half block to the new scene of activity, he held his sopping-wet pants high above his knees, looking for all the world like a Chinese laundryman become somewhat too intimately involved in his wash. There was a look of almost shyness on his features as he walked through the milling crowd of admiring followers, caught in almost too mundane a situation even for one who stretched from heaven to earth.

The final several score of paired feet, of dusty feet, of tired feet, of gnarled feet, of thin feet, of festered feet, of smooth young feet, were washed with despatch. At the last there were almost no bystanders, only the fleet motions of the tin cup as it sloshed, the swiping aside of excess water, the helping of tired eyes and unsure legs in their descent from the low platform. Baba and the *mandali* worked steadily on until the washing of the feet of the poor and the bowing down was done.

"Is Don ready now for the television film? Where does he want it to be photographed? How long will this take?"

Baba had no sooner finished the first task than he was impatient to be on with the next. Everyone asked questions, everyone volunteered answers, almost everyone gave orders. The confusion was uproarious, the good humor and excitement unsurpassed. The idea of participating in a film to be shown to American television audiences could not quite compete with listening to Baba, but it had a zest of the unusual about it, and the *sahvasis* were enjoying the situation to the hilt.

The great dilemma was how to satisfy the needs of the camera for sunlight, and Baba's need for shade. Decisions were made and unmade in rapid succession by everyone but the bewildered cameraman, who clearly was unprepared to cope with the exuberance of two hundred fifty men who had spent three full days in the presence of their master.

Two trials were lost in a babble of confusion and misunderstanding, but the third trial went off without a hitch. For good luck there
was a fourth, and a fifth, all from slightly different angles. Then
Baba held up his hand to signal that the filming was at an end. His
hands gestured quickly, and a smile of mixed amusement and embarrassment broke out on Eruch's features as he said not too loudly,
"Baba says that the next time Don says something will take ten minutes, Baba will know he means thirty minutes."

It was two-thirty in the afternoon of the same great day on which
the feet of the poor had been washed and the television film made.
The lively one and the quiet one were up on their beds having their
usual after-lunch nap. The energetic snores of the former could be
heard wafting out the open windows, sandwiching themselves in
between the low drones and soft clanks and thuds indigenous to the
country on a quiet afternoon.

Down at the bottom of the hill and across the railroad tracks,
where the *sahvas* buildings were located, a low mutter of activity
began to break forth. It grew in intensity, and suddenly the clear
brief honks of the blue Chevrolet could be heard approaching the
hill.

The busy one sprang from his bed with a full-blown snore still
hanging in the air and shook the quiet one.

"On your feet, Baba's coming," and out the door and down the
steps he raced. In a moment he was back.

"Forgot my hat. Come along, now, mustn't be late," and out the
door he clattered again.

Already the car was coming in the gate, and Penta and Pandu and
Sawak were flying about the yard bent on purposes known only to
God.

Eruch addressed himself to the two sleepy-eyed ones.

"Baba wants you to witness the placing of Mildred Kyle's ashes.
Don, you have met Mildred Kyle, and when you go back to America
you must tell them that you have seen Baba place her ashes near his
tomb. A marble marker will be made later to put over them.

"Baba has not allowed any of the *sahvasis* to come up the hill until the ashes have been placed, but after that they will come and he will show them the grounds and the buildings here, and through his tomb."

Without words the small group went out of the yard to the edge of the hill where a squarish, domed white building and an assortment of graves were located. The white building was Baba's tomb, now ready for some years. Around it were buried a collection of well-loved and faithful old followers, as well as several dogs who had burrowed deeply into the lives of all.

At the edge of the modest little row of graves a small stone crypt had been prepared in the ground. One of the *mandali* lifted a large stone slab from the opening, and Baba slowly lowered a small cloth pouch into it. Baba stood thoughtfully under the umbrella, and looked long at the modest remnants of a great and saintly woman.

What was he thinking? What was he feeling?

Was she perhaps happier at that moment than she had ever been while she lived and breathed in that fragile puff of ashes? What had her life really been behind that unassuming exterior? How often had she wished she might break through the impenetrable wall of the otherness of human beings, to find the real self and the simple warmth of oneself in another? Had she perhaps accomplished it? Was she perhaps even now buried more securely in the heart of the one who watched so pensively, than those ashes would ever be in the security of the stone and earth that surrounded them?

Baba twitched a hand, then straightened up soundlessly, and the rock slab was placed over the small opening. Mildred Kyle's body had come to rest.

The first of the main body of *sahvasis* were entering the front gate of the compound. In a few moments all but a few stragglers were inside. Baba and his small group returned to the compound and he began to lead the *sahvasis* around the central building. This was of wood and plaster, built high off the ground atop a massive, sloped stone foundation about eight feet high.

Baba explained that the stone foundation had originally been a water reservoir for a British troop encampment. The troops had subsequently been moved, and so the reservoir had fallen into disuse. In about 1922 the property had been acquired for Baba's work, and the *mandali* had constructed the present two-room dormitory atop the old reservoir in 1938.

The bottom had early been pierced by two doors, one leading into what was now a storeroom, the other into a simple bedroom.

The group then walked to the rear of the structure where a tin-roofed, open-sided lean-to was attached to the old reservoir. Here a dirt floor had been constructed of a mixture of water, cow dung and clay, beat firmly into place and kept slightly moist. The result was a very serviceable, odorless floor. The cow dung, rather than presenting a sanitation problem, was said to have germicidal properties.

In this open lean-to were a dining table, highboy and chairs; here the lively one and the quiet one were served their meals of specially Europeanized food. Baba's younger brother Adi and his wife Freni spent their days here, supervising the guest household, eating their meals with the two occidentals, and making certain that their least wishes were anticipated. At night the husband and wife returned to their home in nearby Ahmednagar.

As the throng of curious *sahvasis* crowded into the sheltered area, Eruch asked them to sit down, while Baba sat back in a jack-knife canvas lawn chair. He was about to start his gestures when he caught himself in mid-air and stared curiously at the hard-packed earth floor. Concern was immediately apparent on his face.

For several moments he kept up a running stream of questions and answers with Eruch, Adi and Sawak, his concern being that someone would catch cold sitting on the damp ground. Then Eruch motioned for everyone to stand up and the party transferred in toto up the stairs and into one of the two dormitory rooms atop the old reservoir. A cool afternoon breeze was blowing through the many windows, from which the shutters had been flung back, and the flagstone floor was cool to the touch of hand and haunch. Here Baba was satisfied, and all faced him attentively to hear what he had to say.

"The five greatest 'thieves' in the world," he began, "are the five living Perfect Masters of their time. They often steal the hearts of people, and periodically they also steal me and bring me down amongst you. Again and again I must become what I am, and each time this is due to the five Perfect Masters. Wherever I may be, at whatever time, it will always be due to those five.

"I never come of my own wish. It is always the five Perfect Masters who bring me down in each avataric period. Those five hold the key to all of creation—which contains a number of universes.

"I have explained in detail in *God Speaks* * how God becomes man as the Avatar (Buddha, Christ, *Rasool*) and men become God as Perfect Masters † (*Sadgurus, Qutubs*).

"It is because of the five Perfect Masters that I appear here before you. They fetch me down, and I experience myself as everything ‡ and tell you that I am everything.

"The state of God-realization cannot be described. It can only be known to those who achieve that supreme experience of the conscious state of God. It is beyond the domain of mind, which persists only through the sixth plane of spiritual consciousness. At that stage God is seen through the mind as being everywhere, all the time. But that is not the supreme experience, as the 'seer' and the 'seen' still remain two.

"The five Perfect Masters are the five persons of their age who not only become God but, after achieving God-realization, also come down to the ordinary normal consciousness of man. Thus they possess simultaneously God-consciousness, plus mental-, subtle- and gross-consciousness. The world is never without the five men-God.

"In spite of appearing as five different men, they are and always remain one God, as each one has exactly the same supreme experience of God-consciousness. Nevertheless, in external relations with the world, each shows a different personality, with his own characteristic traits, tastes, nature, habits and ways of dealing with people.

"For example, both Sai Baba § and Babajan ¶ were very fond of

---

* PP. 143–145.

† PP. 130–131; 172–173.

‡ This statement, although startling, rests upon or falls through a very brief line of reasoning. God is everything. Therefore one who is God, either through descent as the God-man (Avatar), or as a man-God (Perfect Master), must experience himself as everything in God. The burden of proof would then shift to whether Meher Baba were one with God, rather than whether he found himself to be everything.

§ Sai Baba, died October 15, 1918, revered in the Deccan as one of the greatest saints of his age, and the spiritual teacher of Upasni Maharaj.

¶ Babajan died in Poona September 29, 1931 at the reputed age of 133.

hearing *quavwallis* (Sufi songs), and (Upasni) Maharaj * had no taste for them, although he was equally capable of appreciating devotional music.

"Perfect Masters are not necessarily recognized as such in the world. They, too, often meet with opposition and have to share persecution from the masses born of ignorance. However in general they meet comparatively little opposition, particularly when their function as masters remains more or less unknown.

"But the Avatar, who is God-incarnate, must always face the headache of severe opposition. It occurs in every *avataric-yuga* (cycle of divine manifestation). Zoroaster, Rama, Krishna, Buddha, Jesus, Mohammed—all had to face it. The same picture is before my eyes today.

"All the five *Sadgurus* (Perfect Masters) put together mean Baba.† I have come so that you can escape from the cage of *maya,* and experience (know) me in your lifetime. Since the very beginning of the illusion of creation, *maya,* which makes illusion appear as reality, has been hanging around my neck in all of you.‡ That is why I must come (as the Avatar) again and again. That is why I also came back from my New Life,§ so that you might realize that all else—beauty, money, position, worlds, universes—is as valueless as a zero in comparison with God, who alone is worth seeing and becoming.

"Those who live for me and my work, contact me gradually, be-

---

It was she, one of the greatest Sufi saints, who gave Meher Baba God-realization when he was twenty.

* Upasni Maharaj, born May 15, 1870, died December 24, 1941, a renowned Hindu saint, who brought Meher Baba back to gross-consciousness after Babajan had given him God-consciousness. For more details see Appendix II.

† Part III consists of a detailed discussion of Meher Baba's claim to Avatarhood.

‡ This very curious allusion is another direct outgrowth of Baba's frequent statement that he experiences himself as everyone and everything. Therefore the albatross around another's neck is, in Baba's experience, literally around Baba's own neck.

§ In 1950–51 Baba led a small band of his followers about India in what he termed the "New Life". The student of Baba's life must be content to leave this phase in the realm of speculation until someone undertakes the task of researching and describing it.

come intimately connected with me, dedicate their all to me and become my dependents. From time to time, individually or collectively, with me or in accordance with my instructions, they carry out various activities connected with my work. There are a number among them who must necessarily carry out my detailed instructions daily and continuously, living as and where I want them to live.

"For example, at different times in the past there have been various institutions here at Meherabad. There have been a hospital, dispensaries, schools, shelters for the poor, and separate *ashrams* for boys, men, women, the mad and the *masts*. All were run free and were open to people irrespective of their caste, creed or class.*

"I make the best use of money when I have it, and dissolve everything when I have none. Gifts of love I accept with love, and I disburse them with love. I maintain no institutions on a permanent basis, such as those run elsewhere by self-perpetuating organizations. Every heart that loves me continues, regardless of the presence or absence of institutions, to remain my *ashram* for my work.

"Similar processes are repeated in every avataric period, and thus matters proceed, age after age. Among those who are very dear to me there are those whose dependency increases day by day. Eventually they become dependent on me for everything.

"When I first set foot in Meherabad over thirty-two years ago I had nothing, but in the course of my subsequent activities here and elsewhere, over a *crore* (ten million) of rupees must have been spent for my work. Today I have nothing. I give no value to money for the sake of money.

"When I talk of money I come down to your level and say things from that level, but I repeat that I am not in the least concerned with money. I am told that one of you has inquired of Pendu today whether money could be offered to me. This reminds me of the attitude towards money of Sai Baba, one of the five Perfect Masters.

"Sai Baba had exceptionally lustrous eyes and a wonderful personality. He was fond of smoking *chilam* (an earthen pipe) and used to cough and spit freely in the presence of his visitors. He always asked point-blank for money of all those who visited him. In some cases he would ask the same person for money again and again, until

---

* A detailed description of these projects is given in Appendix II.

the visitor was stripped clean, with no money left even for his return journey. However Sai Baba would keep no money and used to give it away.

"*Bhajans* and *quavwallis* were often sung before him by Hindus and Moslems, who revered him alike. But you will never be able to understand thoroughly how great Sai Baba was. He was the very personification of perfection. If you knew him as I know him you would call him the master of creation.

"During his lifetime there were few who *really* loved him, and there were many who could not understand how one who constantly grabbed money from visitors could be a saint! But now you find Sai *mandirs* (temples), Sai match-boxes, Sai 'this' and Sai 'that', mostly made by the same worldly-minded people who mocked Sai Baba during his lifetime.

"Here in my presence you feel like dozing now, but after I drop the body, like Sai Baba, people will begin to understand my divinity.

"During the three years that (Upasni) Maharaj stayed in Khandoba's temple at Shirdi * he lived on water alone under orders from Sai Baba. Maharaj was the only one there who knew who Sai Baba really was. Maharaj himself was so great that if his grace were to descend on a particle of dust, it would be transformed into God.

"But in contrast to Sai Baba, Maharaj for many years chased away those who offered him money. In later years however he began to accept what people offered out of their love for him. That is how the present Upasninagar,† with its temples, residential quarters, etc., has come into being and is maintained.

"Babajan, whom I often call 'the emperor', was really the emperor of emperors. She lived most of the time under a *neem* tree in the cantonment area of Poona, staying there during all seasons regardless of sun, rain or cold. Although wrinkled with age, she remained very energetic to the last, always looking bright, and usually cheerful. She had almost no wants, and there was no question of money in her life, which was that of a real *fakir* (poorest of the poor).

"Among those who were deeply devoted to her was a large number

---

* See Appendix II for details. Shirdi is a village in the district of Ahmednagar.

† Presided over by Maharaj's leading disciple, Godavari Mai. See p. 25.

of Pathan and Baluchi soldiers who would often flock around her seat under the tree. But when, in a mood of *jalal* (divine majesty), she would rise from her seat with a stick in her hand, the strongest men in the group would run away.

"It was Babajan who caused me in less than the flash of a second to experience my most-original state of being the Ancient One (Avatar).

"Narayan Maharaj * had absolutely no physical personality. He was short-statured like Gustadji,† but more lean. He always dressed in fine clothes and used to have a diamond ring flashing on one finger. He lived in grand style in Kedgaon, living a life of routine *arti-puja* (ceremonial worship). He never asked for money directly, but indirectly he used to impress this point upon his visitors and devotees.

"Tajuddin Baba of Nagpur ‡ was completely indifferent to his immediate surroundings. He was *taj* (the crown). You can have no idea who he was. I do know who he is. People used to crowd around him during his lifetime and still flock around his shrine by the thousands.

"All five of these Perfect Masters have brought me 'down', and all that I have become is due to these five. I am made of all the attributes of all five of these Masters, and my avataric state comprises the five states of these five *Sadgurus* (*Qutubs*).§ Naturally, therefore, the qualities of all five are in me.

"Since I began to observe silence (July, 1925) I have not touched money except when I give it to the poor and to the *masts*. Sometimes I ask for money from those who love me. Sometimes I receive money from them unasked. At times I refuse all money offered to me. But I have never obtained money through any such thing as the miracles which the yogis occasionally perform. It is only money offered with love that I accept and disburse for my work.

"At this moment Sai Baba's attribute is uppermost in me. If people

---

* Born approximately 1855, died September 3, 1945, the fourth of the five Perfect Masters of Baba's youth.

† One of Upasni Maharaj's disciples whom Upasni Maharaj told to follow Meher Baba.

‡ Born January 7, 1861, died August 17, 1925, the fifth of the five Perfect Masters.

§ Perfect Master = *Sadguru* = *Qutub*

are to know about me, they should know everything about me. Those who love me should continue to love me. Those who do not love me do not affect me. I am what I am and I will remain what I am for all time and under all circumstances. Money comes, money goes, I remain the *fakir* that I am.

"In order to carry out some important work which I must do, I have a plan. For this I have literally to be free to go where I like and do what I have to do for a period of one year, from February 15, 1956 to February 15, 1957. During this period I wish to receive no correspondence, nor see people or give interviews, and I may not see even those who always stay near me. I have only two months left now to arrange affairs so as to be free from all my apparent bindings.

"All those who contribute whatever they can really spare towards the various provisions I choose to make for the one year, will thereby participate with me in the work I have in mind for that year. But no one should offer money which will increase his own individual burden, mental or financial. It must be done in the spirit of a free offering of love, for love, and must be made with pleasure and without mental reservations.

"To enable all to share equally in the work I will do during the year, I will gladly accept even five rupees. Although it is true that I will regard all contributors as equal participants in my work, regardless of the amount contributed, that fact should not lead one who can easily afford five thousand to give only five hundred, or one to offer only fifty who can offer five hundred.

"Those who cannot spare even a single rupee should not worry. Money has absolutely no connection with love, and love is the only thing of real value. No one could ever win Godhood from me in exchange for all the money in the world, but he who loves me intensely can become God without possessing or giving me a single *pie* (cent).

"Above all else, no one should attempt to raise funds for this project from others, and then remit the total in one or several names. Each one of you is to offer to me directly what you conveniently can, doing so with pleasure and without taking any burden upon yourself, as that would be a burden on me."

Baba then went on to ask the assembled group for volunteers to share more actively in the work to be done during his retirement. To do this, he asked for one man from the group, and promised to select one from each of the other three language groups yet to come, to go into retirement at their homes for twenty-one days.

These four individuals, he explained, should also live indoors during that entire period, on water alone. Further, they were to repeat the two syllables "Ba" "ba" audibly, one on inhalation and the other on exhalation, throughout the period except when dozing. Finally, each of the four was not to lie down to sleep, nor to sleep with his head resting on anything other than his own body, during the entire period!

There was a sense of crisis in the air as Baba outlined the stipulations, but the description had hardly been given when nine of the group rose instantly to volunteer. Baba quizzed each one minutely regarding his ability to carry out the severe conditions. The aged man with thick-lensed glasses and long, flowing white beard, Baba gently thanked and asked to sit down. This the old man did, registering the deepest disappointment.

One of those standing was an emaciated young fellow who looked as though he had just recovered from a long illness. Baba joked with him about the amount of flesh he had on his bones to carry him through the rigorous fast. Nothing Baba could say served to convince him that he was not entirely fit to qualify. Finally Baba told him also to sit down.

Two others who had families and business responsibilities were in turn quizzed and asked to sit down, and now five were left standing. These certainly looked as though they could stand the test of even such an ordeal. Baba seemed undecided which one to pick from among them. As he talked with them and seemed to wrestle with his choice, he began to modify the conditions which were to be observed. First, instead of twenty-one days, the period was reduced to seven: from midnight, February 14 to midnight, February 21. Then, he said that in addition to water they could have each day either one cup of milk or one to two cups of tea, and they should take one teaspoon of a stomach-powder in a glassful of water each noon. Baba then selected all five of the men to carry out the fast. Equal numbers were later selected from the Telugu, Hindi and Marathi groups.

When Baba completed the arrangements for the fast, a gentle-faced man, perhaps fifty years old, rose from among the group and asked permission to deliver some Sanskrit verses. Receiving permission to do so, he recited them so feelingly that apparently the stream broke the flood gates of his heart. He burst into tears, cried out "Avatar Meher Baba-ki-jai" and asked forgiveness for his sins.

Baba motioned the desolate figure into his arms, embraced him warmly, stroked his shoulder and his damp cheeks tenderly and then held him quietly to his chest.

"Don't be afraid," he said. "You need not tell me any more. If I am the Avatar, then I know everything, and everything will be forgiven. If I am not the Avatar, what good will it do you to tell me anything, and what use would it be to ask my forgiveness?"

"Christ often said, 'I forgive you, I forgive you'. Those who loved Christ accepted His *prasad* (offering) of forgiveness. But those who would not recognize Christ naturally could not understand Him. His words were just words to them.

"I can forgive; I have come to forgive. Forgiveness is the highest thing for those who are forgiven. It is not a great thing to me to forgive. In fact, in reality there is nothing to be forgiven, for there is really nothing like good and bad. *You* find them so, and they *are* there in duality, due to your own bindings in duality.

"In the bondage of duality there is good and there is bad, but in reality everything but God is zero. *Maya,* which causes you to mistake illusion for reality, is present for you but not for me. *For me, only I am, and nothing else exists.** It therefore means nothing for me to forgive, and everything for you to be forgiven.

"Forgiveness consists in loosening the bindings of duality in *maya,* which makes you feel and find the One as many. Therefore 'I forgive you' amounts to the loosening of your bindings.

"Although it takes a lot of time to build a big stack of hay, a single lighted match can burn all of it in no time at all. Similarly, regardless of the accumulated dirt and refuse of sins, divine forgiveness burns them away in no time."

The Sanskrit scholar stepped gratefully back into the audience and all rose to their feet, the afternoon now clearly being at an end.

* *I.e.* only God exists.

There was a hush of deep feeling, powerfully generated, which hung over the group. No one wished to break the enchantment of this momentary glimpse into the hidden workings of God and His relation to His creature, man. Without a word, everyone filed out behind Baba and the *mandali* and gathered around the blue car waiting at the foot of the high stone stairs.

It was late. Already the sun was sinking low behind the green hills, and the cowherd children from Arangaon were bringing their charges down from the rolling pastureland to the road that led through the fields of low corn and across the railroad tracks to the village. As the blue car moved slowly down the dirt road the cowherds recognized it, and with shrill cries raced across the fields to intercept it in its course.

The signal of their delighted screams alerted the village. As the *sahvasis* streamed slowly down from Meherabad-on-the-hill they could see the blue car inching through the crowd. Children were trying to reach a hand in through the door, and mothers with shy, black-eyed babes shoved their offspring and their own hands forward in hopes of receiving a rewarding pat. At the railroad crossing, where the car was forced to halt momentarily, a swarm of villagers milled and eddied about the vehicle, threatening to hold it up indefinitely. Finally it made its way through the dense pack and, like a blue arrow bent on racing into the heart of the heavens, it sped into the accumulating sunset.

CHAPTER 5

Lighting the Dhuni

The following morning, which began the fourth full day, the session was underway by eight o'clock. Something of the holiday atmosphere of the first three days had abated and there was more of an air of sober men at work, wrestling with a serious construction problem. The first rash of colds due to the change in climate had begun to dry up, and the regularity of nature seemed to have reasserted itself, judging by the sleep-rested faces.

On this day Baba had promised to hold individual and group interviews, followed at sunset by the lighting of the *dhuni*, a once-a-month ceremonial. But first he must speak his mind on the overall problem of his work, and the participation of his devoted followers in that work.

He picked several people from the group to sit especially close to his great armchair. Again and again on various occasions he made special efforts to show special signs of attention to different members of the group, now this one, now another. The roving finger of favor passed so indiscriminately that no sense of undue favoritism ever seemed to gnaw at the inners of the *sahvasis*. Perhaps the matter never came up because here, for once in the world, there seemed to be a supply of warm love sufficient to satisfy all.

There was a clearing of throats as people settled down into their nesting points. Baba cross-sampled the group with his usual questions on sleeping, eating, elimination and general health. The results were either statistically sound or else he had much on his mind, for this morning he wasted no time in his brief survey.

"Wherever I go, people flock about me by the hundreds and thousands. That kind of love is not what I want. Whether people worship or villify me, I remain what I am. Whether the whole world believes in God or denies Him, God always remains God. I look forward to the love which enables the individual to obey me, so that he may find me and eventually become me.

"Therefore I do not want merely crowds to be attracted towards me. I want really sincere souls. I do not necessarily wait for them to come to me. I often go to them. I can—and do—do my own work. You can—and should—share it too.

"It is easy to collect crowds, and it is easy for crowds to collect. My greatness cannot be established in the crowds and through the crowds, but even a few with love can make the masses feel my greatness, and keep the greatness established in their hearts. One single person who really loves me can move the whole world.

"There is no one here, including myself, who can so love me. If all of you became my real lovers we would need several more worlds for all of you to work in for me.

"My work for you does not consist in your going around beating a big drum for me. Love needs no propaganda. You need love yourself in order to propagate love among others. To spread my love among the people, you have to make them understand me as you understand me. For that you have to bring them to love me as you love me, and that means you have to cause them to feel my love as you feel it. The best way is to show others by your own example how much you love me.

"The world is too full of preachers and teachers. Never forget that I have not come to teach, and I need no preachers.

"In the intimate spirit of the *sahvas* I must be free and frank with you and tell you whatever I feel like saying. Why shout to others, 'Baba says God is the only reality and all else is illusion', when you yourself cannot help whispering to me about your own illusions? There are doubtless many among you here who are sincere and painstaking in your efforts to explain my message to one and all, that they should ignore illusion and awaken to reality.

"Yet these sincere workers do not hesitate to bring to my attention their own tales of illusory woes and worries, such as, 'Baba, I am short of money', 'My wife is not in good health', 'I am about to lose my job', 'There is trouble in my business', and so on.

"Would it be truthful for one of these to tell others, 'Baba says, "Do not worry about illusory things. God knows everything and God does everything" '? Why preach at all what you yourself cannot put into practice? If you do not find yourself free of falsehood, envy, slander, backbiting and hatred, and if you find in yourself lack of love and consideration for others, then instead of telling others, 'Baba says this' and 'Baba says that', you had best keep quiet and not show your face to those whom you would like to win over to me.

"Suppose one of my followers is speaking before a gathering and trying to tell them that Baba is reality and all else is illusion. Suppose that just then a telegram is given to him which tells of a bus accident in which all of his family have been killed. If, in spite of the tragedy and pain of what has happened, he continues to speak with greater conviction, then he has achieved real authority to speak about me and my teachings.

"You win the right to tell others what you first accept in letter and spirit for yourself. Show outwardly only what you have won inwardly.

"There is no doubt, for example, that I am the Avatar, the Ancient One, but how do you know that I am He? You say so mainly because I say so. I say so based on my own living experience of being That. But for you it is just a belief until you become me. Suppose your belief is wrong?

"What I want to impress upon you is this: never give a twist to what you feel deep down in your own hearts. If you feel I am the Avatar, say openly, 'Baba is the Avatar'. If you feel I am a fraud, do not hesitate to say, 'Baba is a fraud'. I remain unaffected by praise or abuse. If you speak what you feel to be true, you have the force of truth to make others accept truth.

"Honest differences between workers laboring in a common cause are signs of the vitality of the work. But a spirit of discipline is also essential in all creative activities of life. How can people work jointly without discipline, and on the other hand, where would there be scope for self-control and discipline if there were no differences between workers?

"Your eyes, ears, nose and mouth are placed in different positions to serve varying purposes. They also appear different in size and shape, and yet all are equally yours. Besides serving specific direct purposes, all your organs are also complementary to each other, and in this respect equally valuable to you. There is no question of one organ competing with another for supremacy of position or service to the body. Each serves in its individual capacity, and all harmonize in the smooth functioning of the whole body.

"Differences between workers who toil in the cause of love and truth can either accentuate or mutilate them for other persons, and for the workers as well. Therefore differences must be properly harmonized and fairly adjusted with the aid of discipline, which is more to be lived sincerely within oneself than enforced upon others. But neither differences nor discipline should ever be raised above love and truth. They should be sacrificed rather than be allowed to mar or cloud the main object. A body without a soul is best buried, burned or disposed of as quickly as possible. No one would like to die to save one's eyes or ears.

"Your love for me should have free expression in the mode or form best suited to you. It should shine through you to others, awakening their hearts to receive this divine gift. Gatherings and meetings in my name should be a channel for the expression of my love, and to give them any other importance is to misunderstand my cause.

"Organizations may be necessary for carrying out work of a routine nature, but if I am the Avatar I need no such things for my own work. Although I would not be worth loving if I were not aware of someone's unexpressed love for me, why should anyone who wishes to express it be compelled to do so through some office or organization?

"My office should be the heart of everyone who loves me. The heart of each should be my shrine, and my lover the priest of that temple of love. Such a temple comes first, and the priest afterwards. A cart placed before the horse can serve no purpose. Love, and the heart which has love, are of greater importance than questions of the position or prestige of those who choose to take up my work.

"A heavy railway train with two engines pulling it in the same direction is quickly moved up a steep grade. But a few cars pulled by two engines straining in opposite directions cannot make progress even on level ground.

"Forget the past and make the most of the present. Keep your own hearts clean. Learn to love each other first before you tell others about my love for one and all. Give love, receive love, gather love; everything else is dissolved eventually in the truth of divine love.

"Let your own life of love for Baba be the message of Baba's love for one and all."

After this Baba retired to the small building which he used so often for his private business, or to rest for a few moments. Soon individuals, and sometimes small groups, were called in to have their interviews. From one conference to the next, no one knew what took place with the preceding or succeeding persons.

The interviews went on all day, with a short break for lunch. As the sun began to sink lower in the hot afternoon sky, Baba and the *mandali* came into the hall. With a few loud cries to round up the *sahvasis,* the group gathered once again in the unusually warm room.

Baba explained to them that they were all very lucky to be there at that time, as it was the day of the month on which they regularly lit the *dhuni* fire. This was a small ceremonial fire, used in a variety of forms in several religions, which was lit in a small brazier just at sunset. Baba adapted the ceremony to his own ends by suggesting that each of the *sahvasis* embody in a small stick of wood one personal attachment or characteristic which he was willing to give up, and then cast the stick into the *dhuni* fire.

The sun seemed to set unusually fast that evening, for as the fire was lit on the edge of the shelter where the feet of the poor had been washed, the figures of Baba and the *mandali* grew into a hazy, unreal backdrop for the tiny, dancing flames. This was the first time Baba had been seen at night, and perhaps that added to the ripe air of mystery which laced the dusty heat of the gathering night.

The *sahvasis* formed into a long, sinuous line leading to the concrete floor on which Baba and the *dhuni* fire sat. Eruch handed each man a small splint of wood, Baba patted or embraced the man, and then the tiny faggot was tossed into the fire. It was quite simple.

The quiet one, who was almost two-thirds of the way down the line, wondered why many of the *mandali* were slipping into the queue to participate in the guileless ceremony. Usually one sensed they had been through these things so many times with Baba that there was little reason for repetition.

The quiet one thought over his personal store of stinky traits, almost tempted to single out the most attractively disgusting one of all, but decided to live with that one awhile longer. Instead, he picked the runner-up: his inordinate sensitivity to criticism. This he determined playfully to embody symbolically in the wood chip. He expected no earth-shaking reaction, and participated in the ceremony more on the basis of "when in Rome", etc.

Well, he learned. He should have taken his tip from the unusual actions of the *mandali,* which would have hinted that something of unusual value was occurring. But no, the sheep calmly walked down the ramp to his slaughter.

As Eruch handed him the wood chip a brief smile of recognition flashed between the two. He moved on two steps to find himself enfolded with unusual tenderness in Baba's embrace, and then he turned around and tossed the stick into the fire. It was done, and he forgot about it as he stumbled on home.

But God and Baba had not. The smoke from that one tiny bit of wood streaked half way around the world, and when the quiet one arrived home a week later all hell had broken loose. Everyone was mad at him for everything he had ever done, and for a few things he hadn't done as well.

After several days of attempting to calm people down and trying to reconstruct his shattered universe he suddenly recalled the *dhuni* fire. What a sucker he had been! Or stop, had he? If the stick tossed into the fire had precipitated all this, then perhaps that loving embrace by Baba held the antidote.

For weeks, as the kettle boiled and sputtered, he thought of the possible mechanics of this unusual thing that he had apparently brought on himself. Through it all however the warm support given at the time it began kept up his nerve. As affairs gradually calmed down again he wiped the mental perspiration from his brow and wondered how many other unsuspecting souls had walked full tilt into a similar blockbuster.

Eruch, next time whittle the sticks just a little bit smaller!

The *dhuni* fire died down, and the blue car sped back through Ahmednagar to Pimpalgaon and the noise of the night preparations of the *sahvasis* began to soak into the desert of stillness of the hot Indian twilight. Hardly a breath of air moved through the leaves and through the corn stalks and through the fingers hanging limply over the edges of mattresses. A long day of heavy work lay behind, and the night was heavy with the static of it.

CHAPTER 6

Some Smiles, Some Tears

As day began to break, the air was chill and the breathless quiet of evening still lay over the rolling hills and valleys. Occasionally a sharp dagger of sound pierced the soft cloak of silence and then was lost as instantly in its folds.

The crackling cough of the night-watchman on the hill rasped now and then, and finally there were whispers in the kitchen as the first of the household staff arrived. The village of Arangaon began to come to life, and the lights of the tuberculosis sanitarium across the valley were switched off. The cooks and the houseboys and the *sahvasis* at the foot of the hill began to cough and talk.

Suddenly, by consent of nature, sleep was at an end and drowsing, sleep-filled eyes were tolerated only in specially set-aside places. It was day, and time for the activities of living. The entire world came alive with a rush and forgot that only moments before its nature had been the blackness and the weirdly-moving forms of a dream within the dream.

Breakfast was served and finished in minutes. Several buses were to arrive at eight o'clock from Ahmednagar to take the entire group to Meherazad at Pimpalgaon, some fifteen miles away, to the north of Ahmednagar. The dusty, rattling contraptions drove up promptly and the *sahvasis* piled in with gay spirits and ample buffoonery.

Down the dirt and stone road between the pleasant shade trees the cloud of dust clattered. Already the road was filling with bullock carts, bicyclists and pedestrians. India is a land of ceaseless tides of restless humanity, her roads glutted by a flood of people moving constantly to markets, to fields, and on business to the next village. But even these understandable pursuits cannot account for the total motion. Millions more must simply be moving for want of a reason or a place to be still.

As the buses carrying the *sahvasis* sped towards Pimpalgaon, an elaborate game of nerves was played occasionally with a vehicle coming from the opposite direction. The opposing drivers would race determinedly down the center of the road, honking excitedly at each other to give way. Inasmuch as Indian roads are often one lane wide, sometimes one and a half, but almost never two, the challenge was to judge at the last possible instant the final intent of the opposing driver. The one who lost must take to the stubble, while the better poker player proceeded on the "paved" section without a moment's let-up on the gas pedal.

The game has many variations and is a fine source of excitement. The surprising part is the unexpectedly low mortality rate in such a hazardous form of roulette. The oriental is by nature a much more intuitive individual than his western counterpart. In some way his intuitional feelers apparently bridge the shrinking gap between the two crash-course vehicles, and in a quick play of personalities the relative force of intent of the two rivals is gauged. As an outcome both drivers are usually preserved to play the game again.

Occasionally the psychic interplay is not concluded until the last possible moment. Undoubtedly this denotes two almost perfectly matched contestants. The result is nerve shattering to the passengers, particularly those unproven in the razor-sharp school. In such cases, driver and passengers alike in both vehicles erupt into a volcano of abuse at the other driver, at his passengers, and at one another.

The bus trip to Pimpalgaon was quite tame in comparison with a real roaring country excursion by auto, but it had its moments of thrill when oncoming buses and trucks chose to exert their claims, or when bullocks too stubborn to recognize any traffic rules heaved to the side at the wrong moment. Even so, it would have been a dull trip if it had not been such a glorious day, and if they had not been going to see some of the most sacred spots associated with Baba.

Just two or three miles short of Pimpalgaon the buses ground to a halt to ford a narrow stream. Shifting into low gear, they grunted and felt their way carefully across the gravelly bottom. The precaution was needed, for occasionally the current would unexpectedly hollow out a deep hole which could easily break an axle.

Beyond the stream and through a bit of forest they broke into the open fields surrounding Pimpalgaon. They curved to the left, the village lying to the right, a low line of small huts and buildings. At last they came unexpectedly to a halt at the side of a collection of strung-out sheds. This was the back part of Meherazad. Strangely standing out from the collection was the blue-painted body of some old passenger bus. Several of the small buildings clearly served as bedrooms, others perhaps as storage sheds, and a garage or two. The whole was too complex to register clearly at a glance.

Baba was there with the *mandali*, waiting for the *sahvasis* to arrive. After exchanging a warm round of greetings, Baba set off at once in the lead to show the *sahvasis* the grounds and buildings. The large party strung out in snake-like form as Baba rounded the end of the protecting barrier of out-buildings which had first been seen, and which shielded from view the two principal dwellings of Meherazad. These were of frame and stucco construction, two stories high, set in a magnificent garden showing clearly the careful attention of one who knew the soul of plants.

There was a further fact which distinguished the garden. Each plant, shrub and tree possessed its own individual dignity. None was banked into an anonymous mass designed to achieve background effect, and yet the overall impression was one of individualism blended into coherent harmony.

Baba led the group into the larger of the two principal dwellings, built in a style which might be described as a combination of Spanish hacienda and California ranch type. The effect was charming, simple and cool.

This was where Baba rested at night. One could not have wished to find a place of more simple, uncluttered taste, and yet showing no semblance of monastic austerity. One could imagine here scenes of simple human jollity, of pathos, of elation, of life lived to its fullest, and yet stripped to its most enduring essentials. This was Baba, but it was also Baba suffused through discerning, feeling hearts and hands.

Why try to describe in exact detail the furniture and the arrangement of the rooms? In this case these are the trivia, and the atmosphere the all. One could feel human hearts opening out in trust, hinges of the human soul creaking into action that had long been immobilized, the weight of human worry lifting as if hollowed from

within to an indifferent weightlessness. Here the process of finding
the divine within could happen even to oneself.

But time did not stand still to allow the formality of endless speculation on the seed. The human tide moved on through the quarters
and around the exterior of the second house, now unused. Here
through the years had been housed many women from the West.
Baba led the line of *sahvasis* out across the corn field and towards an
abrupt hill that rose in back of the property.

As they began to climb Seclusion Hill, one of the young *sahvasis*
struck out from the sinuously winding path and began clambering
directly up through the brush. Baba immediately had him called
back, and then admonished him. "There is no one here who can
beat me climbing this hill, but we are here together to keep each
other company, and not off on an excursion."

As they came to the top of the ridge, two level spots could be seen
which were paved with bricks. One lay at the extreme top of the
ridge, while the other was perhaps a hundred yards back and below. Between the two ran a narrow trail atop the slim spine, the hill
falling away steeply at either side to the gentle roll of the plain
below.

"The two cabins built of asbestos sheets now adjoining the garden
below," Baba explained, "were originally built at these spots. When
I used to remain in seclusion in the cabin on the summit, some of the
mandali would occupy the one on the lower ridge. You can well imagine their problems, especially getting from one cabin to the other
when I summoned them, often at night when the wind would be
blowing furiously over the hill.

"Once I lived here on a few sips of water for seven days. I have
remained fasting and in seclusion for much longer periods, but six
of the days I passed here at that time (1947) were equivalent to six
months of my other fasts and seclusions. When I undergo suffering
for the world, the load I have to bear is gigantic, and affects even my
physical body. I look then as if I had just passed through a severe
illness."

As the *sahvasis* looked about them and at the tiny dots far below,
a sense stole over them of events which towered into the sky, and
they knew, as if the years had suddenly parted into the dim future,

that on these two leveled spots where now only brick floors remained, one day shrines would rise as people commemorated and worshiped the unfathomable.

Here I felt that I would wish to fall down and worship too, for the far beyond was mightily close, and it swept all about one and pierced insensibly to one's soul.

After they had descended, Baba collected the group again in the cool shade of the garden, letting them quiet down of their own wills before he addressed them.

"Tomorrow, when you go from here back to your homes, some of you will take photos of Baba with you, but what Baba wants you to do is to take Baba with you.

"As you leave me you should take as much of me as you can. There is no doubt that I am in you all. However it is up to you to take me with you and to keep me with you.

"To come to me is difficult in itself. Having overcome this difficulty, do not go away from me for anything, or to any other place. When you leave here, go straight back to your homes. You have come for me, and you should go for me. If you leave to visit other places and to do other things, do all that after completing the circuit of coming and going exclusively for me. Whatever you do, do it whole-heartedly. Let there be no half-hearted dealings between us.

"Having come so near to Bombay, one of you has received a number of telegrams from business connections there. But I have asked this person to return home first and then return to Bombay. I don't want you to be half-hearted in your business with me."

At this point Baba apparently recalled that in the newness of the routine of the morning he had forgotten to inquire about their sleep.

"During the past days I have made it a routine of inquiring how you slept and whether you were all right. Some have described visions or other experiences which kept them awake. Some have said that they could not sleep because their immediate neighbors were snoring loudly, and others could not sleep because they were indisposed.

"I have comforted in one way or another those who did not sleep. One person stood up once because he saw that I embraced all those who did not sleep well. Now those of you who did not sleep or who do not feel well should stand up and not hesitate to speak frankly of your troubles."

As a number rose from the group, Baba stood up also as one of those who had not been able to sleep. When the roar of laughter which greeted this died down, the usual person-by-person quizzing went on. One individual had had a vision lasting more than twelve hours. Baba did not allow him to finish his detailed account but motioned to him to sit down, saying that what he had been experiencing was good and that he was not lying. The audience was then told that this man had often been with Baba, since December, 1938, when as a boy in his teens he had composed songs about Baba.

Baba then turned towards him and gestured: "Now listen. Whatever your experiences may be, there is no reason to beat on a tomtom. Listen to me very carefully. When we narrate such experiences we cannot help saying, 'I saw this', 'I felt that', and so on, and so one must take care not to let it get unbalanced and allow the importance to shift to the fact that *I* experienced this or that. For thus the ego is tickled and thereby magnified unnecessarily to one's own detriment.

"One has to go a long, long way to achieve the summit of self-realization. While trying to reach that goal, even *rishis* and *munis* (sages) are apt to fall through expressions of egotism.

"Do not make an exhibit of your love for me. If it is strong enough it will shine through simply and clearly. Of course when I ask you, you must tell me truthfully your feelings and experiences.

"I like you. You possess a pure, innocent heart. Go on loving me more and more. To do that you need not stop taking care of your own family. Also, *do not get upset when your initial state of tranquility is disturbed.*"

As the quizzing about conditions of sleep and health proceeded, the conversation was studded with frequent outbursts of chuckles when matters repeatedly took a light-hearted turn. Although the air of concern of the ill or sleepless one was deftly transmuted in each case into light-hearted acceptance of the situation, there was never the faintest suggestion of lack of full concern on Baba's part. The master psychologist was at work, and out of the dull stuff of human troubles there was produced a leavened loaf of full-bodied optimism towards the future.

The quizzing and the sympathetic jollity came to an end, and Baba turned his attention again to more weighty matters. Each time he prepared to discuss one of these subjects, its start was unconsciously anticipated by the audience, and an expectant hush would steal over them. This would be one of the last, perhaps *the* last, of these discourses, and the men waited in keen anticipation for the subject Baba had chosen.

"Now I wish to talk with you about miracles. This matter is always coming up, and no matter how often I tell people that I have never consciously performed a miracle, these stories still persist. I want to tell you all very honestly again that I have never consciously performed a miracle.

"Ages and ages ago I did perform one great miracle, and the whole of this illusion of creation came from me.* I will perform another such miracle at the time when I break my silence. That will be my first and last miracle in my present incarnation.

"Expect no other miracle from me, and do not associate me with any others. There is a stream of letters from both East and West describing the wonderful experiences of people who say they 'see' me, and 'find' that I do things for them, or 'experience' things which happen through my intervention.

"This is all news to me, as I do nothing of the sort. But there need be no wonder at these things, for people's own love for me and faith in me can do anything.

"Rawalbhai, tell these people what you have personally witnessed when your district badly needed rain."

One of the *sahvasis* rose to his feet and in a few brief sentences told of one of Baba's most ardent followers who had asked in Baba's name that it rain in their parched district. And to the joy of both those who wanted the rain and those who loved Baba, it had rained.

"We need not doubt what Rawalbhai says," Baba continued. "He has witnessed this with his own eyes. But the fact remains that I did not know about this, and I did nothing to bring the matter about.

---

* One must bear constantly in mind the context of "my Father and I are one."

"If I wished, I could make this harmonium dance and play songs all by itself in front of you. Seeing this, you would be sufficiently impressed to obey me, but your obedience would be towards the singing and dancing harmonium, not me.

"You should know two things which have happened during the last two months. In one instance a dead child, whose parents did not love me and who had not even seen me, is said to have come to life again as my name was said over it. In the second instance a young man who loved me dearly and obeyed me implicitly died a tragic death, with my name on his lips to the very last.

"Let me tell you first of the so-called miracle of the dead child returning to life in my name. We recently received a letter from Hamirpur describing this event in great detail.

"A seeker after the truth by the name of Ramdas was directed by his *guru* to call on me at Satara during my last seclusion there. It happened by coincidence that I had sent for all the resident *mandali* to discuss a phase of my work with them. When I inquired if all were there, Eruch had in all truthfulness to tell me about the visitor whom they had left behind.

"I then allowed Ramdas, the visitor, to come to see me, but only through one of the windows, and he was instructed then to go away. Shortly thereafter, he tells my followers in Hamirpur, he saw me in three different forms, as Ram, as Krishna, as —— but I have forgotten the third name given in the letter from Hamirpur.

"Because of the vision Ramdas had seen, he went into the countryside of Utter Pradesh, rather than to Nasik for the *sinhast* (periodic) fair as he had originally planned. In Utter Pradesh he first fasted for some time, and then began to spread my message of love.

"Ramdas selected an area hostile to love and devotion, but he prevailed upon the head of one village to agree to a *kirtan* (discourse on spiritual subjects, accompanied by music) held in my name at the village head's home.

"It is said that he had agreed to this because one of his children was seriously ill, and that his suffering had made him remember God. But let me say to you that one who remembers God in the hour of happiness, remembers God best.

"My worker arranged the *kirtan,* and in the middle of it the sick child suddenly died instead of getting well. Despite the ensuing confusion, Ramdas remained steadfast and, taking the dead child in his lap, continued the *kirtan* with even greater zeal and devotion, meanwhile offering profound silent prayers to me.

"The child returned to life before the *kirtan* was ended."

Baba paused to let the audience absorb the full import of what he had said. Perhaps in some situations a similar group would have cheered, but these men had been long enough in Baba's presence, and become sufficiently conversant with the unexpected nature of his viewpoint, to understand that even this great event was part of illusion. They waited soundlessly for the story to spin on.

"Because of this, thousands in that village and the surrounding countryside expressed their enthusiastic devotion towards me. But I say that this enthusiasm and devotion were not truly for me, but for the incident which had occurred in their village. Regardless of the fervor of their expression, it was not out of love for God, but for love of an additional illusion which had occurred within the illusion of their daily lives."

Baba then singled out the one from the audience who had held the dead child on his lap.

"Listen to me, Ramdas, the child did not return to life because of any miracle on my part. Even granting that the child really revived due to your love for me, this is not a great thing. The really great thing would be for you yourself to die * in your love for me.

"Beware of your 'I'. Never let your ego feed on cheap things. Crowds easily gather around you, but do not let yourself become lost in the crowds, for you would be finished once and for all.

"Now I will tell you of the second miracle which happened only a month ago. Some of you must have seen or heard of Navrozji Dadachanji of Bombay. He and his family love me dearly.

"His son Nozher died recently in a flying accident near Hyderabad. He was a handsome young man, and deeply devoted to me. Besides helping to support his family, he also spent freely from his salary, as an instructor in the Indian Air Force, for my cause and in my name.

"He had called on me at Satara just before he went to Hyderabad.

---

* Not literally to die physically, but to the importance of the world of illusion.

As I had instructed him, he never failed to take my name each time before flying. This he did when he was leaving on a routine training flight. He and one other were in a two-seater plane, and, as things sometimes happen for reasons which will never be known, the plane suddenly dove straight into a lake and both men were lost. Nozher was one of my gems; he died with my name on his lips and has come to me."

The quiet of the group was profound. Baba looked very small for the moment in the silent garden, and yet something akin to a fierce pride seemed to burn in his eyes. One felt very close to the eternal miracle, and the sense of it spilled through the silent audience. The spell of human souls touching, one to another, lasted a full eternal moment, and then Baba roused himself to complete his story.

"At the time of the accident I had gone on to Poona to rest from my seclusion. It was there that Nozher's family sent me a telegram with the news of the accident, expressing their regrets in it for disturbing my rest with the news.

"Such love is what I consider to be the true miracle, the miracle of love."

Again a moment of no speaking, of the quiet even breathing of the *sahvasis*. Again Baba plunged on.

"In reality, there is nothing such as death or birth. I know this, and I say it with the authority of my conscious knowledge. We are all in eternity, and we will always be there.

"Really, none comes or goes, none is born or dies. But to experience this truth we must first free ourselves from the bondage of our ignorance.

"After a hundred years or so you will all have dropped your bodies, and yet you will still exist. Do not think about your bodies, but think only about me. Then, before you drop your bodies, you will be able to remember me.

"My miracle will be to make you become me.

"Although all of you regard yourselves as belonging to different religions, nationalities, etc., to me you are all one. I have not the least objection if you go to meet saints of any religious sect, pay them your respects, and remain in their company. They are all in me. If you feel that a particular being is a great saint worthy of your respect, why should you not revere him?

"But if you want to see God and to become one with God, then the only solution is to catch hold of my *daaman* (hem of garment). If you care only for God, and if you have the one sole sincere desire for union (God-realization), then hold onto my *daaman* exclusively.

"If you want things such as health, wealth, children and other material things, then don't come to me. There are many saints capable of satisfying your desires, and they might be pleased to give you what you want.

"I am what they call in Iran a *shah-saudagar* (merchant-prince). I am neither a wholesale nor a retail dealer. If you're in the market to purchase a pin or a needle you must go to a retail merchant.

"I am not dealing in merchandise such as granting favors. A *shah-saudagar* can and may, if he likes, supply anyone with even a pin, but it would be unthinkable to approach him for such a thing."

With this, Baba rose and walked on through the garden, around the end of the smaller of the two houses placed in its midst, and back to the road beside the long line of sheds and low dwellings. Here the immediate *mandali* slept while Baba was in the Ahmednagar area. Two of the structures, to the rear and set off at one side, were the reconstructed small huts which had been carefully dismantled and carried down from the small mountain.

The blue bus body sandwiched into the line-up, Baba explained, had been used by him and the eastern and western women *mandali* in a long tour of India. Later, at Baba's request, the body had been detached from the chassis and set up at Meherazad, where Baba had spent the forty days of his "great seclusion" in it (June–July, 1949) just previous to the start of the "New Life" phase.

"After that seclusion at Meherazad," he gestured, "it took me and the *mandali* two full months to arrange and carry out at Meherabad the winding up of my old life, and to make preliminary arrangements for the new. Except for my future tomb on Meherabad Hill, I gave up permanently everything which was in my name, utilizing the proceeds for my old life obligations * before launching into the New Life (October, 1949)."

At the end of the inspection of the old bus body, Baba told the

---

* Many old dependents were given gifts in cash or kind.

group they were now to return to Meherabad. He himself would come at two-thirty, and after some Sufi devotional music he would say good-by to each member of the group.

It was mid-afternoon, and the strains of songs from the great Sufi mystics floated from the dormitory atop the old military reservoir. Each one in the room was trying to soak in the last essence of the occasion, to stretch each second of time into an eternity, that body, mind and soul might be wrapped in the endless perfection of the moment.

The rhythms swayed, and the bodies swayed, and suddenly one young man of stolid mien dropped unconscious.

There was a flutter of activity as restorative measures were applied. He was led in a somewhat dazed condition from the hall and the songs went on. India has developed its own knowledge through the centuries of the possible side effects of man's search for his soul. In the West the goal of the boxer is to knock his opponent into physical unconsciousness. In the East the spiritual aspirant might possibly lapse into a similar state of unconsciousness.

The devotions went on, and at last Baba signified that they were at an end. There was nothing left now but to receive the parting embrace of a good-by, and this I shall not tell. There is a time in human fullness, as in human sorrow, when the human soul must be allowed to sit within the privacy of its shrouds and smile or weep or caper as it may.

They walked down the hill, some smiling, some sad, some still gently weeping. They packed their bags and that evening some of them left to go home.

What had they left behind? What was this they carried in their hearts?

For one week they had been with a simple man of great tenderness. He had laughed with them, played with them, prayed with them. He had been father, mother, son and lover. He had played on the strings of their hearts until their innermost beings sang. He had drawn the fullness of feeling from them until they had wept at the tale of Nozher and the real miracle.

This was a man for whom there was no description, who awakened in them things that could not be defined. He was himself, and in that self lay the secret of finding one's own self. No logic was of any use in describing it, discussing it or explaining it. One had only the choice of experiencing it and being lost in the simplicity of it.

Old men became like children, over-awed and delighted by the presence of the true parent, yet the parent who at the same time was the child. Young men became old and wise beyond their years, with penetrating insight into the hidden springs which powered the movements of man in the universe. And they found within themselves the reason to be, and to continue to be, the sparkling streams of assured, unthinking hope, which is always the seal of youth.

Who was this man with whom they had spent this priceless week? He was called "Meher Baba" (compassionate father), and thousands flocked about him at the slightest opportunity. But what did it matter who he was? What did it matter what anyone else thought or said? What *did* matter was this almost overpowering knowledge of having carved through mountains to come back to where one had started: one's own self. Now, it was a self which was real, friendly, believing in itself, no longer disconnected from other selves; a self which felt and lived and vibrated as the quivering reed to the tuning note of the universe.

With its age-old knowledge, India had once more transmuted the individual into the self. A master alchemist had done it. The real miracle was that it had happened today in a busy world of whirling machines and the exploding energies of a giant civilization. But the greatest mystery, that of the self, had been exhibited once more in a timeless process which requires nothing but the touchstone of one who is already one with Himself.

These were the things that Meher Baba said and did with somewhat more than a thousand of his followers in India in November of 1955. If sometimes they have not been told in the same time relationship which they originally bore to one another, then it has been the fault of the one who has tried to describe them, for he too has labored under his own weighty notions of how the story should be told.

All of these things did happen, and within the resources of the memory of Ramju and the quiet one, who were there, and the swiftly moving pencil of the scribes, Faram and Kishan Singh, who were also there, this is a true description of what happened and what was said.

This is a story of the human heart. However the human heart is also closely linked to the human mind, which has a persistent quality of inquiry. Part II is now offered so that the mind may ponder and speculate on matters of great interest regarding the mechanics of creation. It is Meher Baba who now speaks direct.

PART II

Life and the Path

CHAPTER 1

Death and Immortality

The immersion of the individual in the routine of life causes him to be seriously disturbed by the sudden experience of death, particularly when it takes away someone who has been near and dear to him. When the sight of death becomes too frequent, as in time of war or during an epidemic, the individual's mind tends to protect itself by retiring within a shell of habit and routine. Familiar actions, faces and surroundings, which require no thought or adjustment, become at such times a buttress to his emotional balance.

But even this wall of cultivated indifference crumbles when the hand of death snatches away someone who has entered deeply into his inner life—someone who perhaps acted as the pivotal point upon which his emotions turned. At such a time his unquestioning attitude towards life is disturbed and his mind becomes deeply preoccupied with an intensive search for lasting values.

The life of each person is deeply enmeshed in this mystery of death. But it is a mystery which accents thought instead of dulling it, for if anything makes man think intensely about the true nature of life, it is the recurrent theme of death.

As the tale of life is told it pauses frequently to contemplate the gaping holes left by death. There is no way to avoid the thought-provoking impact of that inescapable presence.

Although none escapes the intensive search for the hidden secret to the meaning of death, few can lift the veil and unravel the mystery. For most it remains a soul-searing enigma which causes deep restlessness; for some it offers a wide field for imaginative speculation; for the few, it yields its secret.

Many refuse to accept death as the simple, final extinction of the individual, but this reaction is more often a form of unreasoned wish than a matter of unshakable conviction. Even so, this instinctive rebellion should not be lightly dismissed, for much of the vigor of this blind protest against the seeming fact of death springs from an obscured but still functioning intuition. However, this intuitive reaction does not approach the more secure position achieved through reasoned belief based on faith in the authority of a seer, or on the direct perception of those who know.

When a sensitive individual is first faced by a death of deep significance in his circle of close friends, he is usually struck by the transitory nature of all forms of life. Confronted by the undeniable impermanence of the body, yet unfortified by knowledge of some sustaining permanent principle, he often falls into a mood of deep despair or supercilious cynicism.

If life is inexorably doomed to extinction, he reasons, there can be little meaning in frantic efforts to achieve. In turn, this thought leaves him in a vacuum of purpose which may lead him either to a state of supine inaction, or may precipitate him into reckless rebellion. To him, existence seems to be conditional, intermittent and vanishing, while extinction appears to be unqualified, inescapable and permanent.

When such a grim conclusion has been reached, whether consciously or unconsciously, the individual is tempted to rain death and destruction upon others, or to invite it upon himself, merely because death appears to be more lasting than life. The recklessly destructive desperado and the determined suicide belong to this type. They cannot accept life as having any real value, because their initial, unthinking faith in the value of life has been uprooted by the rude shock of death.

If death is accepted as real, and longer in duration than life, then life is degraded below meaninglessness. Even then, such values in life as truth, beauty, goodness and love can claim some intrinsic worth despite their fleeting existence. But in practical fact, all keenness for the pursuit of even these momentary values is gradually replaced by a sense of hopeless apathy, for one hears constantly a background whisper which says that they too are doomed to vanish one day.

If the cat, while stealthily drinking milk, knows that someone is waiting outside the door with a club, she can hardly relish the flavor of her surreptitious meal. Similarly, a man who comes to know that all his achievements must soon be brought to naught, can hardly have his heart in his efforts. If he stops to reflect that all the people he loves are earmarked for early conversion to dust, then his spontaneous enthusiasm gradually dries up and he is forced to consider what he is striving for. If he tries to cling to these loved ones despite his new awareness, all the desperateness of his ensuing efforts becomes only a sacrifice to vanity.

In order to avoid the pain which he is bound to feel at the inevitable loss of his dear ones, he may try to avoid life by adopting the viewpoint that the living are no more than on a par with the dead. The success of such a game depends upon an exact equation, for if he holds the slightest preference for the living, he will be gravely affected when the living become the dead.

He is forced finally to face the fact that if death means the extinguishing of his beloved brothers in a blind vacuum of eternity, then the entire game of life is a meaningless tragedy. All courage, sacrifice and loyalty to ideals become a farce, and all vital seeking takes on the cast of empty endeavor, of much effort without purpose. Fear of loss treads closely upon all earnest attempts to appropriate and inherit the significance of life, depriving it of all sweetness.

In short, if death is looked upon as mere extinction, man tends to lose his balance and is plunged into perpetual gloom. All his dreams of the enduring reality of truth, beauty and love are refuted and seem by hindsight to have been a blind groping after illusion. His previous ideal of eternal and inexhaustible sweetness, instead of filling him with hope and enthusiasm, now reproaches him with the utter senselessness of all earthly values.

Thus death, when not understood, vitiates the whole of life, and the first impulsive answer of inaction or cynicism, which the individual usually forges to meet the question, strands him in a thoroughly desiccated universe of unrelieved weariness. Nevertheless, this gradually prepares him for another attempt to find a more vital answer to the inescapable query.

The human mind cannot endure such a stalemate for long, as there is an internal force which insists that the inner nature be in motion. Eventually the pressure for such motion breaks through the rigidity of such a negative concept of death. A great flood of new interrogation and discovery often breaks out, and in it the key question now posed by death becomes "What is life?"

The answers supplied are countless, and depend upon the passing moods which spring from the deeply rooted ignorance of the interrogator. The first instinctive answer is "Life is that which is terminated by death". This answer too is still completely inadequate, as it involves no positive principle on which a fruitful life can be based, nor can the individual's need for development be met. Such an answer explains neither death nor life. The individual is driven to try to understand life and death along new lines.

Instead of looking upon death as the opposite of life, he now inevitably comes to look upon it as the handmaiden of life.

He begins to affirm intuitively the reality and the eternality of life. Instead of interpreting life in terms of death, man seeks to interpret death in terms of life. Slowly, event by event, he learns to take life again in all earnestness, with a deeper affirming consciousness. As he does so, he is able to give a more constructive response to the recurring sight of death. The challenge of death is now not only accepted and absorbed by life, but is met by a counter-challenge: "What is death?" It is now death's turn to submit itself to critical scrutiny.

The most unsophisticated answer to this counter-question is "Death is only an incident in life". This simple and profoundly true declaration terminates the unendurable chaos precipitated by regarding death as the extinction of life. Soon it is clearly seen that it is futile to try to understand death without first understanding life.

As consciousness gradually settles into this balanced approach to the problem, it takes on a healthy tone which makes it receptive to the truth concerning both life and death. Direct, undimmed knowledge of such truth is available only to spiritually advanced souls. The seers of all times have had direct access to the truth about life and death, and they have repeatedly given a suffering and groping humanity useful information on this point.

Their explanations are important because they protect man's mind from erroneous and harmful attitudes towards life and death, and prepare him for perception of the truth. Although direct knowledge of truth requires considerable spiritual perception, nevertheless even correct intellectual understanding of the relationships of life and death plays an important part in restoring mankind to a healthy outlook.

Above incarnate life in birth and beyond discarnate life after death, the soul is one indivisible, eternal existence. The gestation of individualization of the soul begins with the evolution of its consciousness. Consciousness begins to evolve in incarnate life, and its evolution becomes complete only in incarnate life.

Simultaneously with the evolution of consciousness through the evolution of forms (bodies), *sanskaras* * begin to accumulate. The evolution of form and of consciousness (and with it individualization of the human ego-mind) is complete when the soul attains the human form for the first time. But because of the accumulated *sanskaras*, the fully evolved consciousness of the soul remains entrapped in illusion and therefore is not directed towards the soul's self-realization (God-realization).

For self-realization, all *sanskaras* must be completely wiped out to enable the soul, as the individualized ego, to be transmuted into the individualized soul in the conscious state of God. Further, the *sanskaras* that began to accumulate in an incarnate life, have to be wiped out in an incarnate life. In order to be wiped out in toto, *sanskaras* must be annulled or cancelled through the process of *exact*-equalization or perfect qualitative and quantitative balancing of *all* opposite *sanskaras*, whether good or bad. This is extremely difficult, for the *sanskaras* have a natural tendency towards preponderance of one opposite over the other.

While unbalance of the opposite *sanskaras* reaches its maximum in an incarnate life, *near* balancing is achieved after death during a period of discarnate life, through the intense subjective pleasure or suffering in the states known as heaven and hell. Each incarnate life is an opportunity for the realization of one's true self. Each death or discarnate life is an opportunity for achieving a semblance of bal-

---

* *Sanskaras* are the habit patterns and the unconscious motivations remaining from previous actions in this and in past lives. They are the propelling forces which so largely determine the actions of the individual, and leave him so little opportunity for positive action aimed at progressive understanding and development of his own nature.

ance to start another birth, with its further chance at self-realization. If the opportunity were fully taken, *one* incarnate life could be sufficient to make the individual realize this goal; but it is well-nigh impossible to attain the initiative and longing to do so without getting involved in the illusory maze of innumerable opposite experiences. The contact of a Perfect Master is invaluable in calling a halt to the dizzy gyrations of incarnate and discarnate lives in illusion, and awakening the individual to the real knowledge of self.

From the psychological point of view, death entails no slightest curtailment of individual existence. This does not mean that the surviving mind remains unaffected by the *kind* of death which severed the individual from the body. Both the condition of the mind as well as its capability to progress further in the life-after-death are often substantially determined by the conditions surrounding the death.

From the standpoint of its psychic after-effects, death can be classified into three broad types, (1) normal, (2) abnormal and (3) supernormal. Normal death follows an illness which ultimately renders the physiological functioning of the body impossible. Generally it involves some kind of warning to the individual, for, if the illness is severe, he often anticipates that death is at hand. Although by no means true of all deaths caused by illness, when the individual has some anticipation of impending death he usually has a chance to tie up loose ends and prepare his mind for this new crisis.

The second or abnormal type of death is that which results from accidents, murder, war and suicide. In accidents and murder there is generally no anticipation of impending death. Being unexpected, death involves in such instances a shock which can shatter the very roots of the *sanskaras* seeking expression through the physical incarnation of the individual.

In unanticipated accidental death, the ordinary ego-mind has a moderate tendency to gravitate towards the gross sphere and cling to it because of the ego-mind's attachment to the gross world.

In anticipated (abnormal) death, when resulting from murder or war, the ego-mind can become bound to the gross world by the chains of unfulfilled revenge. There is less tendency for such binding to occur in death due to war, than in that resulting from murder. In war the combatants on both sides are often impersonal in their actions, and aware that they are fighting for some cause, rather than through personal enmity. If this awareness is clear and steady, death in war does not yield the mental reaction of revenge.

Among abnormal kinds of death, suicide deserves special attention. Suicide may be divided into four grades, (1) lowest, (2) low, (3) high and (4) highest.

The lowest type is a last measure in escaping punishment or ignominy or utter frustration after the individual has tried unscrupulously to satisfy his own selfish desires. Thus one who has committed murder for lust or power may commit suicide when he is caught. Even after leaving the body, such a person does not succeed in severing his link with the gross world for hundreds of years. These individuals live literally as ghosts in the semi-subtle sphere, which lies between the gross and the subtle world. They experience agonizing suffering because of their unfulfilled desires. Due to the link which they preserve with the gross world, they continue to desire various gross objects keenly, a desire which can never be fulfilled. This suffering is even more acute than the intense sufferings in the hell-state * that the individual experiences after he severs his connection with the gross world.

A somewhat less acute class of suffering in imagination is experienced in the hell-state by suicides who have been slightly better motivated, but who are still classified as "low". In this group are those motivated by sheer disgust with life. Thus a person suffering from bad health, or stricken by a loathsome disease, or one who is poverty-stricken and ashamed of being a burden on others, might put an end to his life through lack of will to live.

Since the cause of such a suicide is revulsion from earthly life, the ego-mind does not continue to maintain any enduring link with the gross world beyond the normal three or four days following death. After that normal period, the link is snapped and the ego-mind then begins to experience the intense suffering of its bad *sanskaras*, usually termed the hell-state.

---

* Neither hell nor heaven should be regarded as places. They are mental states, and imaginary in the same sense that the world of duality also exists in the realm of illusion. See below.

Although a ghost caught in the semi-subtle sphere suffers even more acutely than does the ego-mind "experiencing" the hell-state, the latter achieves some exhaustion of evil *sanskaras* while the former does not. Further, the sufferings of the ghosts who maintain their link with the earthly life are more tantalizing, because the link constantly holds before them the prospect of fulfillment of gross desires, without actual means for their satisfaction.

The general belief that suicide is bad is due to the fact that it is usually the result of low motives or a cowardly attitude towards life. When suicide is employed as an escape from dilemmas brought on by failure to cope with the needs of life, it is not only ignoble, but far-reaching as well in its demoralizing effects upon the victim.

The third or high type of suicide is in no way rooted in inferior motives and is therefore free of their deteriorating effects. It is inspired by altruistic motives alone and is a sacrifice made to secure the material or spiritual well-being of others. One who meets death through, *e. g.* a hunger strike, in order to better the welfare of the masses, is a suicide of this high type.

The motives of such a suicide are not far different from those of martyrs who lay down their lives on the battlefield for country, society or religion. The total absence of base motives in this high type of suicide makes it entirely different from the lower grades. As in other noble acts of self-effacement, such highly motivated action entitles the departed individual to the privileges and pleasures of the heavenly state, and also constitutes a definite asset in his spiritual ongoing.

A suicide inspired by ordinary altruistic motives is not the highest type. The fourth or highest class results from intense desire to see God or to unite with Him; this is an extremely rare occurrence. In most cases in which suicide is believed to have been committed for the sake of God, there is an admixture of other motivating factors, such as dissatisfaction with conditions in earthly life.

If and when suicide is embraced purely for the sake of attaining God, it can have the effect of achieving liberation, or *Mukti*. The masters have always warned aspirants against resorting to suicide in the intensity of their longing for union with God, for there is too great room for self-deception and inadvertent admixture of inferior unconscious motivation.

Regardless of the abnormality of the circumstances which may lie back of it, no type of death can really damn the individual forever. It is never more than an incident in his long spiritual journey.

The third or supernormal type of death consists in leaving the body voluntarily. This is done by the advanced yogis who wind up their earthly careers after fulfilling their mission, much as the student locks up his text books after passing his examination. The supernormal or voluntary death of the advanced yogi is definitely anticipated and willed, but is entirely different from suicide insofar as motives, results and manner of leaving the body are concerned.

Friends and relatives of a departed one often are seriously upset by his death, because the dissolution of the form may seem to them to be the extinction of life itself. All of their attachments had been related to the *form*. It was because of the *form* that they had contact with the soul, and it was through the *form* that their various physical and emotional needs were fulfilled. The disappearance of the body that had acted as the vehicle of the soul is therefore often interpreted by them as the annihilation of the individual himself.

From the purely physical point of view, death does not involve annihilation of even the body, but physiologically it has become unfit to be the continued dwelling place of the spirit, and has therefore lost all importance.

From the point of view of the individualized soul as mind, death does not involve any loss whatsoever, as the mind and all its *sanskaras* remain intact. The individual in essence is thus in no way different. He has only cast off his external coat. Nevertheless this severance from the physical body is fraught with two important consequences. It is a means of introducing the individual to a new type of existence, and it is also in itself an incident of the utmost importance because of side effects of the greatest practical consequence.

When others die, the individual loses only one or at most a few friends who have played an important role in his earthly existence. But when *he* dies he loses at one stroke all the persons who had entered intimately into his own life. He also loses all his possessions and is broken away from the achievements on which he had built the very foundations of his sense of accomplishment in life.

As the crowning touch, he must also leave behind the very physical body with which he had identified himself so completely that he was rarely capable of imagining himself as anything but that physical body. This complete annihilation of the entire structure of the individual's earthly existence is therefore a crisis without parallel in his life.

This critical turning point, which occurs at death, is attended by both advantages and disadvantages. The greatest disadvantage lies in the fact that the individual must leave incomplete all the undertakings of his earthly life; he must leave the entire chessboard without taking any further interest in it. The scene of his life is blotted out and the chain of his mundane interests is hacked apart.

From the standpoint of objective achievement, the continuity of his undertaking has undergone an abrupt break. Advancement of the projects he has left behind must come from his previous associates, and can no longer be his concern. It is rare for the individual to be drawn back through a *sanskaric* linking to the identical task which he had begun in a past incarnation, to develop it on from the point where his successors had left it.

It would be a mistake to think that death brings nothing but disadvantages. Death also brings about a general weakening of attachments by shattering all the *sanskaras* which were fed by the earthly objects, because the mind is now torn away from them. While it is true that many of the *sadhanas* * undertaken by the individual during earthly life have the effect of unwinding previous *sanskaras,* still it is only in extremely rare instances that he succeeds in completely erasing the present and future effects of these *sanskaras.* This erasure is effected within certain well-defined limits by the sudden transplanting of the individual that occurs at death.

If the lessons inherent in a single death were to be thoroughly assimilated by the individual, he would benefit by the equivalent of several lifetimes of patient spiritual effort. Unfortunately this does not happen in most cases, because after death the individual usually tries to revive his accumulated *sanskaras.* Through these revived

---

* Devotional and disciplinary practices.

sanskaras he recaptures the experiences through which he has already lived. The period immediately following death usually becomes therefore an occasion for the repetition of all that has previously been lived through, rather than a period of emancipation through understanding all that has been lived out.

Regardless of these shortcomings, death does give a severe shaking to the tree of *sanskaras*—root, trunk and branch—and this impels the mind to revise its attitude towards the objective universe. Death also facilitates a certain amount of disentanglement from the attractive world of form. The individual is never able to go back to earth without some modification of his approach to life.

Life in a new physical body must conform to lines determined by the individual's *sanskaras*. Thus there is often a close resemblance to the past life on earth, but it is not a literal repetition of the past. *It is a new experiment.*

This readjustment of outlook, which is faciliated by the abrupt reorientation involved in death, is particularly helpful when it occurs after spiritual aspiration has been awakened in the individual. In such cases the loosening of all attachment which occurs at death is very conducive to the further flowering of spiritual aspiration. The aspirant now has a chance under fresh circumstances to remodel the entire pattern of his life in line with his spiritual aspirations.

Because of these special opportunities which death offers, the aspirant does not regret his own death. For him, death is not a cloud without its silver lining. The Perfect Master Jalalu'l-Din Rumi has said that he always progressed through frequent deaths. But this cannot justify anyone, and even less a spiritual aspirant, in seeking death for its own sake. To seek death in this manner is to put a false premium upon it. Such seeking of death springs from fear of life and from failure to cope with it, and inevitably must defeat its own purpose.

If death has any value, it is to teach the individual the true art of life. It would be wrong for the aspirant to seek death with the hope of making further progress thereby. On the other hand he should not fear death when it overtakes him. A true aspirant neither seeks death nor fears it, and when death comes to him he converts it into a stepping stone to the higher life.

Some people are particularly afraid of the exact moment of death because they anticipate unbearable pain at that instant. In reality, all physical suffering experienced during illness or just before death terminates at the moment of death. The process of the actual dropping of the body is quite painless, contrary to the superstition that a person experiences indescribable agonies in death.

However the severing of the individual's emotional entanglement in the gross world is not found to be easy. The various religious rites observed after a death have primarily the purpose of helping the departing individual disentangle himself from these ties.

For instance, the repetition of the name of God or of scriptures, often practiced after the death of a person, has a wholesome effect both on those who have been left behind as well as on the one who has passed away, because they help to free both parties of their mutual *sanskaric* attachment to form. On the other hand the lamentation and wailing that is often observed has a degrading and depressing effect both on those left behind as well as on the person who has passed away, for it tends to strengthen mutual attachment to form.

The thought or wish the dying individual holds at the moment of death has special importance in determining his future destiny. If the last thought is of God or the master, the individual achieves liberation.

It is quite common for an individual not to have any specific thought at the moment of death. Even if he has had thoughts or wishes before death, he will tend to forget them at the time of death. At that moment some people hope they may not return to earthly life, but they are not exempted from rebirth by mere wishing. They are reborn, but exhibit a pronounced disgust for life, and tend to lead the lives of ascetics or recluses.

If the good * and evil *sanskaras* of the individual are almost balanced at the time of death, he may take on a new physical body almost immediately. He may even enter a new incarnation as early as the fourth day after death. In such urgent cases of rebirth the individ-

---

* "Good" actions leave *sanskaric* residues in the individual's subconscious as surely as do "bad" actions. Therefore the individual may be bound just as surely by the "golden chains forged by good actions" as by the "iron chains of bad actions."

ual can enliven a ready foetus any time between the sixth and seventh months of embryological development. It is important to note that both father and mother give only *prana* or vital energy to the foetus. In addition to receiving *prana,* it must be enlivened by some individualized soul. Ordinarily this takes place during the later stages of embryological development.

When the individual is ready for reincarnation he is automatically drawn to his future parents by *sanskaric* links. The parents act as a magnet due to their previous connections with the reincarnating individual. Occasionally the strongest *sanskaric* or *karmic* link which the reincarnating individual has with incarnate individuals is not with the parents, but with a brother or sister. It is this link, then, that determines the family in which he takes birth.

In times of emergency, as in wars or epidemics, when thousands of individuals may seek immediate reincarnation, it is not always possible for all to be born into families having strong previous links with them. But if the *sanskaric* status of the individual is precipitating him towards incarnation, his taking on of a body is not postponed merely because parents are not available to provide a suitable previous link. It is possible through the intervention of the Masters to make infinite adjustments through mutual exchanges.

Death is like throwing away clothes which have become useless through wear and tear. Just as a traveler may stop at different places, and at each halt may change clothes according to his needs, so the individual goes on changing his bodies according to the needs of his *sanskaras.*

Death may also be compared to sleep. When a man goes to sleep, he wakes up in the same physical body. When he drops his physical body at death, he wakes up in another physical body.

For most persons the period between death and birth is one of absorption in subjectivity. As mentioned before, after death the ego-mind of the individual normally retains its tie with the remnants of the physical body for three or four days. After this period the connection is completely severed and the individual then exists entirely in the subjectivity of his mental states. This subjective phase is brought about by the resurrection of all the *sanskaras* which the ego-mind has brought along with it after death.

The sudden transplanting of the ego-mind from one sphere to another does wear out the scars of the *sanskaras* to some extent, but for the greater part they remain intact. If death had resulted in the complete wiping out of all the *sanskaric* scars on the mind it would have resulted in emancipation of the individual from all limitation. But this does not happen. Not only are the *sanskaric* imprints retained after death, but they may unroll unhampered in the life after death.

As the *sanskaric* sheet is unwound, the individual experiences in the hell- or heaven-state the sufferings or pleasures embodied in the bad and good *sanskaras*. Every individual has both classes in his store, and his mental state in the life after death is determined by which of these preponderates.

The intensity of the sufferings or pleasures which the individual experiences through these revived *sanskaras* is so great that a greater exhaustion of these *sanskaras* is brought about during a relatively short period than is possible in hundreds of years of suffering or pleasure in the earthly life. It is these posthumous mental states of intense suffering and pleasure which are respectively known in religious literature as hell and heaven. In popular belief they are incorrectly regarded as places or spheres. It is more appropriate to speak of a *hell-state* or *heaven-state,* rather than places.

When there is a preponderance of evil *sanskaras* at death, the individual gradually exhausts the bad *sanskaras* through suffering in the hell-state. The result is that the evil *sanskaras* eventually tend to strike a balance with the good *sanskaras*. It is as if a huge block of ice were placed on one pan of a balance, causing it to sink because of its excess over a smaller weight contained on the counterbalance pan. As the great block of ice is gradually melted and the water spills, there is a tendency for the two pans to come into balance.

Similarly, as the mass of evil *sanskaras* becomes attenuated through suffering, their preponderance begins to vanish and they *almost* come into balance with the good *sanskaras*. This moment, when the two opposite types of *sanskaras* are almost in a state of balance, is the moment when the after-life of the individual terminates and he finds himself precipitating into a new physical incarnation on earth. He is precipitated into a new physical body because no further purpose is served by continuation of his subjective absorption in the discarnate life. He is ripe to accumulate fresh experience in another gross body, and for this purpose he must adopt a vehicle which is suitable for the working out of his unexhausted *sanskaras*.

If the individual soul has been exhausting an excess of evil *sanskaras* and has therefore been undergoing a hell-state, he may jump into a new incarnation in which good *sanskaras* tend to dominate. The cause of this unexpected reversal is to be found in the strength of flow of the *sanskaric* currents. At the time he incarnates, the individual had already been relieved of the excess of his evil *sanskaras*, and the strong tide of his good *sanskaras* was about to predominate. Consequently it is the vigorous current of the good *sanskaras* which motivates him in his new incarnation. Thus a man who had been a profligate in his last life might begin his new incarnation with a marked inclination towards asceticism.

Conversely, a swing over can occur from good to bad when one jumps into an incarnation from a heaven-state in which the preponderance of good *sankaras* had been exhausted through intense imaginative pleasure. The moment of incarnation into a new physical body is precipitated when the good and the bad *sanskaras* have *almost* balanced each other and the tide of the bad *sanskaras* is about to predominate.

A change over at incarnation from good to bad or from bad to good should not be taken as a universal law. Reversal of individual nature is frequent, but cases are also quite common in which the individual remains persistently good or bad for several incarnations. In such cases incarnation occurs before the opposite type of *sanskara* has built up a sufficient current of flow to result in its predominance.

The beginning of the true existence of the individual self * occurs at the moment when consciousness in the course of its evolution

---

* Not to be confused with the manifestation of the individual soul, which occurred at the very beginning of the long evolutive process through the various sub-gaseous, gaseous, stone, metal, vegetable, fish and animal forms. See *God Speaks*, Meher Baba.

adopts its *first* human form. This also represents the terminal step in its *evolutionary* development. This is the moment when the limited individuality is crystallized as the "I" that exhibits the basic characteristic of "self-consciousness". This is the true birth of the individual.

The true death of the individual occurs at that moment when he transcends his limited individuality or separative consciousness by being taken up in the truth-consciousness of the unlimited and undivided being of God. The true death of the individual consists in the complete disappearance of the limiting ego-mind that has created the *sanskaric* veil of ignorance. True death is a far more difficult process than physical death, but when it occurs through the grace of the master it takes no longer than the twinkling of an eye. This dissolution of the ego-mind and the freeing of the soul from the illusion of separative limited individuality are known as liberation.

The *sanskara*-ridden ego-mind can never attain any real poise. It vacillates in constant rhythm to the alternating dominant *sanskaras*. Consciousness can attain true poise only when the ego-mind with all its attendant *sanskaras* terminates. This is effected through the emergence of the unlimited and ultra-*sanskaric* individuality that comes into its own upon the inheriting of conscious, eternal existence, which is true immortality.

The infinite poise of consciousness in realization should not be confused with the semblance of *sanskaric* equilibration that is approached by the limited ego-mind in discarnate life in the hell- or heaven-state. Such ineffable poise is unapproachable by the full consciousness in man as long as it remains clouded by the slightest traces of the limiting ego-mind.

At the time of taking on a new physical body, the good and the bad *sanskaras* of the individual are *almost* in balance. However there is always a slight ascendance at this time of either the good or bad *sanskaras*. They are never in perfect balance, nor do they in any manner overlap or cancel one another. Complete poise can exist only when the two opposite classes of *sanskaras* are so qualitatively and quantitatively opposed that they exactly cancel one another.

When opposite *sanskaras* are not only equal in strength but are also in exact qualitative opposition, they cancel each other and can no longer act as semi-automatic subjective propelling forces, but are transmuted into consummate understanding that is free from opposing reactions to life. This is the state of liberation.

The seeming balance that is approximated by the individual before each birth may be compared to a tug-of-war in which opposite forces are active, although neither may predominate. The matching of forces then has only to be slightly disturbed and the entire situation becomes subject to change. In the same manner, the pseudo-poise of *sanskaras* present at the time of birth has only to be slightly disturbed in order to imprint the *sanskaric* pattern for the individual life.

In the state of realization the opposite types of *sanskaras* interpenetrate each other in such a manner that they cease to exist as opposing forces. The resultant is not a state of *sanskaric* tension, but a state of complete internal neutralization in which the *sanskaras* have ceased to exist as propulsive elements. This is not a mere state of exact mathematical equalization of opposites, but a state beyond the opposites—of true poise rooted in unbroken consciousness of infinite unity.

During the entire long period preceding realization, the mind acts in each single circumstance according to the dictates of the preponderant *sanskaras*. As in a tug-of-war, there is movement in the direction of the greater pull, but that motion represents only a small proportion of the total energy spent, for most of it was used up in the opposition of forces.

In realization there is an entire disappearance or cancellation of the *sanskaras* such as would occur in a tug-of-war when the opposing parties finished the game and stopped pulling in opposite directions. On the other hand, in near equalization of *sanskaric* tension there is only a temporary arrest of express activity. Then, when some new or outside factor upsets this equilibrium, reactions occur which show that the situation had been quiet not because of lack of propelling forces, but rather because they had temporarily cancelled one another. *

---

* This analysis has the greatest possible practical significance in considering the adjustment of the individual to his environment. It often happens that balancing forces in environment tend to bring a very difficult personal situation into temporary equilibrium. At this point the individual tends to regard the situation as solved, because he is no longer

With the annulment of the *sanskaras,* the individual is freed permanently from all *sanskaric* determination. As a consequence, for the first time the individual's life can express itself without latent or patent inhibitions, for it functions in the limitless understanding of truth.

This true poise of realization, which admits no further possibility of disturbance through resurrection of any limiting tendencies, can only be attained while the individual has a physical body. It can never come through the speeding-up processes of one-sided *sanskaric* exhaustion that take place in the hell-state or heaven-state. This is the all-important reason why every individual has to come back to the gross world again and again in physical incarnation, until self-realization is attained.

The alternating links of the continuous chain of individual existence consist of incarnate and discarnate lives, forged from periods of birth to death and death to birth. Only in God-realization can life be freed from the shackles of limited individuality. Only in God-realization does the tenacious chain of recurrent incarnations reach final fulfillment and termination. It is a state of eternal existence, free from birth or death. It is true immortality or deathlessness, by virtue of the fact that it is *above* the birth and death of the body.

True immortality is not the survival of the limited individual in the period following the death of the physical body. It is true that the ego-mind persists unscathed through death, but the individual

---

aware of any intense localized pressure.

However, eventually those balancing forces will shift, and once more the situation will seem to fly out of control. This is usually very discouraging because the sequence may be repeated several times without apparent improvement. The individual then often asks himself why he should continue to try, as he never seems to find a lasting solution to his problems.

But the poise originally established was due only to a happy combination of forces (*sanskaras*) that almost cancelled each other. Final release comes as the basic motivating forces are dissolved and resorbed in the process of ultimate realization.

This may seem a discouragingly remote solution to the pressing problem of the moment, but in such a final solution the answer is complete and the poise absolute, because the forces themselves have been annihilated and lost.

cannot and does not thereupon attain to final freedom from birth and death. *Survival* should not be confused with deathlessness—which is true immortality. The chain of alternating incarnate and discarnate life is only a survival of consciousness-plus-ignorance, and ignorance makes true life impossible.

Life in ignorance is the very negation of existence in truth. It is so basic a curtailment of true existence that, when judged by the standards of the true existence in eternity, it had best be termed a continuous death. Only in realization is consciousness emancipated from the tyranny of this continuous death which nullifies the true life in eternity. And only in liberation can consciousness arrive at that true immortality which lies beyond all curtailment and obscurity.

The individual who has achieved realization of the truth is initiated into eternal and unlimited life, for the limiting ego-mind with all its attendant *sanskaras* has undergone a death that is final. In this process the limited individuality is shed and the soul is invested with unlimited, divine individuality. This may be termed a journey of the soul, but it is by no means the first journey.

The first journey consisted in the evolving of consciousness through the evolutionary process, starting in the most rudimentary subgaseous forms and ending in the attainment of full consciousness in the human form. This journey extends from initial attainment of consciousness by the individual soul to birth of the limited human individuality, in which full consciousness has been achieved, but a consciousness still clouded and ridden with *sanskaras*.

The second journey of the soul consists in the involution of the now fully evolved consciousness through the removal of the clouds of *sanskaras*. The removal requires the effort of numberless lifetimes and lasts from the birth of the limited human individuality to its termination in the unlimited truth. This second journey brings the individual to the unlimited and untrammeled state of infinite existence or immortality and is considered in great detail in Chapter VI. The terminus of this journey is known in Sufi literature as *Fana-fillah*, the final annihilation of the limited ego in the conscious state of God.

At the end of the first journey, the soul becomes conscious of *maya*, or the illusion of duality. This domain of *maya* has only imaginary existence. The entire universe thus in reality is only a zero, but this zero exists for the fully evolved consciousness of the individual human being.

Maya gives to the life of the individual all the meaning that it has, and the imaginary universe of *maya* continues to have a semblance of reality and significance until the wayfarer arrives at the terminus of the second journey, or *Fana-fillah.*

In the state of *Fana-fillah* the universe disappears and has neither existence nor value. This is the true and final terminus point of the great journey. It is reached when the ego-mind has met its total and final death, from which no resurrection is possible. Then only God exists as the supreme and sole reality, and the universe has become a true zero without existence even in imagination.

At this terminus the individual's consciousness is endowed with divine individuality and he is known as a *Majzoob-e-kamil.* At the time of the extinction of the ego-mind (or limited individuality) and the conscious union of the soul in the Over-Soul, consciousness is withdrawn completely from the physical, subtle and mental bodies and these are usually dropped within four days. When the *Majzoob's* body, which for him does not exist, does not actually drop, it is sustained by the devotees or "lovers" who have been attached to him through that body.

When the *Majzoob* was a wayfarer during the second journey he may have had several friends who loved him and expected spiritual guidance from him. The *sanskaric* links thus formed by such friends to the physical body of the wayfarer now cause the body of the *Majzoob* to go on living, even though he is no longer linked in any way with it.

The *Bhaktas* or devotees of the *Majzoob* provide sustenance for his physical body, which keeps on functioning automatically, and by their link with it the devotees derive much spiritual benefit. But all this activity of the body is completely automatic and involves no conscious interest on the part of the *Majzoob.* After the purpose of the *sanskaric* link formed by the *Bhaktas* to the pysical form of the *Majzoob* has been fulfilled, the body of the *Majzoob* ceases to function and is dropped.

When the body of one who has arrived at unlimited truth is automatically dropped at the end of four days, or is dropped after its link to the devotees has been fulfilled, the event can be properly termed neither death nor a journey. It cannot be said to be death, because at the time the body is dropped it has no connection with the consciousness of the person who was once attached to it. The link with the soul has already been snapped and the body continues only on the universal flow of divine benevolence. Death is a severance of the connection between consciousness and the physical body, and since in the two cases just described the body retains no connection with consciousness, they are not properly cases of death.

Nor is it at all suitable to call such deaths "journeys of the consciousness", for the dropping of the physical body makes no difference to the consciousness that was once attached to it. With or without the body, consciousness remains what it had become upon the complete vanishing of separative individuality: abidingly illumined and infinitely absorbed in truth.

If, as occurs in rare cases, truth-realized consciousness returns to normal consciousness of the body and of the universe (without diminution or curtailment of realization), this event is properly described as the third journey. This third journey is undertaken only by the Perfect Masters (*Sadgurus, Qutubs*) who, upon returning to consciousness of body and universe, establish their divine and unlimited individuality in the apparent world of duality. This state of affirmation of unbounded truth in and through the universe of *maya* is known in Sufi terminology as *Baqa-billah,* or abiding simultaneously in God and in illusion.

The apparent universe now has existence for the divine individuality, but at this terminus of the third journey the universe is realized as being nothing and having absolutely no value. The only thing that has real value is God, and the *Sadguru* sees that the entire universe has no reality in itself and exists only as the apparent manifestation of God.

If zeros are placed after the number one (*e.g.* 100000), each zero assumes value not because it has value in itself, but because it is placed after the number one. In the *maya*-ridden state, the relative status of the zeros and the number one are not realized. The two are confused together so that the zeros which constitute the physical universe are taken to have both existence and value in themselves.

In the *Fana-fillah* state of truth-absorption, all the zeros of the entire universe that had been added onto the number one are cut out. Only the one (*e.g.* 1~~00000~~) exists.

In the *Baqa* or *Sadguru* state of truth-affirmation in the universe, all the zeros of the universe reappear, but they are placed from a mathematical standpoint before the number one (*e.g.* 000001). In this manner of reinstatement, the zeros have existence but no value, regardless of how many there are.

In this last case any increase in the number of zeros neither adds numerical value nor alters in any way the value of the number one. The value neither increases nor decreases.

A Perfect Master can perform any miracle. This does not involve any breaking of the law, because he is beyond the domain of *maya* and its laws. Among those who enjoy the *Sadguru* state, the Avatar has unique consciousness. The *Sadguru* experiences the state of "I am God and God is everything", while the Avatar experiences the state of "I am God and I am everything". Man as God (*i.e. Sadguru*) sees God in everything, but God as man (*i.e.* Avatar) sees what God as God sees: Himself in everything. In fact the Avatar not only sees Himself *in* everything but sees Himself *as* everything; not only as being in the many, but as *being* the many in exactly the same manner that He is the One.

When the Avatar or the *Sadguru* drops his body after finishing his spiritual task in the imaginary universe of duality, he retains the God-consciousness that is his continuous eternal state. This fourth and last journey of the Avatar and Perfect Masters is the same as the second journey of the *Majzoob-e-kamil*. Their unlimited individualities suffer no extinction in spite of the fact that they are now removed entirely beyond the world of forms. Their individualities persist because their divine unlimited consciousness abidingly remains as the very inalienable nature of the soul, which requires no form for its *locus standi*.

Sanskaras or the *sanskaric* ego-mind can subsist only by attaching itself to some form, but no expressive medium of form is in any way necessary for the existence of divine consciousness. This, the very nature of the soul, is self-sustained.

The dropping of the physical body by the Avatar or by the *Sadguru* is not death, for even while he uses the body he is in no way attached to it and has no *sanskaric* link with it. Nor does the dropping of the body in these instances involve the usual survival of a limited individuality or ego-mind, for these are simply non-existent in the *Sadguru* and Avatar.

Their dropping of the body also differs from the death of advanced yogis who may voluntarily drop their physical body after completing their work. The advanced yogis cannot discard their ego-mind or limited individuality, which clings fast to them even after severance of their connection with the physical body, but the *Majzoob-e-kamil,* the *Sadguru* and the Avatar embark upon a unique and direct "journey" to the unbounded and indivisible ocean of divinity.

CHAPTER 2

The Cycle of Sleep and Waking

To sleep is to surrender to one of the primary forces of life. Sleep is an inescapable need. There can be no substitute for it, although adjustment within certain degrees to its demands is possible, such as choosing eleven o'clock instead of ten for retiring. Such adjustments can be made only within well-defined limits. There can be no tampering with the strict requirements for sleep over any considerable length of time.

For the average man, prolonged abstention from sleep inevitably results in bodily disorder as well as impairment or even derangement of the mind. The mind loses its normal alertness and deteriorates markedly in its ability to concentrate and work out abstruse problems. Further, it loses its ability to cope with the problems presented by everyday life.

Sleep, being one of the most significant phenomena in the existence of the individual, must be thoroughly understood if the purpose of life itself is to be fully comprehended.

Any attempt to give an explanation of sleep in purely physiological terms will be incomplete and misleading as well. Many people consider sleep to be the inevitable result of the exhaustion of the higher nerve centers of the brain. Some attribute the cause of sleep to the accumulation of metabolic and other deterioration products in the brain. Others regard sleep as the product of the inhibition of higher brain centers by nerve impulses generated in specialized sleep centers.

Still other authorities regard sleep as the natural condition of the brain, and they consider consciousness to be the result of activating the brain through external stimuli. Sleep, in their opinion, is therefore a relapse into the natural state of the brain which occurs on withdrawal of these external stimuli.

The essence of all these physiological explanations is that sleep is a by-product of the physical brain. This is a radically wrong conclusion. A more profound interpretation is required to do justice to the real status of consciousness and its relation to body and soul.

Throughout evolution, consciousness is developed in and through the mind and expressed through the evolving medium of physical form, but *consciousness itself resides in the soul.* The body is only the medium through which consciousness expresses itself.

Through the ages a single life impulse (individualized soul) gradually becomes more conscious as it expresses itself through a myriad of forms. The consciousness thus developed is the possession of the mind and it does not vanish with the disappearance of the physical vehicle.

The physical form also evolves as consciousness unfolds. Bodily forms emerge one after another in continuous and ascending order so that the total consciousness might develop progressively through a fitting progression of form-vehicles. Consciousness is not a coincidental product of physiological processes, but the very reason for the existence of all forms.

Consciousness is the standard by which the distinctions between sleep and waking should be understood. In wakefulness, the mind becomes conscious and expresses itself through the body. In sleep, the mind relapses into a quiescent state of the soul without outer expression. Physiologically, the states of sleeping and waking may be described as the retarding and accelerating of the higher brain centers, but they are more significantly defined as the submerging and emerging of consciousness.

In order to answer the basic question of why consciousness should oscillate between the quiescent state of sleep and the active state of wakefulness, one must attack the problem of the primary origin of consciousness. Before the beginning of all beginnings, the infinite ocean of God was completely self-forgetful. The utter and unrelieved oblivion of the self-forgetful, infinite ocean of God in the beyond-beyond state was broken in order that God should consciously know His own fullness of divinity. It was for this sole purpose that consciousness proceeded to evolve.

Consciousness itself was latent in the beyond-beyond state of God. Also latent in this same beyond-beyond state of God, was the original whim (*lahar*) to become conscious. It was this original whim which brought latent consciousness into manifestation (form) for the first time.

Slowly and tediously consciousness approaches its apex in the human form, which is the goal of the evolutionary process, and thereby an individual mind gradually differentiates itself from the sea of oblivion. However the conscious individual still does not comprehend the truth of the real self. On the contrary, there is produced in man a false sense of limitation and frustration.

The full consciousness that is laboriously produced in the evolutionary process, and that takes the place of utter forgetfulness, remains finite because it is replete with countless impressions (*sanskaras*) of fulfilled and unfulfilled desires that have been acquired while inhabiting the many finite bodies. Originally it was the *lahar* that caused consciousness to manifest. In everyday life it is the impressions (*sanskaras*) that cause latent consciousness in the sleep-state to manifest itself as active consciousness in the awake-state.

Although the sea of oblivion has been swept back through the development of consciousness, yet it has been exchanged for a growing nightmare of ever-increasing futility. Forgetfulness has been displaced by remembrance, but it is a remembrance charged with limitation, helplessness and binding desires.

The full but finite human consciousness struggles to find self-expression and self-gratification, but even these efforts are subject to the *sanskaric* compulsions. They prevent man from recapturing the original truth of his being and subject him to increasing limitation and helplessness. He is like a spider caught in a web of his own making.

As a means of respite, consciousness seeks the oblivion of deep sleep where it again surrenders itself temporarily to the sea of self-forgetfulness—the original beyond-beyond state of God. In sound sleep, consciousness becomes latent for the time being, until the burden of unspent *sanskaras* forces it to manifest again in the awake-state.

In his desperate attempts during wakefulness to overcome his feeling of helplessness and boredom, man may attempt to escape from himself through the exciting emotions of lust or anger. Although drowning oneself in lust or anger may seem to promise escape, the satisfaction achieved is only temporary. Inevitably a strong counter-sense of remorse or depression is induced that is worse than the original sense of frustration. On the collective level, wars provide the exciting avenue of escape that subsequently reacts to numb the spirit of man with an overwhelming sense of burden.

Nature has striven to evolve consciousness through long ages of painful struggle. It is a great tragedy that when consciousness faces an acute need to free itself of entanglement, it should regress instead by resorting to the deadening of sensibility. This expedient is disastrous because it involves a conscious attempt to undo the achievements of natural evolution.

None of man's waking attempts to overcome his feeling of intolerable weariness is wholly acceptable to the soul. All are dissatisfying in the long run. Hence man seeks rest and refreshment by withdrawing temporarily into the oblivion of deep sleep. This psychological necessity for sleep cannot be avoided. Just as the physical body requires alternating periods of activity and rest, so the mind also needs such periods.

Sleep is the means by which the mind withdraws temporarily from the pressure exerted by its age-old load of impressions and desires. Through sleep the mind refreshes itself temporarily for further participation in the game of "becoming self-conscious". If the self were completely aware of its true God-nature during waking consciousness it would find no need to withdraw into the self-forgetfulness of sleep. Its spontaneous joy would be an eternal wellspring of divine refreshment.

When man seeks freedom from the ennui of the waking-state by losing consciousness in the sleep-state, no slightest destruction of consciousness occurs. Deep sleep is an inward withdrawal of consciousness into a condition of temporary oblivion. In this state the mind is completely quiescent. It does not experience the helplessness of finite self-consciousness, nor is it aware of the true self as the illimitable truth. Both the finite illusory world and the real infinite state are forgotten as consciousness sinks into the sea of oblivion. In deep sleep, consciousness exists merely as a latent possibility which must again be aroused to activity.

Sleep stands in the same relationship to consciousness as death does to life. Death is not the annihilation of life, but its transference to another state of being. In the same way, sleep is not the annihilation of consciousness, but its withdrawal into a state of abeyance. Whether latent as unconsciousness or manifested as consciousness, consciousness is always there.

The matter may be summarized as follows:

After going to sleep, when man ordinarily enters the ordinary dream-state:

(a) he has no consciousness of the body;

(b) the link with the physical body remains intact;

(c) pain and pleasure are experienced for a short period;

(d) the man wakes up in the same physical body.

After physical death man also enters a dream-state and:

(a) he has no consciousness of the body;

(b) the link with that particularly physical body is snapped for good;

(c) because the link with the gross no longer exists he experiences pain or pleasure (the states of hell or heaven) far more intensely, whether for a long or short period;

(d) he wakes up in the gross in another physical body.

The passage from sleep to wakefulness consists in the passage from (a) unconsciousness to (b) subconsciousness and finally to (c) full consciousness. Normally, for the ordinary man, these consist of

(a) sound sleep = unconsciousness

(b) dreams = subconsciousness of duality

(c) roused from sleep = full consciousness of duality

When a man almost loses consciousness, as in high fever, he is subconscious as in the dream-state. But if he is rendered unconscious through drugs such as chloroform, he is unconscious as in the sound-sleep-state. Unconsciousness always involves temporary return to the original, beyond-beyond state of God regardless of the cause, whether it be sound sleep, drugs or a physical accident.

Although the subject of the path and its disciplines is considered in detail later, it is of interest to note in this connection that for those on the path the three states are:

(a) beyond-beyond state of God   = unconsciousness

(b) experiences on the path   = real subconsciousness of duality

    (c) roused from all illusion of duality = real full consciousness of God or Self.

Mind seeks the abeyance of its consciousness in deep sleep, but it cannot continue indefinitely to accept this self-refutation. This negative achievement is not an adequate substitute for the final purpose for which consciousness came into existence, *i.e.* for the soul to become fully conscious of itself as the infinite truth. Though man attempts through sleep to escape the burden that consciousness imposes upon him, he is involuntarily drawn back to his waking-state by the impressions gathered in the achieving of the very consciousness from which he sought escape. The old bonds of desires—both fulfilled and unfulfilled—bind him to the world of illusion and propel him again into the maelstrom of finite life.

Although it is only temporary, sleep does give psychological reinvigoration to the mind. If there were not some kind of restoration of psychic vitality during sleep there would be no particular benefit to this oblivion. In spite of the apparent respite, consciousness would remain exactly as it had been at the time of its withdrawal into sleep, and no special gain would be achieved. It would be merely a fruitless interval in a long chain of automatic responses to environment.

Sleep does confer positive benefit. Due to the fact that the separate "I-consciousness" is in complete abeyance during deep sleep, the individual soul is in actual union with the infinite Self. When sleep is dreamless, the individual soul is resting in the undisturbed tranquility of the most-original beyond-beyond state of God. But inasmuch as sleep is a submergence of consciousness into oblivion, it does not bestow upon the soul the *conscious* realization of the truth that the soul will eventually experience when consciousness is freed of all impressions, good as well as bad.

Even this unconscious contact with infinity—the abode of all bliss and power—gives to the mind a new tone and vigor. When consciousness returns to waking functioning it manifests a renewed faith that at some time, in some manner, a final solution to life's complexities will be found.

Although the most important work of consciousness is always done during the waking-state, dreams also play their part in helping consciousness through the maze of problems which beset it. As a rule, consciousness passes through the dream-state during the transition from waking to sleep and while returning from sleep to waking. The dream-state serves as a bridge between sleep and waking, but it is not an inevitable phase. The mind may swing between quiescence and waking without subconsciously passing through the dream phase.

In the dream-state, consciousness is not completely dormant as in sleep, nor is it fully active as in waking. The dream-state is midway between these two phases and it marks a transition from latent consciousness to active consciousness. The unique virtue of the ordinary dream-state is that experiences in it are relatively free from the act of willing as well as from the rigid social demands which prevail in conscious life.

Despite the seeming lawlessness of the dream-state, it is nevertheless subject to the accumulated mental and emotional impressions (*sanskaras*) which function as inexorably in the dream-state as in the waking. Many inclinations and desires which cannot find fulfillment in waking life, seek and find gratification in the self-created, subjective world of dreams. Likewise, many fears and conflicts buried in the subconscious mind inflict upon the dreamer a diversity of suffering which the conscious mind would seek to avoid.

Thus dreamland also invites the experiencing of the opposites. The unique characteristic of dream experiences is that they afford an opportunity to work out a number of the *sanskaric* impressions without creating any new physical bondage. Many dreams have the same force and directive value that inhere in experiences of the waking-state, but these latter are always accompanied by the simultaneous creation of new emotional and mental impressions (*sanskaras*) that prove to be just as binding as the age-old impressions that limit man's consciousness. Dream experiences however result in no such creation of further bindings.

Another interesting aspect of ordinary dreams is that, regardless of what the dream entails, it has no direct effect upon any mind other than the dreamer. This is quite contrary to experiences in the conscious waking-state. These invariably involve and affect many other souls as well, thus complicating many life patterns. The activity of consciousness in the waking state creates a bondage of *karmic* liabilities and assets from which dream experiences are exempt.

The dream world is a type of psychic experimental laboratory, insulated from the demands of physical life and thus possessing some advantage over the waking-state. But because it does not give play to the directive faculty of the will and isolates the individual soul from other souls, it also suffers severe handicaps from which the waking life is free.

In spite of the periodic release and refreshment that deep sleep supplies, the mind continues to be dissatisfied. Driven by need to escape from the burden that finite consciousness imposes upon him, man associates himself with like-minded individuals. By merging himself in a group that has similar problems, he hopes to fortify himself against his growing sense of dissatisfaction.

But his hope is ill-founded. He finds no more redemption by identifying himself with the false "we" than by identifying with the false "I". The increased strength of the group is nullified by increased expectations. Instead of finding his powerlessness mitigated, the individual finds that it is merely shared by many others. His sense of helplessness is accentuated through participation in the group-consciousness, for he shares their collective feeling of helplessness as well as his own.

Although occasionally a means may be found to eliminate some one worry in life, the final solution to recurring problems remains to be found. Suppose, for example, that a man is extremely miserable because others in his office seem to be given better treatment than he. Then suppose that he is suddenly relieved of all his worries by inducing in himself a studied indifference to his surroundings.

This may give him a temporary feeling of release from his problems, but since his troubles are really caused by lack of understanding of himself and environment, his cultivated indifference really leaves the situation completely unchanged. Sooner or later, when his forced indifference cracks and he again becomes emotionally involved, his old worries return to disturb him as before. His attitude of detachment fails to effect a permanent change in his consciousness because it is not based upon the truth that there is but one infinite Self which is the Self of all.

To know oneself honestly and understand one's environment requires a radical change in outlook. Mechanical coercion of the mind into a temporary attitude is not sufficient, for the mind has a tendency to revert to its age-old inclinations (habit patterns; *sanskaric* patterns) and to free itself from any position into which it may have been forced. Unless the mind achieves intelligent discrimination based on lasting values, it is inevitably harassed by its self-created worries. Again and again man must seek the oblivion of sleep as a necessary respite from participation in things of little satisfaction.

Man clings to the palliative experiences of the gross world even though they augment the very worries, sufferings and defeats from which his consciousness desires to escape. Only in the extremity of despair does consciousness gather sufficient momentum to try to break through the constricting web of ego-life and into the life of lasting freedom.

When man realizes at last that his helplessness is the product of his countless cravings, he tries to find peace by renouncing those cravings and accepting life in a spirit of resignation to the divine will. Until that moment of supreme self-determination occurs, however, he finds himself persistently haunted by an overpowering desire to perpetuate his self-created ego-life. Although he tries desperately to break through the self-centered isolation that this life fosters, it is only when he surrenders to a Perfect Master that he is initiated sooner or later into the path of redemptive love.

Surrender to the will of the master is in itself very difficult but it becomes more so under the gaze of friendly onlookers. To them the actions of the spiritual aspirant often seem incomprehensible, as if he were sacrificing his most precious possession—his free will.

Often it seems to the onlooker that the master aims only to increase his own prestige by directing the actions of those who surround him. This falls far short of understanding the work of the master. Just as it is necessary for solder to be fluxed in a salt before it can join the two metal parts together, it is necessary for the soul of the seeker to be bathed through self-surrenderance in the light that the master affords. The master gains nothing; it is not his purpose to gain. Certainly his ego cannot be exalted, for if he is a Perfect Master he has already lost it.

When a man determines to find peace and fulfillment through the renunciation of the cravings of the ego-life, he finds that his new decision is challenged more by the deep-rooted compulsions of his own mind than by any obstructive factors in external environment. Although he now longs to love the master whole-heartedly as the divine beloved, and tries to surrender completely to him, he is far from being master of his own mind. He cannot even surrender the things he regards as his own, despite his sincere decision.

Like Janus, the aspirant has two faces, one looking longingly at truth, the other at ignorance. On the one hand the aspirant yearns for the saving grace of the master and to be completely lost in the unbounded truth that he senses in the master. On the other hand his false, separative ego tries to perpetuate its existence by all available means. But with the first surrender to the master the death knell of the ego-life is sounded, and though it continues to struggle for survival its days of dominance are numbered.

If a person is caught in a quagmire he instinctively tries every means to get out of it, but the very effort he makes thrusts him deeper into it. The more he struggles, the further in he sinks. Help must come to him then from someone who stands on firm ground, and who can only be of help when the struggling man has ceased to struggle long enough to look about for aid.

There is a certain similarity between this situation and the case of the individual who has surrendered his life to the master. The false, separative ego tries its utmost to postpone its own dissolution by resisting the divine love of the master. It struggles in the quagmire of existence, but each act of ego-affirmation invites a reaction of deeper surrender to the beloved's will. This in turn brings with it the clearer realization of the master as being none other than the irresistible truth that is the Self of all selves, and the one reality in the apparent multiplicity of individual souls.

Truth-realization is born of such complete surrender to the engulfing love of God, of which the master is the physical symbol and the channel. The finite self has now not only recognized itself as hopelessly limited, but also as utterly false. It ceases to make any claims or to protest in its own right, offering itself instead to the infinite truth. This offering of purified will redounds to its own advantage.

When finite consciousness of the mind in its stark awareness of futility and falseness capitulates wholly to the infinite truth, the soul becomes consciously one with that truth in self-realization.

Only then can consciousness be said really to have arrived at its final destination. Originally absorbed *in* the infinite, consciousness is now absorbed *by* the infinite, now consciously experiencing its own unlimited power, knowledge, bliss and scope. In being absorbed by the infinite, consciousness is completely freed of one and all illusions and can be called *super*consciousness, in which state its former unlimited helplessness is transmuted into unlimited power.

The aim of life, and the real goal of all creation, is to achieve true Self-consciousness. When the mind of man is transformed into superconsciousness of the soul, it inherits the treasure of omnipotence and there is no recurrence of that sense of helplessness that had haunted his dreaming and waking states. No longer is there need for consciousness to be submerged into the oblivion of sleep in order to achieve unconscious union of the self with the universal Self. The conscious union that the individual self has now established with the universal Self is an unfading attainment that persists forever.

In the unlimited abundance of superconsciousness, the freed soul experiences no curtailment or cessation. In superconsciousness the soul experiences itself as all-mighty, its bliss is unbounded and its continuous awareness of itself as the infinite truth admits no slightest interruption by the self-forgetfulness of the ordinary sleep-, dream- or wake-state.

Ordinary waking consciousness of the mind is not only incapable of realizing the true Self, but is deluded to accept the false, limited self and the false multiplicity of the phenomenal world as real. It is therefore a form of ignorance. Superconsciousness may be termed "supra-waking", because this state has transcended all normal limitations and has become truly whole in the sense that it retains no element of illusion. It is the opposite of ordinary sleep, for oblivion of the truth is complete in ordinary sleep, while awareness of truth is complete in superconsciousness. When waking consciousness invades and consciously illumines the depths of forgetfulness, ignorance and illusion, it becomes transmuted into supra-waking consciousness.

CHAPTER 3

Origins and Effects of War

The basic causes of the social turmoil that often precipitates into war, may be found in the individual, the social whole, the functioning of *maya* and in the very intent of God's will. Inasmuch as these are essentially one in the final analysis, this means no more than that war is a part of the divine pattern. Insofar as war affects the individual, however, it must be understood at all the levels within illusion from which it is precipitated.

The first is the level of the individual himself. It may readily be seen that most persons are immersed in their own egos and selfish viewpoints. This is the life of illusory values in which men are caught. If man were to face the truth he would understand that all life is one, and in this understanding, forget the limiting self.

But man does not face the truth, regarding himself as separate from and competing with the rest of mankind. This attitude often breeds a concept of personal happiness that creates lust for power, unbridled greed and unrelieved hatred.

Ignorant of the real purpose of life, many persons sink to the lowest level of culture, burying themselves in and contributing to the decay of forms lingering on from the dead past. Bound by material interest and a limited viewpoint, they forget their divine destiny. They have truly lost their way, and so they lay savagely about themselves, for their hearts are torn by fear and hate.

The second level from which wars are bred is that of the social whole. Here, economic pressures are often cited as a major cause. Also, resistance to aggression seems a reasonable cause.

It would be an illusion within illusion, however, to claim that wars arise merely to secure material adjustment. They are more often the product of uncritical identification with narrow interests which, through association, finally come to be regarded as one's sole rights. To profess that humanity's problem is merely that of bread is to re-duce humanity to the level of animality.

If man chooses to set himself the limited task of securing purely material adjustment, he must understand and be guided by the spiritual ramifications of this simple goal. Economic adjustment cannot be divorced from a spiritual context. Economic adjustment can be achieved only as people realize that there can be no planned cooperative action in economic matters without the replacing of self-interest with self-giving love. Failing this fundamental requisite, the attainment of the highest efficiency in production will only lead to a further sense of insufficiency and new conflict. A profound spirit of self-giving love must underlie all effort to solve and remove the economic pressures leading towards war.

While material adjustment can only be regarded as a part of the wider problem of spiritual adjustment, spiritual adjustment in turn requires the elimination of self. It must be removed from all those phases which affect the intellectual, emotional and cultural life of man.

It may readily be seen then that a solution to the individual and social factors underlying war rests upon the spiritual enlightenment of the individual. This need not mean that wars are inevitable as long as the ego-self of the individual continues to ride rampant in the cultural and economic areas of life, for war is only the most explosive gross manifestation of the combined egocentricity of mankind. But conflict of one sort or another is inevitable until the ego-self is finally tamed and eliminated.

As man faces the truth and begins to appreciate that all humanity, nay all creation, is one, the problem of wars will commence to disappear. Wars must be so clearly seen by all to be both unnecessary and unreasonable that the immediate problem will not be to stop wars, but to wage them spiritually against the attitude of mind which generated them.

In the light of the truth of the unity of all, a cooperative and harmonious life becomes inevitable. Thus the chief task for those who set out to rebuild humanity after a great war is to do their utmost to dispel the spiritual ignorance that envelopes humanity.

The disease of selfishness in mankind will need a cure that is not only universal in application, but drastic in nature. Selfishness is so deep-rooted that it can be eradicated only by being attacked from all sides. Real peace and happiness will dawn spontaneously when selfishness is purged. The peace and happiness that come from self-giving love are permanent. Even the worst sinner can become a great saint if he has the courage and sincerity to invite a drastic and complete change of heart.

The levels from which war springs have not yet been exhausted. The third is that of *maya*. When truly understood, all conflicts and wars are also seen to be a part of the ·divine game. They are thus a result of the divine will, which finds expression in the world of manifestation, through the medium of *maya*—the cosmic power that causes the illusory world of duality to appear as real.

The purpose served by *maya* is twofold: (1) it can be instrumental in trapping the mind in the duality of illusion, and (2) it can also be instrumental in freeing the mind from the grip of spiritual ignorance and bondage. *Maya* should not be ignored; it must be handled with detachment and understanding. Wars are the work of *maya,* and are either spiritually disastrous or beneficial depending on whether they are based on attachment to or detachment from the hold of *maya*.

The final level from which the causes of war spring is no level at all, for it is a part of the divine plan of God to give to a hungry and weary world a fresh dispensation of the eternal and only truth. During war, great forces of destruction are afoot which at times might seem to be dominant. But constructive forces for the redemption of humanity are also released through various channels. Though the working of these latter forces is largely silent, eventually they are bound to bring about the transformations that will render safe and steady the further spiritual progress of humanity.

Regardless of the political and economic factors described by the historian as he looks at war in retrospect, from the spiritual point of view this sanguine phenomenon is a cyclic divine ferment over which no earthly power has control.

There are always two aspects of Divinity that are eternally active in the affairs of the world. In Persian, the destructive aspect of Divinity is termed "self-glorification", and the constructive aspect "self-beatitude". When the "self-glorification" aspect of God predominates, there is destruction and suffering on a colossal scale, as in the last world war. The aspect of "divine beatitude" on the other hand brings peace and plenty. These are usually the golden ages of civilization.

During the phase of "self-glorification", Divinity repels Itself, so to speak, through Its own creation, while in the phase of "self-beatitude" Divinity attracts or loves Itself through Its own creation. The former is a negative method, the latter positive. Both must be regarded ultimately as instruments of divine wisdom to rouse humanity to its divine heritage of self-realization. When the individual or the race is about to lapse into bestiality, it is suffering that rehabilitates them.

Both the "self-glorification" and "self-beatitude" phases of God are exerted in cyclic waves and affect individuals and the race with similar intensity. As the destructive phase now begins to weaken, the constructive cycle of "divine beatitude" will gradually make itself felt.

Just as the recent world (war) catastrophe overwhelmed the innocent as well as the guilty, so in the approaching "self-beatitude" phase the undeserving as well as the deserving will have equal chance of receiving divine grace provided they are awake to the situation, so full and unique a cyclic dispensation it will be.

Ethics in time of war can only be judged by the degree to which they reflect the divine plan. In war there are two kinds of forces operative: (1) those which make for love, justice, harmony and the well-being of all mankind, and (2) those which work in alliance with narrow racial and national loyalties towards the selfish exploitation of others. Nevertheless, although the last great war brought great suffering and destruction upon millions of people, it was not in vain, for out of its chaos there will emerge a new world of freedom, happiness and understanding.

He who would wage war must search his heart and make sure that the ends for which he is fighting are a reflection of the divine plan. His actions will be justified only if they help to lead humanity to spiritual brotherhood cemented by an inviolable sense of the unity of all human beings, regardless of class, color, nationality, race, religion or creed.

One might ask how it is that at one time the causes of war seem rooted in individual human selfishness, at another in racial and economic pressures which transcend the individual, and at still another in the divine plan of God. And how can the individual help by striving to whittle down his own ego, if the outlines of war already exist in God's text of the past and the future?

The answer to this sincere query had best be offered by means of an analogy. One's eyes see that an apple has a rosy color, and it is said that the apple is red. One's nose may savor the aroma of the apple, and the apple is said to smell fragrant. When one takes the apple in one's hands, its skin is found to be smooth and cool, and when one bites into it, the apple is found to be sweet and succulent.

All these sensations are coordinated in some fashion by one's consciousness into the notion of *one* apple that has *many* attributes. Its succulence is no more to be denied a place in the "reality" of the apple than is its aroma or its color. It is recognized intuitively that all traits belong to the same apple, despite the fact that the sensations enter consciousness through different windows. Whether the object exists partially or totally in the realm of reality, or only in illusion, is of little interest for the purposes of the analogy.

The "reality" of the apple, then, has many separate facets, as interpreted by one's senses. One suspects that it would have even more if only the mind were not limited in its perceptual capability by the types and location of the "windows" that open into it.

Just as the apple possesses a variety of unarguable properties, all of which belong to the same object, so other objects and organisms often give evidence of numerous aspects of reality. The same fact in life looks different therefore to different people, its appearance being determined by the particular window of the spiritual nature from which the individual looks.

From this emerges one vital principle: each person must look at cause and effect from the window that is natural to him. To try to see through all windows is to risk stagnation in the complexity of a whirlpool of intellectual facts that can never be integrated by intellectual means. To try to argue another out of the seeming world of reality that he sees from his window is to argue the unarguable. Roundness is as real to the apple as is fragrance, until one day both are lost in perception of the entirety.

So also it will seem to some that the causes of war lie wholly within the responsibility of the individual. For others, society will be the cause. Still others will see the hand of *maya,* and some will see the will of God.

During a war there are persons who unveil their inherent higher self through the endurance of pain, and by acts of bravery and self-sacrifice. It is better that such unselfish action be released under the stimulus of danger than not released at all. It is better that men forget their petty selves under the pressure of collective calamity, if need be, than remain permanently absorbed in fear and greed.

Great suffering awakens great understanding in man. Supreme suffering fulfills its purpose when it awakens him finally to genuine longing for real understanding. Unprecedented suffering leads to unprecedented spiritual results. It contributes to the basing of life on an unshakeable foundation of truth.

The individual must understand fully his identity with the supreme universal Soul. Having perceived this truth, he will find that his life rearranges spontaneously so that his attitude towards his neighbor in everyday life becomes different. Then he will act upon the spiritual value of oneness, which promotes true cooperation.

Brotherhood is a spontaneous outcome of true perception. The new life for the individual is based upon spiritual understanding and is an affirmation of spiritual practicality in the truth.

Just as war is not an unmixed evil for the individual, so it may have certain forward-propelling effects on humanity as a whole. The destructiveness of war tends to bring humanity to a spiritual crisis born of the physical nightmare. Inevitably suffering and misery pose the question of what it all leads to, how it will all end. Gradually people become sick of wanting and sick of fighting. Greed and hatred finally reach such an intensity that everyone becomes weary of them. Then mankind begins to suspect that the only way out is through selflessness. The only alternative to war and its suffering is seen to be to stop hating and to love, to stop wanting and to give, to stop dominating and to serve.

Wars require the exercise of cooperative functioning, and in this resides one positive result. Still, the value of this cooperation should not be overestimated, for too often it is artificially restricted by identification with a limited group or ideal.

Often wars are carried on by a form of love, but a love that has not been properly understood. In order that love may come into its own it must be free, untrammeled and unlimited. Love exists in all phases of human life, but usually it is latent; or it is limited and poisoned by personal ambition, racial pride, narrow loyalties and rivalries, and attachment to sex, nationality, sect, caste or religion. For the resurrection of humanity the heart of man must be unlocked so that unadulterated love may be manifested in it—a love uncorrupted and free from "me" and "mine".

People who make unlimited sacrifices for the sake of their country or political ideology are also capable of the same sacrifices for God and the truth. As war teaches that even the man in the street can rise to the greatest heights of sacrifice for a selfless cause, it also teaches that all the mundane things of the world—wealth, possessions, power, fame, family and even the very tenor of life on earth—are transitory and devoid of lasting value.

In this manner the incidents of war also win man over for God through the lessons they bring. It is now high time that universal suffering should hasten humanity to the turning point in its spiritual history. It is now high time that the very agonies of our times should become a means for the bringing of real understanding of human relationship. It is now high time for humanity to face squarely the true causes of the catastrophe of war. It is now high time to seek a new experience of reality. It is high time that men have a fresh vision that all life is one in God, who alone is real and all that matters. God is worth living for, and He is worth dying for; all else is a vain and empty pursuit of illusory value.

War is a necessary evil that is in God's plan to awaken humanity to its destiny as the new humanity. The time is now ripe. Men are ardently seeking to contact the embodiment of the truth in the form of a God-man, through whom they can be inspired and lifted into spiritual understanding. In this critical time of universal suffering men are becoming ready to turn towards their higher self and to fufill the will of God.

They will accept the divine guidance and love which alone can bring about spiritual awakening. Divine love will perform the supreme miracle of bringing God into the hearts of the new humanity and of establishing them in a true, and therefore a lasting, happiness. Divine love will satisfy the greatest longings of mankind, make men selfless and helpful in their mutual relations, and ultimately resolve all problems. The new brotherhood on earth will be a fulfilled fact, and nations will be united in the fraternity of love and truth.

What will be some of the characteristics of the new humanity that will emerge from the travail of the present? It will of course heed science and its practical attainments. It is a mistake to look upon science as opposed to the spirit. Science is a help or hindrance to spirituality depending upon the use to which it is put. Just as healthy art is the outflowing of spirituality, so science when properly handled can be the expression and fulfillment of the spirit.

Scientific truths about the physical body and its life in the gross world can become a medium for the soul to know itself. However, if they are to serve this purpose, they must be fitted properly into a greater spiritual understanding that includes a steady insight into true and enduring values. In the absence of such spiritual understanding, scientific achievements are likely to be used destructively, thereby strengthening rather than weakening the chains which bind the spirit. The balanced progress of humanity can be assured only if science and religion proceed hand in hand.

The coming civilization of the new humanity will not be ensouled by dry intellectual doctrine, but by living spiritual experience.

It will be free from a life of limitation and will enjoy unhampered the creative life of the spirit. It will break away from attachment to external form and learn to live by the claims of the spirit. The limited life of illusion will be replaced by unlimited life in the truth, and the limitations by which the separative self lives will wither away at the touch of true understanding.

Spiritual experience has a grip on deeper truths that are inaccessible to intellect. Spiritual truths can often be stated through the intellect, and intellect is certainly of some help in the communication of spiritual experience, but by itself the intellect is insufficient to bring spiritual experience to man or to allow him to communicate it to others.

If two persons have had headaches they can use the intellect to discuss their mutual experience. But if one of them has never had a headache, no amount of intellectual explanation will ever tell him what a headache is. A man must have had a headache to know truly what it is, and in order that he understand it, he may have to be hit on the head. Intellectual explanation can never be a substitute for spiritual experience. At best it can only prepare the ground for that experience.

The fact that spiritual experience involves more than intellect alone can grasp is often emphasized by calling it a mystical experience. Mysticism is frequently regarded as opposed to intellectuality— obscure, confused, impractical, unconnected with reality—but in fact true mysticism is none of these. There is nothing irrational in true mysticism when it is, as it should be, a vision of reality. It is a form of perception that is absolutely unclouded, so practical that it can be lived in every moment of life, and so deeply connected with experience that, in a sense, it is the final understanding of all experience.

When spiritual experience is described as mystical, one should not assume that it involves something unnatural or beyond the grasp of consciousness. The only implication is that the experience cannot be comprehended by the limited human intellect unless it transcends its limits and is illumined by direct realization of the Infinite.

The spiritual understanding that will enliven the new humanity can never fail to accept the stern realities of life and its demands. Those who cannot adapt readily to life tend to recoil from it and to look to a fortress of self-created illusions for protection. Such a reaction is an attempt to perpetuate one's separate existence by protecting it from the demands made by life. At best this can only give a seeming solution by providing a false sense of safety arising from a false sense of self-sufficiency. It does not even constitute progress towards a final solution. On the contrary, it is a sidetrack from the true path.

Again and again, fresh and irresistible waves of life will beat upon man and dislodge him from the illusory shelters within which he hides. He will only invite fresh forms of suffering upon himself by trying through escape to preserve his separative existence. Only when he faces about, awakened and supple, will he find himself clothed in the security of the inner self.

Just as the individual may try to preserve his sense of separative individuality by escape, so he may also try to retain it through an uncritical identification with forms and rituals, or with traditions and conventions. All these are preponderantly fetters which restrain the release of infinite life. If they were a plastic medium that might be readily molded and suffused by unlimited life, they would be an asset in fulfilling the divine life on earth. Generally, though, they tend to gather prestige in their own right and to develop independently of the life they were intended to express. When this happens, all attachment to them eventually entails a drastic restriction of life.

Even as the individual may try to hold onto his separative existence through escape into self-created illusions, so he may also attempt to hold onto it by identification with some narrow class, creed, sect or religion, or by division based upon sex. He may seem to have lost his separative existence through identification with a larger whole, but more often this identification becomes a means of expressing his separative existence. This he accomplishes through feeling separate from those who belong to another class, nationality, creed, sect, religion or sex. Thus his sense of separation from the contrasting group is more fundamental than his sense of identification with the members of his own group.

The strength, in fact the very being, of separative existence is derived from identification of the self with one of two opposites. This results automatically in distinction from the other opposite. Real merging of the limited self can only be achieved in the ocean of universal life. This involves the surrender of all sense of contradistinction in form, belief or action, the surrender of all separative existence in all categories.

The large mass of humanity is deeply enmeshed in these separative and assertive tendencies, and one who looks on at this spectacle is bound to feel the blackest despair. It is true that the readily observable forces of lust, hate and greed cause incalculable suffering, but even in the most passionately disruptive forces there is some form of redemptive love. Buried in the muck of human misery are seed pearls of the greatest perfection, and these precious gems of individual action and feeling are not lost, but require only threading on the strong cord of spiritual knowledge.

Those who despair for mankind, and particularly in time of war, should know that real possibilities for the new humanity exist, and they will come into being through a release of love in measureless abundance. This release of love can come through spiritual awakening brought about by the masters.

Love can never be born of mere determination; through the exercise of will one can be dutiful at best. Through struggle and persistence it is possible to mold external action to conform to one's concept of right, but such results are spiritually barren because they lack the inner warmth of real love. Love and coercion can never sit side by side holding hands.

Love springs spontaneously from within, but although love can never be forced from or upon another, it can be awakened through love itself. Essentially, love is self-communicative: those who do not have it catch it from those who have it, for one cannot absorb love without making a response. Regardless of the barnacles which may cover the surface, the response is stamped by the nature of love.

The secret of true love is that it is unconquerable and irresistible. Even the one who resists its approach is lost as he springs to plug the hole through which it is flowing past the walls of his heart. It races behind him and he turns only in time to find himself surrounded and born aloft on its irresistible might.

True love gathers power and spreads itself until it transforms everyone it touches. Humanity will attain to a new mode of life through the unhampered interplay of pure love, as it spreads from heart to heart.

When it has been recognized that there are no claims greater than those of the universal divine life that encompasses all, then love will establish peace, harmony and happiness in all of the social spheres, and it will shine forth over all in its own unequalled purity and beauty. Divine love cannot be dimmed by the clouds of duality, for it is an expression of Divinity Itself.

It is through this very divine love that the new humanity will tune itself to the divine note. Divine love will not only introduce imperishable sweetness and infinite bliss into personal life, but it will also be the means by which the new humanity will be made possible. Through divine love the new humanity will learn the art of cooperative and harmonious life; it will free itself from the tyranny of dead forms and release the creative life of spiritual wisdom; it will shed all illusions and become established in truth; it will enjoy peace and abiding happiness; it will be initiated into the life of eternity.

It has been said that war cannot be considered entirely bad, although it can hardly be considered entirely good either. There are deep-seated reasons for the occurrence of war, and when one finds oneself in the middle of the holocaust, it is helpful to have a few guiding principles.

People should face the circumstances of war with courage and the faith that no sacrifice is too great when the call of duty is clear. In the event of aggressive attack, all must resist it by direct combat if there is no alternative. But as each individual makes such resistance, he must be certain that he is motivated solely by a sense of duty, without hatred or bitterness towards the aggressor, who has acted out of spiritual ignorance.

Further, he must not be insensitive to the suffering inflicted. On the contrary he must render every possible aid to the victims of war.

The fact that a person is a spiritual aspirant does not release him from his duty to the social whole. This may involve some deep soul searching, because spiritual aspirants tend to be indifferent to war on the grounds that most wars are actuated by purely material considerations.

It is a mistake to divorce spirituality from material considerations, for the latter have some spiritual importance. It is not by ignoring human suffering but by handling it with creative love that the gate is opened to life eternal. It is not through callous indifference, but by active and selfless service that one attains the transcendental and illimitable truth that lies at the heart of the illusory universe.

Spiritual aspirants are rooted in the conviction of the reality and the eternity of the infinite Soul. It should be easy for them then to stake life itself on the performance of a duty that springs from the claims of the spirit.

The duty of the spiritually enlightened one is an extension of the duties of the average person and of the spiritual aspirant. He is alive to the truth that all souls are one, and the role he must play in this game of God's is necessarily determined by the spiritual illumination he has. He performs his duty in cooperation with the divine will. Being in tune with the infinte truth, he is not only free from all thoughts of selfish gain, but also from the backlash of hate, malice and revenge.

War cannot create any real cleavage, even between the people who are fighting against one another. These people seem to be different from one another because they have different minds and bodies, but when judged from the point of view of their souls, all differences are not only secondary but simply false. The spiritual unity of all souls remains inviolable in spite of all wars, and from the point of view of ultimate reality, no soul is really at war with any other soul.

There can be a war between ideologies, which may extend to and involve the minds and even the bodies of the people, but the undivided and indivisible Soul remains One in Its unimpeachable, integral unity.

All those who must undergo the rigors of war have great need for equanimity. It will be profitable to remember that the soul remains unscathed by the destruction of material things, and death itself is only a gateway to further life. Therefore those who would play their part well in the divine game should remain unmoved by bereavement and loss, imparting to others a spirit of cheerful resignation to the divine will.

Due to lack of spiritual insight, sufferings of war inevitably embitter many persons, and they need to be helped to recover a sense of the unspoilable sweetness of life. Those who have been initiated into the eternal values of inner life must assume the responsibility of driving away unwarranted gloom and depression and cheering those who are in deep sorrow. When crisis is upon one, let one's thoughts not be for self, but for others—for the claims of the divine Self which exists equally in all.

War cannot be justified merely because it brings certain spiritual qualities as by-products, for these qualities can also be developed in time of peace. It is time now for humanity to develop a spontaneous spirit of love and service, rather than require the stimulus provided by danger to precipitate unselfish action.

All should face the crisis of war with patience, fortitude and self-sacrifice, never forgetting that the redemption of a distracted humanity through divine love is much closer than one dreams at such a time.

CHAPTER 4

The New World Culture

The East has had, and will continue to have, great influence on the spiritual heritage of the world, and therefore upon the outlines of the new humanity. For all its material backwardness, the East remains spiritual. For ages it has been the home of avatars, prophets, masters, seers and sages whose contribution to the spiritual evolution of humanity has been unparalleled. It is essential that the spiritual atmosphere of the East be maintained even at the cost if necessary of material unhappiness. If the East's spiritual power and value are retained, the suffering of her people will finally be supplanted by happiness.

The current problems of the East are more complex in some ways than those the West is required to solve. Men of all races, creeds, cults and religions are to be found in the East. Although this lack of racial and cultural uniformity has presented difficulties in developing solidarity in the national life of the East, it must not be regarded as being an unrelieved handicap. The various streams of culture pouring into the life-history of the East in particular, and of the world in general, have added to the wealth of its resources. They have not only created a suitable opportunity for the generation of a new cultural synthesis, but have *required* its emergence.

Under deft and creative leadership, such conflicting elements can bring a rich new culture into existence, capable of rejuvenating and harmonizing the life of the whole world.

A new, cohesive, vital culture cannot be brought to life by a purely mechanical combination of isolated elements selected from present cultures. This could only result in a vague patchwork with no spontaneous life of its own. Such a hodgepodge of assembled ideas can never be a substitute for that essential element from which a new culture must be generated: a direct, fresh perception of the goal. The new world culture must emerge from an integral vision of truth, springing independent of existing traditions, and unrelated to any laborious compilation of historical values.

The new world culture, born from the new humanity and its integral vision, will automatically involve a cultural synthesis. The vision that inspires the new culture will be comprehensive. It will not deny the value of diverse traditions, nor will it merely accord them patronizing tolerance. On the contrary, it will entail active appreciation of the diverse religions and cultures.

This vast vision of truth cannot be limited by any creed, dogma or sect. It will actively help men to transcend these limitations, not by blind negation of the value of the existing creeds, but by discovering, accentuating, unfolding and cherishing the facets of truth which are in them.

Another task which confronts the creative leadership of the East is to strive for political poise in spite of the difficult position the East occupies in international circles. The East can never make its full contribution to the world unless it is free from external political domination and fear of foreign aggression. Insistence upon this fundamental point though should not disturb its political poise, nor push it into a vitiated and reactionary isolationism. On the other hand, any future discharging of the clear duty to resist foreign aggression should not involve it in a sense of hate, malice or revenge.

This in turn raises the perplexing question of the utilization of non-violence, which has been such an active tool in India's recent past. Aggression must be met with resistance, and in such case non-violence is impractical. Pure non-violence, or incorruptible love, only comes spontaneously when duality has been completely transcended in the realization of the last and only truth. Even non-violence of the brave is possible only for advanced souls who have eradicated all forms of greed and hate from their minds through rigorous discipline.

For the masses, it is undesirable to adhere to external non-violence when it is a question of clear duty to resist aggression in their own defense or in defense of weaker brothers. Insistence upon universal non-violence can only lead the masses to a cowardly, irresponsible and inert attitude.

True love is no game for the faint-hearted and the weak. It is born of strength and understanding.

In its enthusiasm for the highest ideal, wise leadership can never afford to lose sight of the relative and practical. Human evolution proceeds by gradual stages from selfish violence to unselfish violence, and then from non-violence of the brave to the pure and incorruptible non-violence of truth as infinite love. Each individual exists at some point in this succession, and his duty in time of war is indelibly determined by that position.

All narrowness limits love. In the East, as in the rest of the world, humanity is breaking itself into narrow groups based upon caste, creed, race, nationality, religion or culture. All this is due to ignorance, prejudice and selfishness. It can only be mended by fostering a spirit of mutuality which will derive its strength from a sense of the inviolable unity of all life.

Creative leadership will have to recognize and then emphasize the fact that all men are already united, not only by their co-partnership in the great divine plan for the earth, but also by the fact that they are all equally the expression of the one life. No line of action can be really fruitful unless it is in complete harmony with this truth.

There must be love for friend and foe, good will, patience and forebearance. Man must try to remedy his own defects instead of clamoring about the faults of others. The world will soon realize that neither cults, creeds and ceremonies on the one hand, nor passionate striving for material welfare on the other, can ever bring about real happiness—but that selfless love and universal brotherhood can accomplish it.

The future of humanity is in the hands of those who have this vision, and the role of the East in that future will be an irreplaceable one if it knits its spiritual and human resources together into a creative synthesis of its ancient heritage.

CHAPTER 5

Notes on Freedom

Throughout the ages, the voice of mankind has been lifted up in a great clamor for freedom. The love and quest for freedom are principal characteristics of humanity, regardless of race, time, nationality or geography. But in spite of the fact that freedom has been the watchword of groping mankind for so many thousands of years, there are very few persons who really understand the full implications of true freedom. There are many, though, who struggle to attain a relative freedom dictated by their partial understanding of the nature and conditions of true freedom. Thus different persons long for different kinds of freedom according to the different things they have come to value.

Relative freedom, which is the brand of freedom usually involved, is sought in all phases of life, and is usually related to the type of existence people wish to lead. For instance, those who identify themselves with their country instinctively work for national or political freedom. Those who are motivated by economic considerations strive for economic freedom. Those who are inspired by religious drives work towards religious freedom. Those who espouse some sociological or cultural ideology promote freedom of movement or speech.

The localized freedom which grows from these limited goals is illusory and can only be termed a contrasting state in which the reverse of the discomforting situation prevails. It is a freedom of ignorance in which there is at best transitory peace and plenty, and passing relief and enjoyment.

Regardless of the material bindings of the good and the bad, spiritual freedom is always at hand, ready to be grasped by man. This is true because man's inherent spiritual freedom of the soul is eternal, infinite and changeless, regardless of whether it is experienced with full human consciousness or not.

Few realize that this is the basic freedom. It alone can give the stamp of true value to the different kinds of relative freedom, for, in the long run, they are all dissolved in it. Even when the external conditions of a free life are completely fulfilled and guaranteed, the mind of man will still be in a straight jacket if man has failed to win spiritual freedom.

External, relative freedom is inevitably restricted by contact with other individuals. Therefore external freedom is subject to redefinition and restriction within the limits imposed by group, communal and national living. Inevitably national rights in turn become subject to adjudication or violent readjustment because of the overlapping "rights" of other nations. The constant adjustment of these so-called rights at all levels is completely incapable of final solution within the spheres of interest and controlling principles natural to them. Consciously or unconsciously, individuals as well as nations must draw upon a more reliable concept of freedom within which those rights may be resolved.

National, economic, religious and cultural freedoms are the reflection of the duality of existence. They exist only in varying degrees, subject to constant discordant adjustment. Even when won through persistent effort, they cannot be permanently maintained because the external conditions upon which they have been constructed are themselves subject to deterioration.

Only spiritual freedom is absolute and unlimited; when it is won through persistent effort, it is won forever. For, although spiritual freedom can and does express itself in the duality of existence, it is grounded in and sustained by the realization of the inviolable unity of all life.

One important condition of spiritual freedom is freedom from all wanting. It is *wanting* itself which chains life by attaching it to the conditions in environment which would fulfill that want. If there is no wanting, there is no dependence, and therefore no limitation.

The individual never achieves true freedom until he is no longer pushed or pulled by any inner compulsion. When he has worked through all the desires and worn them so threadbare that he can be, or not be—have, or have not—then he is free. It is here that the

Perfect Masters are indispensable in helping to lighten this crushing burden of trying to wear out and discard the wants.

When the individualized soul breaks through the encasing steel armor of wanting, it emancipates itself from its illusory bondage to bodies, mind and ego. This is the spiritual freedom which brings with it the final realization of the unity of all life and puts an end to all doubts and worries.

Fully conscious, eternal experience of spiritual freedom is the inevitable and final destination for all life and for each individual being.

The method for abandoning the hold which duality has on consciousness is not simple. The more comfort and pleasure available to man, the less his chance for a strong enough push to force him to give up even the temporary happiness of his achievements. And yet he must eventually do this (internally) to bring the full focus of consciousness to bear on the experience of the eternally inherent self or soul, with all its blissful freedom of real existence.

This is why God loves most the so-called destitute and helpless. The greater the helplessness, the greater can and should be the dependence upon God for His help, which is ever more ready than are the sincere and earnest wishes for it. The greater the bindings, the greater the chances for quick, permanent relief, through fully conscious experience of man's own original and everlasting freedom. The unlimited and everlasting spiritual freedom of the self or soul exists eternally and infinitely in one and all, and is equally available to every man and woman irrespective of class, creed or nationality.

Spiritual freedom can and does transcend all the illusory phenomena of duality, because divine Oneness is always divine Oneness, before the beginningless beginning and beyond the endless end. Contrarily, the illusion of all material binding from first to last is always illusion, and even its illusory existence depends upon the play of the eternal spiritual freedom of the soul.

It is only in spiritual freedom that one can have enduring happiness and unhampered self-knowledge. It is only in spiritual freedom that one finds the supreme certainty of truth-realization. It is only in spiritual freedom that there is a final end to sorrow and limitation. It is only in spiritual freedom that one can live for all, and yet remain detached in the midst of all activity.

Any other lesser type of freedom is like a house built on sand, and any lesser attainment is fraught with fear of decay. There is no gift greater than that of spiritual freedom, and no task more important than helping others to find spiritual freedom. Those who have understood the supreme importance of spiritual freedom must not only strive for it themselves, but also share the God-given duty of helping others win it.

Regardless of whether a man is wealthy or poor, highly educated or illiterate, the only real help is to give him the perfect hope that everyone has a really equal opportunity to achieve everlasting freedom from all bindings.

Helping others achieve spiritual freedom is very different from rendering other types of help. For the hungry, one can provide food, and they have only to eat it. For the naked, one can provide clothes and they have only to wear them. For the homeless, one can provide houses and they have only to live in them. But for those who experience the agonies of human bondage, there is no ready means of providing immediate relief except by the grace of God.

As a rule, spiritual freedom must be won through watchful and unfailing war against the lower self and its desires. Those who would help shoulder the load in the cause of truth have not only the responsibility of attaining the goal for themselves, but of extending love and understanding to others in every step which they take towards that attainment. There is no other way of sharing their burden.

Real help in achieving the perfect hope of attaining spiritual freedom can only be given by the Perfect Master who has achieved with full consciousness the freedom of the self, and at the same time continues to be entirely conscious of the illusion of duality. From him, true and great help can be obtained, for he has experienced one hundred per cent of the truth of spiritual freedom, and is one hundred per cent confident that the truth is real. Such a Perfect Master can give relief to humanity from "immediate ignorance", as well as relief to the individual from "continual ignorance".

But direct help from a Perfect Master is rarely available, and so each individual must help others in every field of life to the utmost of his capacity. First, however, he must take every possible precaution against the development in himself of a sense of obliging, or of obligation in the receiver. This is best achieved by a feeling of pure love between man and man.

Such selfless love springs from the profound understanding that each individual, on achieving full human consciousness, has arrived at the same threshold of infinite divine Oneness. Each human being does possess therefore a truly equal spiritual opportunity to achieve the oneness of spiritual freedom, which is potentially as complete in himself as in the other.

Even though one may have tried to take every precaution to avoid any sense of obligation in the help one gives, undoubtedly there is every chance of this element entering to some extent through either giver or receiver. Still, this should be no cause for hesitation in rendering whatever relief one can provide. Although extending help to others is fraught with the danger of endlessly multiplying misery for both giver and receiver, man must nevertheless help his fellow with the same care that he meets his own needs.

There are further questions of great importance in rendering help to a suffering humanity, such as temporary versus permanent relief. Often a sharp choice must be made. When immediate relief is likely to turn a curable case into an incurable one, or to spread the infection to others, insistence upon immediate relief and refusal to try for a permanent cure is unthinkable.

Similarly, there is no real value in helping if one robs Peter in order to pay Paul. There is no point in giving relief at one end by creating misery at the other.

The question of pity for the suffering and downtrodden is also a moot one. Such expressions of pity in themselves are an expression of ignorance, as pity itself is invariably based on unconscious denial of the equal capacity for everlasting freedom of the self. There is no truth in the myth that the well-fed, well-clothed, well-educated can best find God. On the contrary, the so-called rich are comparatively more handicapped by fleeting comfort and mercurial resources than are those who feel chained by their material needs.

Since God loves the afflicted ones most, to emphasize their helplessness is to act in ignorance of their true state of grace. Instead of making them think more and more about their helplessness, they must be made to come nearer and nearer to God.

Instead of stressing the limitations of some men, the emphasis should be placed on the limitations of all men. Instead of stressing the need that "I" help "you", or "you" help "me", it should be "we" helping "us". Instead of making ourselves and others helpless minded, we should become and help others to become helpful minded.

The relative difference between man and man in material resources or physical endowment becomes lost like a mote of dust in the infinitely greater resources of the inner self—the treasure house of all. It must be impressed constantly upon humanity that the real birthright of every man and woman is to achieve his own original freedom, that it *can* be achieved, and that sooner or later it *must* be achieved. Without this, there is no lasting escape from the day-to-day problems born of duality.

Men must be made to understand clearly that their present life is a chain of continuous strife, that this chain is composed of links of the opposite experiences of virtue and sin, service and tyranny, etc., and that the chain can never be permanently ended as long as ignorance is not eliminated by achieving the eternal experience of one's own self.

Except in cases of complete physical helplessness, help can best be given by offering the individual work, and making him feel that he is fit to do work. Yet even this help is superfluous when judged from the standpoint of spirituality. Real help that can be rendered humanity is to make man feel his inherent divinity, and to cause him to see that the only purpose of life is to love God in order to become one in full consciousness with Him.

No sacrifice is too great to set man free from spiritual bondage and help him achieve spiritual freedom. This alone can bring peace to all, sustained unfailingly by an unassailable sense of universal fellowship and cemented by an ungrudging love for all as expressions of the same reality.

CHAPTER 6

The Ways to the Path and Its States and Stages

Truly happy people are rare in spite of the smiles which are usually the brave front for varying degrees of internal misery. Yet everywhere and in every walk of life, man is longing for happiness and searching desperately for some means of breaking out of the trap which his life has become.

It is not his fault if he assumes that the solution to his deep dissatisfaction lies in a sensual life, or in achievement in business or the social world, or in a life of exciting experiences. Neither is it his fault if life is not usually long enough to teach him factually that he would find even more profound disillusionment if these goals were to be fulfilled to the hilt.

If he would suspect that his ideas of achieving a successful and happy life were wrong, and that he must try some new way of living, then the stalemate might be broken. A new line in the divine picture is sketched only when some individual takes life forcefully in his hands, breaks up the old patterns and insists on creating something new by his own inner vision.

Progress in the inner life of the individual is accomplished by such a breaking with the old and venturing forth into new ways. True happiness can come only to one who will find the courage to strike free of the attachments which he has formed throughout a sterile lifetime. If he will not do this, then he is shackled endlessly to the treadmill of oppressive action in which happiness is so transient that it has almost disappeared the moment it is experienced. After it has disappeared, there is left only the persistent, bottomless vacuity of mind which strangles life, regardless of repeated efforts to fill it with endless experiences.

Such suffering comes from blunt ignorance or persistent attachment to illusion. The average person plays with illusion as children play with toys. It is not easy for little children to give up their toys, and it is equally difficult for adults to relinquish the mental and emotional toys to which they have become habituated. The mind of the individual is very old, and through the ages it has become deeply engrossed in playing with illusion. It has become addicted to this self-created spectacle, and has had no thought other than to go on watching with fascination through cycles and cycles of creation.

During this period of rebirth in cosmic illusion, the individualized soul becomes identified with the physical body due to the limitations imposed upon consciousness by the impressions (*sanskaras*). Its knowledge of reality is therefore necessarily restricted to the products and inferences of sense-perception. Information so obtained is completely inadequate and even misleading insofar as the true nature of reality is concerned.

The quest for happiness is irretrievably enmeshed in the problem of the illusion of the world of form with which the individual self has become identified through the body. If this illusion can be shattered, the shackles which bind happiness are automatically shattered as well. But how to shatter the illusion?

An individual who mistakenly believes that he is a coward may live a lifetime of misery during which all his actions are shaped by this incorrect belief. But if some event in his life challenges him so deeply that he unthinkingly strides forth with great courage, then the illusion will suddenly vanish and he will see himself as a different being. Often it takes real crisis to bring out a sure knowledge of the real inner self, and it is always a creative knowledge.

Even as the individual can be wrong in his convictions regarding his own nature, so he is often quite wrong about the nature of the world around him. In reality, it is a world of illusion that separates him from his true birthright of freedom and happiness in oneness with the One.

Actually, no individual is entirely devoid of some real happiness in some form, for God as an endless and fathomless ocean of bliss is also within every person, and no one is entirely cut off from Him. Pleasure sought in illusion inevitably results in endless perpetuation of that very same false life of the ego, which leaves the individual exposed to intense suffering.

The whole play of illusion and the suffering it engenders functions by the divinely established law of *karma* (cause and effect). Therefore suffering must be accepted with grace and fortitude. It must be remembered that one's own actions are the cause of much of one's suffering, and therefore wise action can minimize it. But real alleviation of suffering requires spiritual enlightenment, and for that man must turn to the Perfect Masters and the God-man (Avatar).

If the world of form is only an illusion in reality, and if its harvest is such a rich one of misery, then why should its experience be required of the soul?

Life in the world of matter is an unavoidable phase in the progress of the individual, inasmuch as it provides the field for *action*. Action is the expression and therefore the focusing of the mental and emotional impressions (*sanskaras*) which impel the individual. As the individual acts, other motivating forces incompatible with that momentary effort are withheld.

Action is the paramount means through which the individual exercises discrimination in choice and adjustment between the many claims exerted upon his consciousness. Action also links a large number of individuals together through the innumerable *karmic* ties which have arisen out of past service and bondage. The material world offers the necessary environment for this interchange and interdependence.

On one hand these *karmic* ties trap the mind in a complex web. On the other hand they facilitate collective life with all its opportunities for exercise of love, sacrifice, service and mutual help. Through the negative lessons of hate and malice, as well as the positive lessons of love and service, the individual finds himself compelled to participate in collective effort. The mind's seeming isolation is continually invaded by the life-streams of other minds, ultimately enabling the individual to abandon entirely the illusion he had entertained of being separate. Thus he gradually comes to realize the unity of all life.

In spite of the suffering entailed, experience in the material world of action is thus not without compensating value. It constitutes a necessary phase in purifying the consciousness of the mind from all illusion in order that it may be transmuted into the consciousness of the soul.

One sees then that the material and spiritual worlds of lower and higher illusion play an irreplaceable role in the divine game, which has as its goal that man shall become consciously aware of his own divinity. The positive values derived from the divine sport in illusion cannot be harvested without simultaneous collection of the residual by-products of the coming-to-consciousness, termed "impressions" or *"sanskaras"*.

A newly constructed building is not considered to be really completed until the debris of construction has been cleared away. Similarly the fully developed individual consciousness is not available for union with the Divine until these residual products have been cleaned away and there is left only the completely untrammeled, unitary nature of the individualized soul, now fully conscious of self. As discussed earlier, in the processes of both sleep and death the individual returns unconsciously and briefly to the beyond-beyond state of God. In it the soul achieves refreshment before it returns first to the subconscious state of ordinary dreams or the intense subconscious state of heaven or hell, and then to the ordinary conscious state of wakefulness or reincarnate life.

The individual cannot remain in the beyond-beyond state of God for long for very important reasons. The goal is to achieve the full awareness of consciousness, which is fully achieved when all of the residual impressions have been dispelled.

Full consciousness is achieved in the first human form, but remains captured, so to speak, by the residual impressions, which continue to exist regardless of the waking or sleep state of the individual mind. It is as if they continued to stand as the unpaid balance of the price of consciousness. It is due to the standing impressions or *sanskaras* that individual consciousness must return again and again from oblivion to square its account with illusion, in illusion.

However consciousness must eventually disengage itself from enmeshment in the material realm of action, for in the long run all activities of the worldly man are like the movements of someone on the surface of the ocean. He develops some knowledge of the ocean of life through those activities, but only as much as is obtainable through exploration on the surface of the ocean. The time inevitably

comes when he wearies of surface-wanderings and makes up his mind
to plunge into the depths of the ocean of life.

Thereupon he becomes deeply concerned with the riddles of
"whither" and "whence", and this fact constitutes his spiritual birth,
by which he is eventually ushered onto the path.

The path of divine knowledge has both beginning and end. In rare
cases, a pilgrim may be very advanced due to efforts in previous
incarnations. In such case he may attain divine knowledge instanta-
neously as a gift bestowed upon him through the grace of a master.
In most cases, though, the pilgrim has to travel the path by stages,
attaining this knowledge gradually.

The understanding of God which the average person attains
through belief or reasoning is so far removed from true understanding that it cannot be called inner knowledge.

Such true knowledge (gnosis) does not consist in the construction
or perception of an ideology. It is the product of ripening experience
that attains increasing degrees of clarity. It consists in man's consciousness becoming more real and participating increasingly in the
truth, until there is nothing more to become, and nothing more to
assimilate.

The devotional rituals followed in religions do not lead the seeker
to the true inner journey, for in greater part they are mechanical
observances barren of the redeeming experience of divine love.

Nevertheless, regardless of how rudimentary these types of belief
and devotional observances may be, they do contain in latent form
the future inner knowledge.

As the aspirant struggles through the obscuring fog of mental and
emotional tension his consciousness becomes more one-pointed,
forming a spearhead that eventually pierces through the curtain to
the inner path of divine knowledge. Even the early glimpses of this
knowledge which the pilgrim gets are a great advance over understanding that rests solely upon faith or reason.

As the aspirant advances towards the path he undergoes a significant change of direction that might be compared to a somersault. He
is now more concerned with the inner realities of life than with their
outward expression. As the emphasis shifts from the external to the

internal aspects of life, the deepening of consciousness is greatly accelerated. Now consciousness is no longer committed primarily to external incidents or routines, but is directed towards the deeper and truer aspects of being that demand greater integrity of thought and feeling.

Caught up within this deeper awareness of the self is a concurrent deepening of perception into the workings of the world. A refocusing of consciousness occurs which is far-reaching. All the avenues through which the individual conducts his search are radically transformed by the sincerity and concentrated purpose of his effort. The increasing depths of his internal understanding suffuse every aspect of life, giving it new form and meaning and causing him to hasten his exploration with the greatest exhilaration.

Poise of mind born of the pilgrim's new understanding automatically and unwittingly brings about a readjustment of material surroundings, and he finds himself at peace with the world. Conservatism, intolerance, pride and selfishness are shed, and everything takes on new meaning and purpose.

Sinner and saint appear to be waves on the surface of the same ocean, differing only in magnitude, each the natural outcome of forces in the universe rooted in time and causation. The saint is seen to have no pride of position and the sinner no stigma of eternal degradation. Nobody is utterly lost and nobody need despair.

The "internalizing" which is the real basis of entering upon the path should not be confused with the purely intellectual discovery that there can be an inner life. Nor should the gradual and natural shift from participation in external events to a focusing on inner development be confused with the limited intellectual detachment some persons achieve. Since such detachment is only intellectual, it brings freedom only in the realm of limited intellect and is usually characterized by a sort of dryness of being.

The intellectually detached often try to shape the present in the light of knowledge of history, as well as through their insight into the possibilities of the unborn future. At best, such a purely intellectual perspective inevitably remains partial, sketchy, incomplete, and in a sense even erroneous. Further, the intellectually detached are almost never in vital communication with the elements which so largely shape the course of the present. Therefore their beliefs, even if transformed into effort, rarely produce marked results. The limited intellect is not competent to grasp qualities which are beginningless and endless.

Intellectual perspective is workable and even indispensable for planned action. Yet in the absence of the illuminating wisdom of heart and the clear intuition of spirit, intellectual perspective gives only relative truth bearing the ineradicable stamp of uncertainty.

So-called intellectually planned action is really the product of weighty subconscious forces which have not yet risen to the threshold of consciousness of the planner. Thus, planning often leads to many results entirely unanticipated in the so-called planning. In other words, "planning" turns out to be planning mostly in name only, containing only sufficient conscious participation by the planners to satisfy their need to feel that they have a real share in the whole game.

Intellectual perspective, intellectual planning and intellectual detachment therefore should be carefully separated from the robust exploration of the inner self and the internalizing of the facts of existence that characterize the individual who has set foot on the path.

Although the unfurling realization of divine knowledge is often figuratively described as "traversing the path", this analogy should not be taken too literally. There is no ready-made road in the spiritual realm. Spiritual progress is not a matter of moving along a line already laid down and unalterably defined. Rather, it is a creative process of spiritual involution of consciousness, and this process is better described as a "spiritual journey" than as the traversing of a path.

The journey is comparable in fact to a flight through the air, and not to a journey upon the earth, because it is truly a pathless journey. It is a dynamic movement within the consciousness of the aspirant that creates its own path and leaves no trace behind it.

The metaphor of "the path" is helpful to the aspirant in the early stages of his development because it gives him the sense of new phases of consciousness to be experienced. This anticipation is stimulated further by accounts of others who have completed the spiritual journey. This makes the pilgrim's ascent easier than if it depended solely upon his own unguided efforts to visualize the probable path.

While trying to understand the path as described by the masters, the aspirant must also make use of his own imaginative faculty, but within the constructive bounds defined in the master's spiritual guidance. Actual spiritual experience is as far removed from uncontrolled imaginative expectation as reality is from chaotic dreams. Though the imagination of the pilgrim is inevitably determined by past experience, it must offer no resistance to the directional suggestions of the master.

In fact, increasing surrender to the guidance of the master involves drastic curtailment of deceptive imagination—the roots of which are deeply embedded in the mental and emotional past of the pilgrim. With the gradual transmutation of the aspirant's imaginative faculty into divine consciousness, the veil of ignorance becomes steadily less opaque. In the end, all imagination comes to a standstill and is replaced by the true everlasting realization of God as the sole reality. Thus "the journey", like everything else in duality, is also an imaginative one, but it leads ultimately to final and enduring knowledge unclouded by any kind of imagination or transitory fantasy.

As the aspirant progresses on the spiritual path, a fundamental modification in the structure of his *sanskaras* begins to occur. Whereas, before, the expression of one *sanskara* in the world of form resulted in the inevitable creation of fresh *sanskaras,* this self-perpetuating process now begins to draw to a close. As the aspirant's assertive lower self begins to be removed, the tension of the existing impressions can be released or expressed without the creation of fresh *sanskaras.*

At first slowly, but with gradually increasing speed, the old *sanskaras* are spent with less and less attendant creation of fresh *sanskaras.* With final cessation of formation of fresh *sanskaras,* all past impressions naturally unwind to the finish and then, free of all impressions, the soul stands fully Self-conscious forever.

The various routes by which the individual may start on the journey are many indeed. Several of the principal ones are referred to as *Dnyana Marga* or the way of knowledge, *Karma Marga* or the way of action, *Bhakti Marga* or the way of devotion, and *Yoga Marga* or the way of mental and physical discipline. Each of these paths may be regarded as a routine, dutifully followed and unthinkingly executed, or it may be transmuted into a path of living discovery by having become the focal point of the aspirant's entire being.

Dnyana Marga or the way of knowledge, may consist in the pursuit of speculative philosophy, either through independent thinking or in the study of existing systems of philosophic thought. Or it may be transformed through concentrating the mind and the entire personality on the truths hitherto mentally grasped. Such deep meditation on spiritual realities is aimed at assimilating their inner meaning, and results in lifting them out of the category of intellectual playthings into animating principles which invade and gradually transmute the innermost core of the aspirant.

Karma Marga, or the way of action, may normally consist of a life of service to humanity, a life in which effort is expended to improve the well-being of people through social, political or physical projects. In such service the motivating factor is usually a sense of duty, but often it is corrupted by the desire to achieve power, fame or other personal gain. Regardless, the way of action creates in its wake many joys and many sorrows, much exultation and much disillusionment. It often creates further bindings for the soul and is frequently fraught with nagging restlessness due to the worker's expectation of specific results. As often as not, it results in enlargement of the ego rather than its deflation.

On the other hand, internalizing this same way of action renders it pure, safe and spontaneous. In such case the aspirant may still be engaged in humanitarian work, but that work is no longer entangled in personal ambition.

Such service is not a mechanical response to a sense of duty, but a spontaneous expression of voluntary love. Through it man gradually becomes purer, is freed from many limitations, and finds peace of being as he becomes wholly detached from the results of his actions. Under the enlightening influence of inner understanding, the life of action helps in the elimination of the ego-mind and quickens the pace to attainment of truth-consciousness.

The inner spiritual path is irreplaceable because of the welling up of divine love which occurs during its course. Even in *Bhakti Marga* as the ordinary religious man of the world practices it, this up-welling of love is absent. It is only in the inner transformation of the way of devotion that the aspirant is initiated into that spontaneous love which needs no outer observance for its realization. Such love springs up spontaneously in the heart under the quickening touch of the master's grace.

Yoga Marga, or the way of mental and physical discipline, is also capable of producing a complete transformation in the aspirant by unfolding the inner path of gnosis or *Irfan* in him. In his attempt to gain control over mind and body, the worldly man often resorts to these yogic practices and austerities to achieve the discipline he covets.

There are three main systems of yoga: (1) *Hatha Yoga* which consists of self-mortifying asceticism and physical austerities; (2) *Raja Yoga* which is the process of mental self-denial through resistance to all desires; and (3) the positive system of *Pranayama,* which consists in the awakening of the *Kundalini,* and meditation through an ascending order of exercises.

It is characteristic of all the different systems of yoga that they emphasize the purification and preparation of bodies or vehicles of consciousness, rather than concerning themselves directly with the onward movement of consciousness itself. The contribution of yoga is comparable to that of the physician who removes the ailments which have developed in the functioning of the internal organs of the body.

Of the different systems of yoga, *Hatha Yoga* is the most superficial. The self-imposed austerities represent in a sense a pressuring of God, or of a God-realized Master, for either power or realization. It is a kind of bargaining in which penance is undertaken with an ulterior motive. It can hardly be called self-sacrifice, for the things apparently denied oneself are denied in order that one might have something else. Ultimately it reduces to intelligent selfishness.

Spirituality, as love, can never be achieved through any type of coercion. If spiritual attainment should be sought in this manner, the person invites harm upon himself rather than spiritual benefit, and restriction of power rather than expansion. In brief, he gets exactly the opposite of what he had sought.

The yoga of mental self-denial through resistance to all desires (*Raja Yoga*) is chiefly negative in its method. It consists in a concentrated attempt to be freed from all good and bad wants which plague the mind. In following this method the individual attempts to avoid all wants and desires. This in itself is a form of wanting, for it is wanting a state of wanting nothing. However, this form of yoga, when carried to its extreme limit, can result in the subjective annihilation of the ego-structure of desires.

The positive system of yoga consisting in the practice of *Pranayama* (breathing exercises), gives increased control over *prana* or the vital energy. It also includes the awakening of the *Kundalini* or the latent spiritual power in man, and is supplemented by an ascending order of meditation exercises. But in this yoga there is the danger of the aspirant having a "fall" and retrogressing spiritually if he misuses his awakened occult powers. This he inevitably does if these powers are awakened before he is spiritually ready.

The aspirant is therefore well advised *not* to take up this positive system of yoga except under the direct supervision of a master. When aroused under the proper guidance of a master, however, the awakened *Kundalini* can lead the aspirant to the occult *Riddhi-Siddhi* powers of the fourth plane which is described later.

In any case, the highest attainment possible through *Pranayama*, the breath exercise phase of the positive system of yoga, is that of the objective or semi-illumination of the fifth plane.

Both the fifth and sixth planes of gnosis are states of illumination, but they may be either subjective or objective, depending upon the manner in which the illumination has been achieved. The positive systems of yoga lead to objective illumination of the fifth plane, but such objective illumination can only be termed "semi-illumination", for in it God is experienced as *without*, and therefore sight of Him is eclipsed or obscure.

In contrast, subjective or full illumination is brought about through the inner path of love, which brings about a blending of devotion, knowledge and action. Such subjective illumination in the fifth and sixth planes has absolutely no element of obscurity, because God is experienced *within*. In a sense, God is nearer the subjective realm than the objective, although ultimately He is inclusive of both, as well as beyond both.

Such are the traditional paths by which the aspirant may launch upon his quest for realization. The particular route by which the worldly man will start his search is determined by his temperament and environment. But when he enters the inner spiritual path he seeks the truth of consciousness as it *is*. This quest for the real compels him to transcend the obscurities of the mind and the twistings which arise from temperament and environment. Even as the inner truths unfold, these factors continue to limit his consciousness, but he is now impelled to make a conscious effort to free himself from their entanglements.

The first evidence in the aspirant of freedom from limitations imposed by the subjective mind is that he begins to understand without prejudice his own nature and environment. To react intelligently to environment is impossible unless its true meaning is understood.

For example, a man habitually inclined to react cynically to all that is good in other people, inevitably fails to appreciate the latent good in those whom he contacts. Consequently he not only misses the pleasure of harmonious relationship with them, but is also prevented from utilizing the potential value of such experience for the good of others.

Similarly, if a man erects his projects on an incorrect evaluation of environment, the energy which he invests in them may be wasted in spite of his enthusiasm. Correct judgment of environment and people is an important requisite of fruitful and right action. It requires in the aspirant both the capacity to rise above his personal prejudices and, more important, to understand them. Judgment befogged by personal bias renders right action impossible.

To illustrate further, if the individual projects the content of his own subjective desire upon another human being, seeing in that person the fulfillment of his emotional longings, and if he acts under the impulse of that blind driving force, then disappointment is inevitable. He has only seen in the other what is in himself.

There can be no adequate response from the object of one's desire under such emotional compulsion, and therefore no fulfillment. So true understanding of environment is as necessary for attaining soundness and depth of feeling as it is for engendering efficient, creative action. Such true understanding is achieved only when the aspirant frees himself from temperamental compulsion.

The personal factors which cause the worldly man to look upon the various approaches towards truth as widely divergent or even mutually antagonistic, are gradually transcended on the path. Eventually the ways converge, and their interdependence is revealed to the aspirant. He sees that each way implements the others.

Bhakti or devotion becomes the expression of truth through feeling. The way of knowledge becomes the assimilation of that same truth through understanding, and the way of action is seen to be the result of the will being actuated by that very same truth.

In the worldly stage man is drawn more to one way than to others because of the particular limitations of his character and environment. On the path they blend with each other as the aspirant gradually succeeds in emancipating himself from the specific restrictions of mind and heart. Even the dry, self-imposed asceticisms of yoga flower as the individual realizes divine love as he follows the inner path.

It is possible by following any of the ways just discussed to lose the individual mind, the lower self, and yet retain complete consciousness. However this is true only when the zenith is reached through the inner path.

The easiest and safest way to lose one's finite ego is by surrendering completely to the Perfect Master or to the God-man (Avatar), who is consciously one with truth. In them the past, present and future of the individual are drowned and during his implicit obedience to the master he is no longer bound by those actions, good and bad. Such complete surrenderance is in itself complete freedom.

Of all the high roads which take the pilgrim directly to his divine destination, the quickest lies through the God-man (Christ, Messiah, Avatar). In the God-man, God reveals Himself in all His glory, with His infinite power, unfathomable knowledge, inexpressible bliss and eternal existence. The path through the God-man is available to all those who approach Him in complete surrenderance and unwavering faith.

To the one who has unfaltering love for the God-man, the way to abiding truth is clear and safe. Such a one must waste no time playing with things that do not matter. Loyalty to the unchangeable truth, guided by enduring love, is the simple way that leads to God and abiding peace.

Although God is more easily accessible to ordinary man through the God-men, yet God also reveals Himself in His *impersonal* aspect, which is beyond name, form and time. Regardless of whether it is to be through His personal or His impersonal aspect, it is necessary that the aspirant seek Him and surrender to Him in love.

When the aspirant *contemplates* only God without a second there is no room for love for God or longing for God. The individual has the intellectual conviction that he is God.

Yet in order to experience that state in actuality, the aspirant goes through intense concentration or meditation on the thought "I am not the body, I am not the mind, I am neither this nor that. I am God". In exceptional cases the individual may experience through meditation what he has assumed himself to be. This mode of experiencing God is not only difficult but dry.

Progress is more realistic and enjoyable when there is an ample play of love and devotion to God. This postulates temporary and apparent separateness from God and longing to unite with Him. Such provisional and apparent separateness from God is reflected in the Sufi concepts of the states of *"Hama az Ust"* or "Everything is from God", and *"Hama Doost"* or "Everything is for the beloved God".

In each of these concepts the individual perceives that his separateness from God is only temporary and apparent, and he seeks to restore this lost unity with God through intense love, which consumes all duality. The only difference between these two is that, whereas the individual who follows the concept of *"Hama Doost"* rests content with the will of God as the Beloved, in the concept of *"Hama az Ust"* he longs for nothing but union with God.

Since the individualized soul which is in bondage can be redeemed only through divine love, even Perfect Masters who attain complete unity with God and experience Him as the only reality, apparently step into the domain of duality and talk of love, worship and service of God.

Divine love, as sung by Hindu masters like Tukaram, as taught by Christian masters like Saint Francis, as preached by Zoroastrian masters like Azer Kaivan and as immortalized by Sufi masters like Hafiz, harbors no thought of the self at all. It consumes all frailties which nourish the illusion of duality, and ultimately unites the individual with God. The awakening of this divine love in the heart of the aspirant and the cleansing of his being is one of the functions of the God-man and Perfect Masters.

The life of love of a Perfect Master is unperturbed by desires or duality. Once the mind of the aspirant gets a glimpse into this life of true values it protests against the bondage of desires and the cage of the separative ego-life.

The Perfect Master acts from the truth with which he is one, and not from any limited ego-consciousness. Hence his help is more effective than all the unaided effort the aspirant himself can make.

The Perfect Master does not give something which is not already within the aspirant in latent form. He unveils the real self of the aspirant and enables him to come into his own rightful divine heritage.

Complete surrenderance to the God-man is not possible for one and all. When this is not possible, the other high roads which can eventually win the grace of God are:

(1) Loving obedience to and remembrance of the God-man to the best of one's ability;

(2) Love for God and intense longing to see Him and to be united with Him;

(3) Being in constant company with the saints and lovers of God and rendering them whole-hearted service;

(4) Avoiding lust, greed, anger, hatred and the temptations of power, fame and faultfinding;

(5) Leaving everyone and everything in complete external renunciation and, in solitude, devoting oneself to fasting, prayer and meditation;

(6) Carrying on all worldly duties with a pure heart and clean mind and with equal acceptance of success or failure, while remaining detached in the midst of intense activity; and

(7) Selfless service of humanity, without thought of gain or reward.

In the end, all walks of life and all paths ultimately lead to the one goal, which is God. All rivers enter into the ocean regardless of the diverse directions in which they flow, and in spite of the many meanderings they may take. The high roads are important because they take the pilgrim directly to his divine destination, avoiding prolonged wanderings in the wilderness of complicated byways in which the traveler is so often unnecessarily confused.

The various states and stages through which the pilgrim passes on his journey to God-realization may be broken down into three phases which the Sufis call *Tariqat, Marifat* and *Haqiqat*. In the first, divine knowledge is experienced on the planes of energy as inner intuition, inspiration and conviction.* In Sufic terminology this glimpse of divine knowledge is known as *Tajurbat-e-Tariqat*, and represents a transition from ordinary understanding to a condition of inner experiences of smell, sound and sight.

During this first stage of unfolding knowledge there is a far deeper conviction about spiritual realities than is possible through the usual understanding of the worldly man. However, even this conviction is not unshakeable. It bestows only a mild and wavering degree of divine knowledge. The pilgrim has now only started on his spiritual journey and must face many trials.

While becoming established in the first stage, many aspirants are unable to cope with the ordeals they encounter as inner sight is opened. Whatever the pilgrim encounters here is for his good, and if he has a master's guidance he need not fear that he will be lost, although at the climax of the first phase (*Tariqat*), which is the fourth plane, the one real danger of risking a fall does occur through possible misuse of the extraordinary powers associated with this plane.

During this first phase the aspirant is disengaging himself from enmeshment in the material realm of action, and ascending to the realm of energy. This is accomplished through the gradual dissolving of the multitudinous desires which chain his consciousness to the ma-

---

* Not to be confused with ordinary intuition, inspiration and conviction, as *inner sight* is not to be confused with ordinary sight.

terial world. Although the individual is now constantly dependent upon the finer realms of energy, mind and divine consciousness, even while immersed in the realm of matter, still he cannot live freely in these realms because of his continued enslavement to the gross world.

Moreover, he cannot receive in any appreciable measure the renewal which divine consciousness would pour into him, due to the resistance offered by the entanglements of the dense material plane upon which he lives. Nevertheless it is these divine radiations, meagerly felt though they be, which enable the matter-ridden mind to face suffering and make the effort to rise in the higher realms of energy and mind.

At last, weary of enslavement to the gross world, the individual decides to free himself from the enticements of matter. In this moment of irrevocable decision the individual cuts himself loose from the bondage of gross desires and ascends to the realm of energy. His will now reinforced, the individual prepares for a release of vital force far greater than was ever available to him during his bondage to the gross. The activities of the individual are now more powerful, for his actions are unhindered by the low voltage characterizing the energy of the gross realm.

Often the aspirant becomes absorbed in the new powers now available, and he realizes that he can perform miracles and other phenomena. The tendency to wish to perform miracles, or to judge spiritual developments by the performance of such spectacles, may persist for some time. Even spiritually advanced persons find it difficult to outgrow this habit of playing with illusion. It should be clearly understood that attachment to miracles is only a continuation of the habit of playing with illusion. It is not miracles, but inner illumination which will one day bring true freedom.

In the realm of energy the increased capacity of the individual to receive the downpouring of divine radiation gives him a greater sense of spiritual power, a larger measure of knowledge and a deeper sense of fulfillment, although these are as yet intermittent and fragmentary. The individual continues to carry on the physical plane activities of eating, drinking and other automatic activities of physical life. But he is now no longer the tormented slave of unfulfilled desires rooted in the physical functions, although a recrudescence of desires in a milder form is still possible.

He is now subject though to new forms of restlessness. In desperate search for enduring peace he determines to ascend to the still higher mental sphere, upon which the realm of energy fundamentally depends for its sustenance.

Having crossed to this realm, the pilgrim is now at the second phase of the journey, in which he begins to see the light of God. Unfolding divine knowledge now amounts to real illumination, and the aspirant is given knowledge of the past, present and future. He is now firmly established in the divine path, and there is no longer any risk of his "falling" or losing his true illumination. There are still many trials, but he faces them with conviction, confidence and resolution.

This second phase occurs at a point which is called *Qubuliyat*, or "God's acceptance of the pilgrim". Here, being endowed with illumination he knows what trials lie ahead of him, but he also knows that he cannot fall from this fifth plane, and is aware that he can meet any situation adequately.

At a certain time the pilgrim passes to the point described by the Sufis as *Marifat*, and sees God as He is. This is spoken of as being the sixth plane of ascent of the individual in his conscious return to the One. It is in the mental sphere, as was the fifth plane.

In the sixth plane the freedom, joy and illumination that the soul experiences are all greatly enhanced, as the mind is in direct contact with transcendental divine consciousness. The bliss experienced in this higher realm surpasses all possible pleasures experienced in the realms of matter or energy. There is now absolutely no resistance to the direct infusion of the unceasing radiations of light, power, wisdom and bliss that overflow from the Godhead. The individual's happiness is unutterable, his vision undimmed, his power unrestrained, his peace undisturbed, and his understanding suffers no slightest momentary impairment. He knows no lack of any kind; he continually sees God as He is.

All that the individual enjoys in the mental realm is still not *self*-sustained, but is continually supplied by the never-failing emanations from the transcendental Godhead. Although the mind is completely surcharged with the heavenly abundance which descends upon it from God, nevertheless it constantly recognizes its utter dependence upon the renewal which comes to it from above. The higher realm of mind is no less dependent upon the transcendent Godhead than are the lower realms of energy and matter, for the individual, though enjoying perpetually the free life of the spirit, still has not attained *unity* with the Godhead. He has not yet transcended duality nor realized himself *as* the Infinite One.

In short, man on the gross plane makes indirect use of energy and mind through the gross sphere, and he can experience only such joy, power and knowledge as the limitations of the gross permit. Man on the subtle plane uses *energy* directly but uses *mind* indirectly, *i.e.* through the subtle plane. Also his joy, peace and understanding are still severely curtailed by the fact that he cannot make direct contact with the mind itself.

Man on the mental plane can use energy as well as mind directly. Thus he enjoys immeasurable power, knowledge and bliss, but inasmuch as these are gifts from the Godhead, he still has a sense of dependence. He experiences the attributes of divinity as reflected in the mental spheres, but they do not originate in him.

Even when man is able to make direct use of the mind, he falls short of that ultimate experience of knowing himself as the infinite Godhead. Although the individual experiences uninterrupted self-fulfillment owing to his absorption in the replenishing divinity, still he must transcend the mind completely if he chooses to realize himself as the unlimited and eternal truth, power and bliss of God.

At this stage the traveler sees God as the sole reality, but he may remain absorbed in this sight of sights, or he may cross the final gulf and become one with God.

In the final and third phase of the spiritual journey, called *Haqiqat*, man becomes one with God as the infinite truth. This realization is *self*-sustained. Man's consciousness is now completely one with the illimitable truth of the conscious God. The individualized soul has completely transcended the mind and established unity with the Godhead, thereby realizing itself to be the fountainhead of infinite love, infinite peace, infinite bliss, infinite power and infinite knowledge.

These attributes are now no longer received by the individualized soul as emanations from the transcendent Godhead, but are experienced as being the soul's own inalienable characteristics. Nor is this state of superabundance merely one of self-sustained and unmarred spiritual self-sufficiency. It is a spontaneous overflowing in which divine consciousness sheds the glory of its superabundant life upon one and all. In this state God knows Himself as God. The goal has been reached.

To recapitulate, the realization of God *as He is* has required the complete surrenderance of the false individuality of the separate "I". All sense of separateness and duality is only illusion, sustained by the *sanskaras* (impressions) of the ego-life and expressed through lust, hate and greed. Through a pure life of selfless love and service and the grace of God or a Perfect Master, it is possible to brush away these limiting *sanskaras*. By transcending the illusory veil of separateness, the individualized soul comes to know itself as identical with God who is the sole reality. God-realization, which is achieved at the end of the last phase of the first journey and on the seventh plane of consciousness in which the mental sphere is completely transcended, is the goal of all life. It is the reason why the entire universe came into existence.

God-realization is sometimes mistakenly considered to be the selfish aim of the limited individual, while in reality there is no room for any selfishness or limited individuality in God-realization. On the contrary, it is the final aim of the limited and narrow life of the separate ego. God-realization not only results in the attainment by the individual of an inviolable unity with all life, but also in his dynamic expression of this final realization of truth through a spontaneous and undivided life of love, peace and harmony. The life of the God-realized is a pure blessing to all humanity.

Within this state of God-realization, God is known and experienced to be the only reality, and as there remains nothing further to know, one aspect of this divine consciousness is omniscience. Since God is experienced as being the only One without a second, having no rival to overcome and no limitations to transcend, the individualized soul realizes a second aspect of supreme consciousness to be omnipotence. Since God is also experienced as unconditional and spontaneous joy continually welling up within the soul, the third aspect of divine consciousness is realized to be unlimited bliss.

These attributes of omniscience, omnipotence and unlimited bliss are not divisible parts within infinity, but differentiated qualities of one indivisible infinity. Being indivisible, no one of them is in any way curtailed by another. Since they interpenetrate each other completely, none can or does exist without the others.

In God-consciousness, to *know* is to exist as blissful power; to exist as power is to know oneself as unbounded bliss; and to experience bliss is to be permeated by divine knowledge in which knower, known and knowledge are all one. Any existence in which power is limited, knowledge imperfect or joy beclouded, is a product of false imagination and cannot satisfy the earnest seeker after God.

Thus in the truth-consciousness of *Haqiqat*, God knows Himself as having infinite attributes, but He has no consciousness of the universe. In a few cases, consciousness of the universe returns to the God-realized soul without in any way obscuring the totality of his divine knowledge.

This first affirmation of God-consciousness in the universe may be said to constitute the first journey of complete divine knowledge, known as *Baqaiyat.** Conscious now of the universe through the being of the *Jivan-Mukta* or *Azad-e-Mutlaq* or *Baqa-billah*, God does not regard it as other than Himself. Not only is His knowledge not handicapped by consciousness of the world; it (God's knowledge) uses the shadow (creation) which it has itself created as a medium through which it finds expression.

In this state of *Baqaiyat*, God not only knows Himself as God but also as everything. He now experiences His own infinite attributes of omniscience, omnipotence and unbounded bliss also in and through the consciousness of the universe. God knows Himself as being everything, and everything as being Himself. His knowledge of Himself includes the knowledge of everything in illusion.

God enjoys the same infinite and unlimited attributes as in the first state of *Haqiqat*, but their expression within the illusion of duality

---

* This is the state of the *Jivan-Mukta*. A more complete integration into activities in the world of duality is achieved by the Perfect Master in the state of *Qutubiyat*, described below.

is naturally determined by the earthly vehicle in which the individu-alized soul functions. The God-realized *Jivan-Mukta*, though living in a world of duality, is aware only of the unimpaired unity which sustains and pervades the universe. Such a one experiences con-stantly the love which knows no limitation through time, circum-stance or mood.

Though the *Jivan-Mukta* lives and functions in the world of dual-ity, his consciousness dwells beneath the appearance of things in the underlying reality of his self (in God). In this manner such a soul creates no cleavage between the illusory and the real world, nor does being in the world constitute for him any limitation on the spontane-ous flow of divine love. On the contrary, the world with all its dual aspects becomes the medium through which his infinite love operates automatically.

In this phase of realization * the individual enjoys the limitless at-tributes of God but does not feel impelled to use them for the benefit of others. He has become fully conscious of his impersonal divinity which automatically permeates and controls all aspects of the uni-verse, and therefore he does not feel moved to intervene in the affairs of the world.

Active interest in cosmic processes or activities of the illusory uni-verse is possible only when the third journey from *Baqaiyat* to *Qutu-biyat*, or the *Sadguru* (Perfect Master) state is completed. In this state the fullness of divine knowledge, power and bliss is not only experienced completely, but is also dynamically expressed. Here the unlimited individuality of the Perfect Master participates fully in the life of the entire universe. In this state God not only knows Him-self as God and lives as God, but *works* as God, coordinating the truth He has realized with the processes of the universe.

Thus, at the end of this third journey of divine consciousness, God takes active interest in the spiritual yearnings of other souls, and ex-tends His help in their onward ascent. In this state as the Perfect Master, He is no longer detached from the happenings of the world,

---

* *I.e.* the *Jivan-Mukta* state. The soul has returned to consciousness of the world of duality, but the focus of consciousness of the *Jivan-Mukta* wanders between duality and God-absorption. See *God Speaks*, pp. 171–172.

and the cosmic processes and events of the world are no longer left solely to the direction of impersonal divinity. God Himself has become a person who is simultaneously fully divine and fully human, and He takes under His personal and conscious supervision the groping, struggling life-streams within the universe. The *Qutubiyat*- or *Sadguru*-state (Perfect Masterhood) is truly a state of personal Godhood.

His omniscience and unlimited love impel the *Qutub* or *Sadguru* to use his unlimited power freely for the spiritual benefit of all who deserve his grace. He goes halfway to meet aspiring souls and he accentuates their progress, communicating to them his boundless, overflowing love to the extent that they are capable of receiving it. This is a state in which God offers Himself to himself in measureless abundance, in and through the universe of duality.

Throughout his expression of personal interest in the life of the universe, the *Sadguru* never becomes entangled in duality. He is never bound in any way to the world of form in which he is expressing his dynamic and unlimited personality. When his divine game in the world of form is over he drops the link to his own bodies —physical, subtle and mental, and with the universe—without sense of loss or pain. He withdraws from the scene of his divinely expressed life in illusion and draws to a close his creative manifestation in the universe.

Withdrawal from participation in the universe of duality does not in any way impair his consciousness of divine knowledge, nor his conscious, constant and unbreakable experience of infinite power and bliss. He continues to remain conscious reality. Activity in the world constituted only action in an illusory universe. Withdrawal from it is only withdrawal from the unreal, through which he chose to manifest for the liberation of those still in bondage, and is termed the fourth and last journey.

CHAPTER 7

Attitudes for Aspirants and Other Groups

In previous chapters general outlines have been given of the sufferings which finally impel the individual to embark upon the journey. In addition, the major paths and high roads were described by which a great majority of the seekers travel, and the states and stages through which the aspirant gradually progresses were briefly sketched.

The entire spiritual process should never be regarded as one that can be described in intellectual terms, grasped by the mind and followed as a personal discipline. In many ways it constitutes the abandoning of all the previous means by which the individual had thought to achieve lasting peace. In other ways it is the essentializing and enlightened use of those same methods, but with a new sense of their utility.

The spiritual attitude represents nothing essentially new in the material life of the individual, but is rather a reorganization and reinterpretation of all that has existed in his life, and an infusion of new meaning into the present and future. In achieving this reorientation the aspirant often finds himself temporarily confused.

One of these points of confusion concerns his attitude towards intellectuality, science and technology. If the spiritual quest is to be real it cannot be deflected by an obsession with this vital nerve network of modern civilization. In some way the aspirant must place it in proper perspective with the totality of human development, and thereby be neither hypnotized nor repelled by it.

Intellect is reserved so to speak by nature for man. To have intellect one must be a human being. Regardless of how keen and quick that intellect may be, though, it will always remain just one of the stepping stones to wisdom, inspiration, illumination, knowledge, and at last, realization of truth. To keep playing on the stepping stone, however polished it may be, is like sitting tight on a heap of hoarded treasure.

Like everything else, intellect can be used, as well as misused. The deeper the intelligence, the greater one's responsibility to discriminate between essential and nonessential, service and disservice, progress and retrogression. The task of the aspirant is to use intellect as a tool, not to be overcome by it.

Often one hears in religious discussion of the opposition between matter and spirit. There is no fundamental opposition between matter and spirit. Like the closely knit elements of life and form in a person, the spiritual and material aspects of human life are closely united. Realization of this would eliminate erroneous contrasting concepts such as God and man, one and many, light and darkness, etc., all of which spring from the illusion of duality.

The fundamental link between spirit and matter can be seen in the necessary connection between ideas and deeds. Mere playing with spiritual ideas without putting them into action is as unproductive as emphasizing the material at the expense of the spiritual. The simplicity of the real solution to all problems makes that solution increasingly baffling. The real solution lies in the elimination of all *self*-interest; this makes man practical in the truest sense of the word and gives him strength to face the facts concerning body and soul.

The aspirant need not worry about the opposition between spirit and matter, but should rather concern himself with the proper use of the one as the vehicle of the other. Then he will realize the higher ideals which relate to the actions of everyday life. The living spirit behind love, service and brotherhood then blossoms out in accomplished deeds and is no longer empty words and academic theories reserved for armchair practice. God's infinite beauty, power and bliss are experienced with full consciousness in art, science, literature, nature and all walks of life.

Although the unconscious slavery of modern man to the industrial age is a serious matter, the emancipation of mankind from physical and economic slavery is a comparatively easy affair. The real slavery, because it is the most cruel and destructive of all, is the intellectual bigotry which claims to possess an exclusive monopoly on all truth. It is people obsessed by such a belief who, when they happen to be in a position of material power, hasten the downfall of a laboriously built civilization or the disintegration of a living religion.

Man can be redeemed from all types of bondage—physical, mental, spiritual, social, political, moral—sooner or later. But the redemption of man from the self-imposed shackles of intellectual self-sufficiency, uncritically accepted ideals and a dry religious heritage is a task which is well-nigh superhuman. Here is the real task of the aspirant: to pierce through his own layers of self-imposed self-sufficiency and insensitivity so that he may expose a layer of vital awareness to the world about him, which would teach him if it could.

Often the aspirant is concerned in the early phases of his awakening by his attitude towards established religions and their rituals. All of these have a tendency to encourage the spirit of love and worship, and as such they help to a limited extent in wearing out the ego-shell in which human consciousness is caught. But if they are followed unintelligently and mechanically, the inner spirit of love and worship dries up. Then they harden the ego-shell instead of wearing it out.

Rituals and ceremonies cannot carry one very far towards the path, and if they are unintelligently followed they bind as much as any other unintelligent action. In fact, when they are deprived of all inner life they are in a sense more dangerous than other unintelligent action, because they are pursued in the belief that they help towards God-realization.

Due to this element of self-delusion, lifeless forms and ceremonies become a sidetrack to the path. Through mere force of habit one can become so attached to these external forms that intense suffering may be required to dispel their imaginary value.

Often the aspirant becomes discouraged when he begins to understand how very long and difficult the path is. But these are persons who are concentrating only on jumping to the final goal and have not yet been caught up in the absorbing challenges which call for the greatest ingenuity at every step of the way.

When the aspirant meets the challenge of life's game, it becomes so exhilarating that there is little inclination to worry whether the goal is one or a *crore* of lifetimes away. A healthy approach to life contains the automatic answer to pessimism over the distance to be traveled.

The man of the world believes that to have understood a thing intellectually is to have learned it. The true lesson in action, though, involves the wearing out of the *sanskaras* and the "wants" they engender.

To learn in this sense it is not enough to comprehend intellectually. Learning may be a lengthy process which moves slowly through many, many repetitions of difficult situations. Learning has not been accomplished until one has been freed from all emotional entanglement. This is almost—if not entirely—impossible without the aid of a master. It is for this reason that when the aspirant realizes the master's true contribution, he greets the master with much joy.

All action, except that which is intelligently designed to attain God-realization, binds consciousness. It is not only an expression of accumulated ignorance, but also a further addition to that accumulated ignorance. Sometimes the pilgrim becomes so weary of recognizing that each act, instead of unwinding a knot in the inner being, has only tightened it harder, that he wonders whether it is wise to continue a life of action.

In many ways, inaction is preferable to unintelligent action, for it has at least the merit of not creating further *sanskaras*. Even good action creates *sanskaras* and adds to the complications created by past actions.

All life is an effort to achieve freedom from self-created entanglement. It is a desperate struggle to undo what had been done in ignorance; to throw away the accumulated burden of the past; to seek rescue from the debris piled high from temporary achievements and failures. Life strives to unwind the limiting *sanskaras* and find release from the mazes of its own making, to ensure that its further creations might spring directly from the heart of eternity and bear the stamp of the unhampered freedom and intrinsic richness of being that knows no limitation.

Action that is aimed at attaining God is truly intelligent and spiritually fruitful because it brings release from bondage. It is second only to that action which springs spontaneously from the state of divine knowledge itself. All other forms of action (however good or bad and however effective or ineffective from the worldly point of view) contribute to bondage of the soul and, as such, are inferior to inaction.

Inaction is less helpful than intelligent action, but it is better than unintelligent action, for it amounts to the non-doing of that which would have created a binding. The transition from unintelligent action to intelligent action (*i.e.* from binding *karma* to unbinding *karma*) is often through inaction. This is the stage when unintelligent action has stopped because of critical doubt, and intelligent action has not yet begun because adequate momentum has not been achieved. This special type of inaction, which plays a definite part in progress on the path, should not be confused with ordinary inaction that springs from inertia or fear of life.

The state of inaction that springs from critical doubt gives way sooner or later to intelligent action, and intelligent action in turn is dissolved in the final goal of perfect inaction. Perfect inaction does not mean inactivity. When self is absent, one achieves inaction in one's every action, however excessive it be. Various of the yogas, such as *Karma Yoga* and *Dnyan Yoga,* can be instrumental in achieving the end of all action by practicing inaction in the midst of intense activity.

The only way to live a life of absolute inaction is to surrender completely to a Perfect Master. Then one dies entirely to oneself and lives only for the Perfect Master, acting and fulfilling the dictates of the beloved one.

Each age group, each profession, each race has its own problems in pointing itself towards the beginning stages of the path. The following brief messages are intended for various of these groups.

Message for Youngsters

I remember very well when, not long ago, I was just like one of you. You little ones are especially dear to me. Children are innocent and free from vain egotism. Children have no low desires. When, after becoming free of all childishness, a man really becomes childlike, he realizes God.

Whether you like it or not, you must soon grow up and cease being childish. More and more you must enjoy letting your teachers teach you and your elders lead you while you are growing into men and women. Unless you are willing to learn and ready to obey, they cannot help you as they would like to do.

The whole of life is like playing the game of hide and seek, in which you must find your real self. I give you my blessings, that you may succeed in this realization that life is all-time play. God alone is real, all else is false, and so you must try to love God who is within us all. To gain this love you should try to be honest in your thoughts, words and actions.

To Youth

It is the privilege of youth to be full of energy and hope. Not being caught in any ruts, your dreams of the future have the advantage of being inspired by an unfettered imagination. In the glow of a new-born love or in the warmth of a newly-caught enthusiasm, you are quick to respond to the call for action and self-sacrifice.

Life would be poorer without these qualities that are predominantly present in youth. But if you are to derive the full benefit of the qualities with which you are abundantly endowed, you must also try to acquire some other qualities which are rare in youth.

Hope should be fortified by a courage which can accept failure without upset. Enthusiasm should be harnessed by the wisdom that knows how to wait with patience for the fruit of action. Idealistic dreams about the future should be balanced by a sense of the realities of the present. And the glow of love should allow itself to be illumined by the full exercise of reason.

It is easy for youth to be so absorbed in realizing the ideal that it becomes bitter against the present and the past. But it is as well to cultivate a spirit of idealizing the real, while being appreciative of the heritage of the past. The world as it is may not seem to conform to the pattern which youth adores, but you must never forget that it is always good enough to merit your most loving attention. In your desire to improve the world, do not, by becoming bitter, surrender your right to be happy.

Youth loves freedom and therefore has a natural impulse to rebel against all authority. This is well and good, but you should make a real effort to keep free of the many illusions to which youth is particularly susceptible. True self-expression need not include irreverence for others. True criticism need not involve snobbishness or cynicism. True freedom need not manifest hostility or separateness.

Freedom without responsibility is a doubtful boon. Freedom is worth having only where there is self-restraint and willingness to cooperate with others. Youth is always willing to act and take risks. It should be allowed to yield freely to this fearless and imperative urge of life within. But while engaged in action, youth must take every care that it is creative, and not destructive. Let your watchwords always be LOVE and SERVICE.

To Students, Artists, Social Workers and Public Institution Servants

Literacy is not education and education is not culture, and all these together do not constitute "*Dnyan*" or gnosis. This stands in a class by itself, independent of any concomitant factors. Illiteracy and ignorance invite exploitation, but literacy can also become a willing tool in the hands of those who exploit. Education devoid of culture is inherently destructive, although on the surface it seems to represent progress.

Since all types of people have claimed that their greatness constitutes "culture", the word has become indefinite in the minds of the public. True culture is the result of spiritual values assimilated into life.

Therefore you must keep before you the ideal of that spiritual culture which, once developed, imparts life and beauty to all undertakings—educational, technical, industrial, social, moral and political —and pierces through their differences to produce unity. This results in the development of the highest character in the life of a nation or individual.

All men in the flesh are unquestionably equal, yet no two men are equal. Despite the fact that one sun shines on the one world, sunshine is not the same the world over. In their hopes and their fears, men are the same everywhere, yet at a given moment this one is antagonistic to that one.

Love for God, love for fellow beings, love of service and love of self-sacrifice—in short love in any shape and form—is the finest "give and take" in existence. Ultimately it is love that will bring about the much-desired equating of human beings all over the world, and without necessarily disturbing the inherently diverse traits of mankind.

It is infinitely better to hope for the best than to fear the worst. Time is composed equally of night and day. In its inevitable course of ups and downs the world is fast approaching once again a glorious dawn.

My blessings to you all.

To *Harijans* and Laborers

To think that birth or profession is the basis for difference between men is to dream in the past and remain dead to the present. In those things which represent true value in human heritage, all men are equal. Cleanliness of mind and body have never been and never can be the monopoly of any one class or creed. They should be aspired to and can be achieved by everyone. At the same time it should be recognized that to maintain such purity in the face of increasing opposition from various directions will entail suffering.

The spiritual status of any people is in direct proportion to its ability to suffer. Suffering should be intelligent and deeply penetrating. When a people develop their spiritual outlook on life they automatically increase their capacity to suffer.

Selfishness multiplied by population results in war, exploitation, persecution and poverty. Selflessness multiplied by population brings about peace and plenty.

All the modern fads rampant in the guise of politics, economics, materialism, communism, nationalism and socialism must be judged by the criterion of selflessness. Whether you are religiously suppressed or politically oppressed, whether you are exploited economically or sweated industrially, the suffering you endure will determine your spiritual position.

Man-made differences, like all other things made by man, take no time to change in changing times. A great change-over is approaching in which rights must and will be restored, and in which responsibilities must also be shouldered.

It is indeed great to be a man, but it is far greater to be man-to-man.

Irrespective of birth levels and belief tables, my blessing to all those who feel themselves oppressed, depressed or suppressed for any cause whatsoever.

General Message

What is wrong with the world today? Such questions are bound to arise in thinking minds, but often the answers given are not completely honest. Diagnoses given and remedies adopted have all been biased and so the situation remains vague and unresolved.

The crux of the matter lies in the correct reinterpretation of the ancient word "religion". The West has very little religion, and whenever one hears of it, it is either subservient to politics or at best an adjunct of material life. The East is suffering from an overdose of religion, and consequently it hankers desperately for a material antidote.

Religion in the West is synonymous with scientific progress, which is distinctive in its manifestation. Religion in the East, and in India in particular, has gone underground and been replaced largely by crude ceremonies, vague rituals and lifeless dogmas. Instead of nourishing the seeds of peace and plenty, this subterranean religion tries to propagate communism, fanaticism, nationalism and patriotism, which have now become bywords associated with leadership and greatness, suffering and sanctity. In short, religion as a living force has become obsolete.

The urgent need of today to resuscitate religion is to dig it out of its narrow, dark vault and let the spirit of man shine out once again in its pristine glory.

The most practical thing in the world is to be spiritually-minded. It needs no special time, place or circumstance. It is not necesssarily concerned with anything out of the ordinary daily routine. It is never too early or too late to be spiritual. It is just a simple question of having the proper mental attitude towards lasting value, changing circumstance and avoidable eventualities, as well as a healthy sense of the inevitable.

Spirituality is not restricted to, nor can it be restricted by, anyone or anything, anywhere, at any time. It covers all life for all time, and it can easily be achieved through selfless service and that pure love which knows no bondage and seeks no boundary.

A mighty surge of this spirituality is about to sweep over the world. My blessings to you all.

There is no more ready means by which the first outlines of the inner self can be known than through complete honesty. Honesty with one's fellow beings is the beginning step; from this there cannot help but come honesty with oneself.

It is heartening to find that even the worst of one's nature is not frightening, and that the very fact of having faced the worst in oneself gives the courage to look at the challenges of life and the path. Having achieved honesty and found courage, the sustaining self begins to reveal itself.

To be honest is certainly not easy, for never before has dishonesty and hypocrisy been so rampant in the world as today. If the least hypocrisy creeps into one's thoughts, words or deeds, God, who is the innermost Self in us all, keeps Himself hidden.

Hypocrisy is a million-headed cobra. Today there are so-called saints in the world who tell people to be honest and not hypocritical, yet they themselves are deeply involved in dishonesty. If you cannot love God and cannot lead saintly lives, then at least do not make a pretense of it. The worst scoundrel is better than a hypocritical saint.

Honesty is not only a light on the inner path, it is also one of the most effective means for relief of the suffering which afflicts all—man or woman, rich or poor, great or small. Relief from all kinds of suffering is within ourselves if, in all circumstances and in every walk of life, we try to think honestly, act honestly and live honesty.

Infinite honesty is one of the aspects of God, and therefore the least hypocrisy in ourselves keeps us aloof from God.

Simplicity and all it implies is another great aid in the development of human love. Simplicity springs from humility, and humility is often confused with modesty. Modesty is weakness, but humility is strength. Therefore a world of difference separates the two. The moment you say "I say in all humility—" the very use of the expression betrays your ego. Even though you believe that you are being humble, you are expressing your egotism.

The difficulty is not resolved even if you try with true honesty to express true humility. Inevitably, obstacles arise, such as the thought of what others may think of your expression of humility.

No sooner is humility given expression than it is no longer humility. It is nonsense to give deliberate expression to humility. A life of humility is lived spontaneously, and should not give rise to thoughts of either humility or modesty.

As an example, suppose you start to clean a latrine, but you cannot help noting the smell. A janitor who has cleaned them all his life remains unaffected. The person who parades humility is like the one who notes the smell while cleaning a latrine. The person who *lives* the life of humility is like the sweeper who is immune to the odor and completely unworried about what others think of him. He actually lives the life of a janitor.

To have to try to be humble is also nonsense. You must be so natural that your life becomes humility personified, which means all strength freed from all weakness.

So, whatever you are, express it unmindful of public opinion and the reaction of others. Be natural. If you are dishonest, do not try to hide yourself behind the curtain of honesty. This does not mean though that you should be dishonest.

Above all else, be content with your lot, rich or poor, happy or miserable. Understand that God has designed it for your own good, and be resigned to His will. Remember the present in the frame of the past and the future. You eternally were and always will be. You have had innumerable forms as man and woman, beautiful and ugly, strong and weak, healthy and sickly, powerful and helpless, and now you are here again in another form.

Until you gain spiritual freedom you will be invested with many such forms, so why seek temporary relief now which will only result in further bindings later? Do not ask God for money, fame, power, health or children, but seek His grace and it will lead you to eternal bliss.

One of the greatest things to possess is faith, which ultimately leads to conviction; and from conviction one day arises realization. There are no two kinds of faith. Faith is the last thing to be labeled. The only question is whether one has strong faith or weak faith. Some manifest faith only to the point of acknowledging forms and ceremonies, while some go beyond this to seek the kernel and eschew the hull, believing either in the impersonal infinite existence or in the personal existence of one's own master.

Thus it is only a question of degree of faith. In whole-hearted faith, relief will be found from the many sufferings which afflict man. We are already in possession of infinite power and happiness, but it is our way of life which prevents us from enjoying these eternal treasures of God. Faith can provide a key to attain them.

Eventually, faith must give way to conviction, for after all, faith is only faith. There are two kinds of experience—external and internal. External experience can result through the gross media. What we actually see of the gross world through our gross eyes gives us conviction of a sort, but there are occasions when even this conviction is based on incorrect analysis.

Thus, if we see a man drinking milk from a bottle under a toddy tree,* we assume unconsciously that he is drinking toddy, which is incorrect. What is seen with the inner eye gives absolute conviction and can never be false. Such is the case, for example, when one sees with the inner eye that God is the Infinite Existence.

Therefore what is really needed to give eternal conviction is not mere theorizing or reasoning, or even faith, but actual (inner) experience.

Once God has been realized, there is no question of faith or even of conviction, just as there is no question of a man's needing faith to believe that he is a man. Having transcended the boundaries of faith, one finds oneself identified with the infinite and the one Self manifested everywhere.

---

* A cheap, intoxicating drink is commonly made in India from the sap of the toddy tree.

CHAPTER 8

Love and God

There can be no greater folly than that the aspirant quarrel with another over the pros and cons of this way or that, instead of concentrating on his own onward march. One road may be steep, another full of potholes, a third torn by racing rivers. Similarly, one man may walk best, another may be a good runner, a third a fine swimmer. In each case the things that should really count are the destination and the progress that each individual makes. Why should one who runs like a hare come in the way of another who is more likely to succeed at the pace of a snail?

Spiritual progress is like climbing through hills, dales, thorny woods and along dangerous precipices to attain the mountain top. On this path there can be no halting or return. Everyone must get to the top, which is the direct realization of the supreme Godhead. All hesitation, sidetracking or resting in halfway houses, or arguing about the best route, only postpones the day of final fulfillment.

The aspirant cannot be too alert about the path. The slightest lingering in the false world of shadows is inevitably an invitation to suffering that could have been avoided if the eye had been steadily fixed on the supreme goal of life.

The best of all forces, which can overcome all difficulties on the way, is the love that knows how to give without need to bargain for a return. There is nothing that love cannot achieve, and there is nothing that love cannot sacrifice. There is nothing beyond God and there is nothing without God, and yet God can always be captured by love. All other essential qualities will come to the aspirant if he follows faithfully the whisperings of the unerring voice of love that speaks from his own heart, shedding light on the path.

To lose hold of the mantle of this guide is to find only despair. The heart without love is entombed in unending darkness and suffering, but the heart that is restless with love is on its way to realization of the unfading light that shines on the unfathomable sweetness of life divine.

Pure love is matchless in majesty; it has no parallel in power, and there is no darkness it cannot dispel. It is the undying flame that has set all life aglow, yet it must be kindled and rekindled in the abysmal darkness of selfish thoughts, selfish words and selfish deeds. As it is fired anew it bursts out in magnificent light to serve as a beacon for those who still grope in the darkness of selfishness, be that darkness deep blue or all black.

Human love, regardless of its limitations, should never be despised. It is bound eventually to break through all limitations to initiate the aspirant into eternal life in the truth. Then the lover may lose his separate, false self and become united with God, who is the one matchless and indivisible ocean of unsurpassable love.

God does not listen to the language of the tongue and its *japs*, *mantras*, devotional songs and so on. He does not listen to the language of the mind and its routine meditations, concentrations and thoughts about God. He only listens to the language of the heart and its message of love, which needs no ceremony or show, only silent devotion for the Beloved.

This love can be expressed in various ways, all of which ultimately result in union with God. The practical way for the average man to express love is to speak lovingly, think lovingly and act lovingly towards all mankind, feeling God to be present in everyone.

Love is dynamic in action and contagious in effect. It is only the spiritually alive and enlightened who can feel the significance of the ancient adage, so cheaply bandied about by some preachers and philosophers, that "love begets love".

The way of love is not free from sacrifices. Just as heat and light go hand in hand, so do love and sacrifice. The true spirit of sacrifice springs spontaneously, like humility, and cannot be aware of itself nor reserve itself for particular objects and special occasions.

Love means suffering and pain for oneself, and happiness for others. To the giver it is suffering without malice or hatred. To the receiver it is a blessing without obligation.

Just as it can never be too early or too late to learn to love for the sake of love, so there can be nothing too small or too big to be sacrificed or sacrificed for. The flow of life, the flow of light and the flow of love are as much in the drop as in the ocean. The smallest thing is as big as the biggest and the biggest thing is as small as the smallest. It all depends upon the particular yardstick used.

The spirit of true love and real sacrifice is beyond all ledgers and needs no measure. A constant longing to love and be loving, and a noncalculating will to sacrifice in every walk of life—high and low, big and small, between home and office, streets and cities, countries and continents—are the best measures man can take to be really self-ful and joyful.

Love is different from lust. In lust there is dependence upon the physical object, and thus spiritual subordination of the soul to it. Love puts the soul into direct, coordinate relation with the reality which lies behind the form.

Therefore lust is experienced as being heavy, but love is experienced as being light. In lust there is a narrowing down of life, while in love there is an expansion in being. To have loved one soul is like adding its life to your own. Your life is multiplied and you live virtually in two centers. If you love the whole world, you live vicariously in the whole world. But in lust there is an ebbing of life and generation of a sense of hopeless dependence upon a form which is regarded as *another*.

Thus in lust there is accentuation of separateness and suffering, but in love there is a feeling of unity and joy. Lust is dissipation, love is recreation. Lust is a craving of the senses, love is the expression of spirit. Lust seeks fulfillment, but love experiences fulfillment. In lust there is excitement, in love there is tranquility.

Divine love is qualitatively different from human love. Human love is for the many in the One, and divine love is for the One in the many. Human love leads to innumerable complications, but divine love leads to freedom. In divine love the personal and impersonal aspects are equally balanced, but in human love the two aspects are in alternating ascendancy. Human love in its personal and impersonal aspects is limited, but divine love with its fusion of the personal and impersonal aspects is infinite in being and expression.

If, instead of seeing faults in others, we look within ourselves, we are loving God.

If, instead of robbing others to help ourselves, we rob ourselves to help others, we are loving God.

If we suffer in the sufferings of others and feel happy in the happiness of others, we are loving God.

If, instead of worrying over our own misfortunes, we think of ourselves as more fortunate than many, many others, we are loving God.

If we endure our lot with patience and contentment, accepting it as His will, we are loving God.

If we understand that the greatest act of devotion towards God is not to harm any of His beings, we are loving God.

To love God as He ought to be loved we must live for God and die for God, knowing that the goal of all life is to love God and find Him as our own self.

Therefore let us become the soldiers of God. Let us struggle for the truth. Let us live not for ourselves, but for others. Let us speak truly, think truly and act truly. Let us be honest as God is infinite honesty. Let us return love for hatred and win others over to God. Let the world know that above everything the most dear to our hearts is God—the supreme reality.

Besides keeping God before ourselves in our daily lives and loving Him by loving our fellow men, we can love God by surrendering to the *Sadguru* or Perfect Master who is God's personal manifestation, or to the God-man, who is God descended directly into form. To surrender to any of these is to surrender to God Himself.

This is my song:

> For the rich, I am the richest;
> For the poor, I am the poorest;
> For the literate, I am the most literate;
> For the illiterate, I am the most illiterate.

> Thus I am one of you, one with you
> And one in you, and we are all one.

To have my real *darshan* is to find me.
The way to find me is to find your abode in me.
And the only one and sure way to find your abode in me
Is to love me.

To love me as I love you, you must receive my grace.
Only my grace can bestow the gift of divine love.
To receive my grace you must obey me whole-heartedly
With a firm foundation of unshakeable faith in me.

And you can only obey me spontaneously as I want
When you completely surrender yourselves to me
So that my wish becomes your law
And my love sustains your being.

Age after age, many aspire for such a surrender
But only very few
Really attempt to surrender to me
Completely as I want.

He who succeeds ultimately
Not only finds me
But becomes me
And realizes the aim of life.

The final way to realize God is to love Him and to lose oneself in Him through intense longing for union with Him. To love God whole-heartedly is to lose oneself eventually in the Beloved and enter the eternal life of God.

Like a tree, such love has branches—branches of whole-hearted devotion, perfect selfless service, self-denial, self-sacrifice, self-renunciation, self-annihilation and truth. In this love are embodied all the yogas known to saint and seeker. The highest aspect of this love, which surpasses love itself, is that of complete surrender to the will of the Beloved. This means complete obedience to His wishes regardless of the cost.

The Perfect Masters are always immersed in the joy of this union with God and can never be snared in the mazes of the illusory universe. Therefore they do not ordinarily pay any attention to the universe other than to divert the attention of humanity from the shadow to the substance.

Divine love makes the individual true to himself and to others. It makes him live honestly, comprehending that God is infinite honesty. Divine love is the solution to all difficulties and problems. It frees man from all bindings. It makes him speak truly, think truly and act truly. It makes him feel one with the whole universe. Divine love purifies the heart and glorifies one's being.

When one truly loves God, that love is based on the desire to give up one's whole being to the Beloved. When one loves a Perfect Master, one longs to serve him, to surrender to his will, to obey him whole-heartedly. Thus pure, real love longs to give and does not ask for anything in return.

When the individual truly loves humanity he longs to give all for its happiness. When he truly loves his country he longs to sacrifice life itself, without seeking reward and without the least thought of having loved and served. When he truly loves his friends he longs to help them without making them feel under the least obligation. When he truly loves his enemies he longs to make them his friends. True love for parents or family makes him long to give them every comfort at the cost of his own.

Trust God completely and He will solve all difficulties. Faithfully leave everything to Him and He will see to everything. Love God sincerely and He will reveal Himself. And as you love, your heart must love so that even your mind is not aware of it. As you love God whole-heartedly and honestly, sacrificing everything at the altar of this supreme love, you will realize the Beloved within you.

CHAPTER 9

Help to Others

On the path, the most important condition of discipleship is readiness to work for the spiritual cause of bringing humanity closer and closer to the realization of God. Enough has been done to make people food-minded, now they must be made God-minded. The downtrodden and the poor must understand that from the spiritual point of view their misfortunes and miseries can be made into weapons in the struggle for truth. They should be helped to see that these miseries can be counted as gifts from God and, if bravely and cheerfully faced, can become the gateway to eternal happiness.

Because of its paramount importance in promoting the true well-being of humanity, spiritual work has a natural claim on all who love humanity. It is very necessary to be quite clear about its nature. The whole world is firmly established in the false idea of separateness and is therefore subject to all the complexities of duality. Spiritual workers have to help redeem the world from the throes of imagined duality by bringing home to it the truth of the unity of all life.

To review briefly the problem of the redemption of mankind as it has been set forth in the preceding parts of this work, the root-cause of the illusion of manyness lies in the soul's identification with its bodies or with the ego-mind. Both the gross and subtle bodies, as well as the ego-mind of the mental body, are only media for experiencing the world of duality. They are not the media for knowing the true nature of the soul, which is above them all.

By identification with the bodies or the ego-mind, the soul gets trapped in the delusion of manyness. Actually, the Soul in all bodies and ego-minds is just one undivided Existence, but as It becomes confused with these bodies and ego-minds which are only vehicles, It considers Itself to be limited and looks upon Itself as being only one among the many of creation.

As a consequence, most souls are unconscious of their true nature as God, who is the oneness and the reality of all souls. Thus God-realization is present in them only in latent form, inasmuch as they have not yet experienced that oneness consciously.

On the other hand, those very few who have cast off the veil of duality experience the soul itself without confusing it with any medium or vehicle, and in this experience the soul consciously knows itself to be identical with God. In the realization of the truth of this oneness, life finds freedom from all limitation and suffering, for it is the self-affirmation of the Infinite as infinity. In this state of spiritual perfection the ego-life has been finally and completely surrendered in the experiencing of divine truth. God is known and affirmed as the only reality.

To realize God is to dwell in eternity. It is a timeless experience. But spiritual work concerns itself with souls who are caught in the complexity of a creation which is knit by time. Therefore spiritual workers cannot afford to ignore the element of time and the importance of its flow in creation. To ignore it would be to ignore the spiritual work itself.

The task for spiritual workers is to help in the universal dispensation of truth to a suffering humanity. They have both to prepare humanity to receive this truth and become established in it themselves. It is extremely important to remember that in helping others leave behind the illusion of duality and attain spiritual freedom, it is necessary to live and act constantly in the principle of unity. The spiritual worker will be working for others who are inclined to create divisions where they do not exist, and who will allow him no respite to recoup himself.

The minds of people have to be purged completely of all forms of selfishness and narrowness if they are to inherit life in eternity. It is by no means an easy task to persuade people to give up these traits. It is not by accident that people are divided into the rich and the poor, the pampered and the neglected, the rulers and the ruled, the leaders and the masses, the oppressors and the oppressed, the high and the low, the winners of laurels and the recipients of ignominy. These differences are created and sustained by the spiritually ignorant, who are so attached to difference that they are not even conscious of its perversity.

They are accustomed to look upon life as divided into separate, watertight compartments and are unwilling to give up this separative attitude. When the worker launches upon his spiritual work he enters a field of divisions to which people cling desperately, which they accentuate and fortify, and which they strive consciously or unconsciously to perpetuate.

Mere condemnation of these divisions will not enable the worker to destroy them. Divisions are nourished by separative thinking, and they yield only to the touch of love and understanding. People must be won to the life of truth; they cannot be coerced into spirituality.

It is not enough for the worker to have unimpaired friendliness and untarnished good will in his own heart. If he is to succeed in his work, he must give people the conviction that he is helping them to redeem themselves from bondage and suffering, and to realize their rightful heritage of the highest. There is no other way to help them attain spiritual freedom and enlightenment.

To render spiritual help one should understand clearly the following four points:

(1) Apparent descent to a lower level:

It may often be necessary to descend apparently to the level of those whom one is trying to help. Though one's purpose is to raise people to a higher level of consciousness, they may fail to profit by what is said unless talk is in terms they understand. What is conveyed through thought-feeling should not go over their heads. They are bound to miss it unless it is adapted to their capacity and experience.

However, while doing this, it is equally important not to lose one's own level of understanding. Approach and technique will be changed gradually as those being aided arrive at deeper and deeper understanding, and one's own apparent descent to the lower level will be only temporary.

(2) Spiritual understanding ensures well-rounded progress:

Life must not be divided into departments, which are then dealt with separately and successively. Departmental thinking is often an obstacle to integral vision. If one divides life into politics, education, morality, material advancement, science, art, religion, mysticism and culture, and then thinks exclusively of only one of these aspects, the answers that are brought to life can be neither satisfactory nor final.

If one succeeds however in awakening spiritual inspiration and understanding, then progress in all these departments of life is bound to follow automatically. Spiritual workers will have to aim at providing a complete and real solution to all the personal and social problems of life.

(3) Spiritual progress consists in the spontaneous growth of understanding from within:

Spiritual workers have also to remember that the spiritual wisdom which they wish to convey to others is already present in latent form and that it is only necessary to assist in unveiling that spiritual wisdom in them. Spiritual progress is not a process of accumulation from without, it is an unfoldment from within. A master is necessary for anyone to arrive at self-knowledge, but the true significance of the help given by the master rests in his ability to enable another to come into the full possession of his own latent possibilities.

(4) Some questions are more important than answers:

Spiritual workers must not lose sight of the real work which should be accomplished. When it is clearly understood that spiritual wisdom is latent in all, the worker will no longer be anxious to provide others with ready-made answers. In many cases he will be content to set up a new problem or to clarify the nature of a problem already faced.

He may have done his duty if he asks someone a question in a practical situation which that person would not have asked himself. In some cases the worker will have done his duty if he succeeds in putting another person in a searching attitude so that he begins to understand and attack his problems along some more fruitful line.

The questions the worker may help to formulate should be neither theoretical nor unnecessarily complicated. If they are simple, direct and fundamental, these questions will answer themselves and people will find their own solutions. Nevertheless, indispensable service will have been rendered for, without tactful intervention, the individual would not have arrived at the solution of his various problems from a spiritual point of view.

The spiritual worker necessarily is confronted by many obstacles, but obstacles are meant to be overcome. Even if some of them seem insuperable, he must do his best to help others, irrespective of results or consequences. Obstacles, their surmounting, success, failure —all are illusions within the infinite domain of unity, and the worker's task is already done when it is done whole-heartedly.

Work must be performed without worrying about consequences, regardless of success or failure. One may be sure that work done in this spirit and with this understanding yields inevitable results. Through the untiring activities of spiritual workers, humanity will be initiated into the new life of abiding peace and dynamic harmony, unconquerable faith and unfading bliss, immortal sweetness and incorruptible purity, creative love and infinite understanding.

PART III

Avatarhood

CHAPTER 1

Personal Relationship

How can one being assess another who is entirely beyond his level? How can an ammeter measure a current beyond its capacity? How can a drop measure the ocean?

These questions are inevitably raised as one reads Parts I and II of this book. It has not seemed honest to pose them without at least giving recognition to them, and some signposts suggesting their solution.

I am one of many persons who have asked these questions repeatedly of themselves. It has seemed both strange and important that the answers we have found have so often been the same.

Therefore this final section is framed from my own thoughts, self-arguments and gradual conclusions concerning my personal relationship to Meher Baba.* Undoubtedly this is a rash approach, but I know no other way to suggest the profound effect Meher Baba has on the life of another human being, of the questions he raises, of the support one receives from him in the solution of those problems, and of the conclusions one gradually draws from these experiences.

I intend to avoid any attempt at a scholarly comparison of Baba's traits with those of Krishna, Buddha, Jesus, Mohammed and other personages historically less well-defined. I am not a theologian nor a student of comparative religion.

Further, I live too close to the lifetime of Meher Baba and the swirl of human events generated by his powerful personality to try to express any part of the opinion of posterity. My only honest basis of expression is as one human being who has lived initially in the intense subjective experience of deep questioning which Meher Baba so frequently generates. Later, I have lived in the air of calm

---

* An independent viewpoint on this subject is given by Irene Conybeare in the closing portions of her *Civilization or Chaos?*, Chetana, Bombay.

which seems equally to flow from him.

Both the confusion as well as the clarities must be described, because one forms the warp while the other forms the woof of the fabric of spirit which is woven. It is important to give full recognition to both, because we in the western world have inherited a confusing attitude towards this essential interplay.

Religion, philosophy and mysticism have come to mean a last possible antidote to the pains of life. When life becomes unbearably distressing, the contemplative arts are looked to for an alleviant. Therefore it is assumed that they must not produce pain in themselves, and that those teachers who use them must provide only solace and healing. Why resort to them otherwise?

However this allows no real scope for the surgeon's skill. Often he must cleanse, cut and cauterize, and if the patient withdraws at the first sign of pain, it is doubtful that the source of disease can always be reached and the trouble remedied.

The East has learned perhaps more than we that there must be great effort, and there may be great pain, in man's coming to grips with himself. Yet many pursue the matter, regardless of these deterrents. They recognize that the conscious, head-on attack is far more bearable in the long run than to allow the unconscious teacher, nature, to continue its painfully tedious tutelage.

Thus there is some tradition in the East that the best course is to come to grips with the great central problem, and to accept the disciplines necessary to its solution. In the West there is the unconscious opinion that help should consist in soothing ointment applied by the gentle touch of a healer. This notion is almost fatal to the progress of the intelligent, seeking western mind.

Hence it is necessary to recognize the important role that conflict and confusion play in human development, and to construct gradually our own tradition of their acceptance. To develop such a tradition it is necessary to accept, recognize and preserve the facts of trial, difficulty and pain in the lives of our own great seekers. When this has been done and accepted as a positive instrument through which divine grace often works, it will be of the greatest help in assisting the seeking individual to persist through the first difficult steps.

I was entirely unprepared for the questions which were raised in full cry when I first heard Meher Baba discussed. My first feeling was that people were speaking in his name who seemed poorly equipped to do so. Surely, if he were indeed a great man, he must know about their activities and that they were not doing his cause much good.

Logic led from this observation to the inevitable conclusion that Baba was probably either a fake or a fool. There seemed no easy way out of it.

Further, undertaking silence, and then using the subterfuge of an alphabet board for communication, seemed childish.

Next, there was the very troublesome fact that he seemed on occasion to interfere grossly in people's lives and finances, asking them to do things which disrupted the normal pattern of life. What if I should gradually become entangled with him and he should ask me to give up my present way of life?

And then there was the equally troublesome question of what one's friends and one's business associates would think.

Finally, there was the almost indigestible fact that he let himself be called the Christ of our times, even allowing the statement to get into print. True humility would seem to avoid such assertions even if by some chance they were true.

With a net strike-out record such as this there seemed no possibility that Meher Baba could legitimately be a great spiritual teacher. And yet one of my closest friends and spiritual guide of some years' standing was convinced that Meher Baba was the greatest spiritual teacher of our age. I could not shrug off this fact, and yet I could not accept the one who was at contest.

For five years Meher Baba was the central question mark in almost every day of my life. Out of loyalty to my friend I could not reject Meher Baba even in the privacy of my own thoughts. Yet equally I could not honestly accept him because of the matters which weighed so heavily against him.

I was forced to do something which I have never been able to duplicate. I constructed a watertight dam around all the black negation that wanted to flow out of me, and then camouflaged it so completely that I could walk casually by it several times a day. The feeling was entirely dammed off, but I did allow myself a dry intellectual recognition of the issues still unsolved.

My first object lesson in the questions I had raised came from my business life. I think no one is given any organizational responsibility without concluding very quickly that the job must be done with the material available. Further, if there is one human crime greater than that of making blunders, it is failing to try to help and support the people who are doing the blundering. There is certainly a time to prod people into better performance, but the horse carrying the load does not live on prods alone. Further, many mistakes can be forgiven if they have been made with honest intent.

Within two years these things had been made crystal clear. I began to suspect that perhaps Meher Baba found himself in the position in which every other boss finds himself, of having to make the best possible use of the resources at hand.

Once having come to this conclusion, the rest of the answers began to come quickly. I met several people who had been with Meher Baba, and it was readily apparent that generally they were of unusual caliber. My first point definitely had been off base.

The question of observing silence was also soon parried into neutrality. An unusual series of drains on my energies left me completely knocked out for several months, and when I was at lowest ebb I tried speaking just as little as possible. To my astonishment I found that it was of marked help. From this point it was an easy step to realize that a great spiritual teacher might easily wish to conserve energy for vital spiritual activities. My answer might be wrong, but at least I could see a ray of reason.

I began to feel better. The dull feeling of heaviness at the pit of my stomach began to lighten and I could feel that one day I would be able to exhume the whole matter and work it out.

As I read more about Baba and talked with people who knew him, it began to be clear that, while he sometimes asked people to do very difficult things, he did not do so unless they were ready.* This

---

* It is an interesting fact that Baba has asked only a very small number of persons in literal fact to give up all and follow him. The situation is more frequently the reverse, in which an individual begs to be allowed to give up his current life in the world of affairs to be with Baba, and

realization still provided scant comfort. It is difficult to be shivering in one's boots, and yet try to imagine oneself completely able to cope with a problem which now produces only fear. The fear must be met over and over again, and faced in so many ways that it becomes a familiar face; then it begins to wither.

As for friends and one's business associates? Well, people of good caliber are surprisingly tolerant of another person's odd problems. Their caliber is usually built solidly on their recognition of their own profound needs. They stick by one. All in all, it is surprising how little a crisis is involved in accepting someone such as Meher Baba as one's guide, and to allow that fact to become known.

This left one final question: the Christhood of Meher Baba. Was he really the Avatar of the age? If he was, how could I know it?

I believe that I cannot *know* until the day I too have finally achieved the Godhood within me, for only perfection can know Perfection.

Nevertheless it is important that I work constantly at this question, and it is important that others work hard at it also. It cannot be sloughed off on the basis that it is a matter of no real concern for oneself. It is the most supremely important question which anyone can ask, because in it lies the ultimate question: "Why am I here?"

My original distress at Meher Baba's unusual way of working was typical of, although perhaps more acute than, the difficulties many people have. But such upset is only the introduction to the man himself. Once the barrier of conventional prejudice has been broken down and the individual has established his own contact with Meher Baba, then the real work within the relationship begins.

I have already described elsewhere my initial reactions to Meher Baba on first meeting him.* His entirely unexpected impact on my internal functioning, which resulted within two days in virtual elim-

Baba insists that he remain at his post.

For the great mass of people, the call to "give up all and follow me" means, "give up all attachment to your present worldly life and follow my way". However it is only truthful to point out that there is always the minute percentage who are apparently intended to take the command quite literally, but they are not the ones who are frightened by its conditions.

* See the Introduction to *God Speaks*.

ination of my strong tendency to worry, was only a clue to what was to come.

During the next four years, 1952–1956, I was with Meher Baba first for two weeks in India, and then for somewhat longer in America. This is not a large total, but it would be more accurate to say that I was with him all the time, for I felt constantly and powerfully his guiding influence.

This is a fragile point which I wish to reinforce. I have never felt as if Meher Baba were looking down the sights of the gun-barrel of my life as I aimed at one point and then another. I am sure I would be annoyed by such supervision of my moves.

It is as if he busies himself quietly with setting parts of one's nature into motion that had either stagnated or never been in motion, rescues other parts from whirlpools in which they had been caught, supplies energy and direction to get these things moving properly, and then calms overwrought nerves too long jangled by futile endeavor. Having done this, he makes no effort to jump into the driver's seat, but allows the individual to use or abuse his overhauled engine as he wills.

It is only fair to point out that that "will" has meanwhile undergone some modification as well. One has the feeling of being able to listen intently and pick up a soft but distinct direction signal that has started. There is nothing compulsive about this signal, for I can and often have overruled it. But I trust it, and I listen for it, because I find that the results make me a happy and a unified man.

There is another important characteristic of this direction signal. It works equally in the messy parts of life. As a developing human being I have a number of very problematical sides to my nature. I'd just as soon they weren't there because they are a real drain.

The truly astounding thing about one's relation to Meher Baba is that nothing is rejected or suppressed. I can think of none of the awkward, discouraging, embarrassing sides of myself which I would not show to Meher Baba. However the matter is even more intimate than this. One has the instinctive feeling that Baba already knows the worst which can be known about one, that he has accepted it, forgiven it and gone about its constructive reclamation, *not rejection*, in the flash of an eye.

These are not idle words of praise. Here one finds not just compassion, but real forward motion. This knowledge provides a great feeling of hope and courage. It is truly astounding to have lived for weary years with certain basic problems, to see them under the best of circumstances move in hesitant, grudging starts, and then, suddenly, under the unspectacular impact of a silent man from India, to find them all moving vigorously ahead.

Much of the sickness at heart, discouragement and bitterness in living comes from the gradual eroding away of a sense of hope. As a child, or even in early adult life, the individual unconsciously expects the best of life and of himself. Then it begins to be clear that neither is he, nor can he expect, the best.

This is usually known as "coming to grips with reality". No doubt reality is a good thing, but it is unfortunate that in the soil of "reality" lie the seeds of the destruction of hope. Slowly one seems to grind to a halt and to accept with resignation the barriers of habit, character and circumstance.

This is oldness, true oldness.

One of the greatest gifts received from Baba is the renewal of spontaneity, for as he sets one's nature incomprehensibly back into motion, life again becomes an adventure. There is newness, unpredictability, hope, sustainment around each corner in time. The soul becomes once more like a child, and one is struck by the lightness of one's heart. Life is no less complex, there are no fewer problems to be solved, one's consciousness of the tragedies of life has not been dulled. But the greatest tragedy of all—the loss of hope—has been wiped out. No wonder there is room for happiness.

The deep loyalty, devotion and trust which Meher Baba's adherents give to him is based in part on this relief from stagnation which he provides.

It is also based on another factor: a certainty of support in crisis. Of all the intangibles in which Meher Baba deals, this is perhaps the most difficult to fathom. One day there is not the courage to face certain things in self and in the world. The next day the courage is there. Meher Baba has come into one's life in the interim.

This is not a solitary observation based on one person's experience. It would be remarkable even if that were the case. It is the experience of thousands and thousands who have had personal contact with the silent man.

It is possible to speculate indefinitely on how the transformation is accomplished. One cannot help but think of the tales of the Christians who faced the lions in the Roman arena with smiles on their faces. There apparently is such a thing as supreme courage, and it is apparently based on supreme certainty. But how is supreme certainty suddenly achieved? I have no way of knowing, but I do know that I can now face things in my life which would have sent me hiding behind a wall of frustration a few years ago.

It may be in the long run that it is this complete acceptance of oneself by Baba which does it. Ordinarily the human being never seems free of some sense of insecurity in his human relations. People have an awkward way of suddenly becoming very much apart. Sometimes they do it out of simple selfishness, sometimes in carelessness, often in the name of righteousness.

The net effect is that one is alone. No one is able to feel alone, and at the same time full of the warmth and satisfaction of life.

Much of oldness also comes from having tried again and again to spin a bridge of trust and affection across to another human being, and having seen it smashed each time. Finally one begins to feel that perhaps there is no such thing as being truly united with another being, that at best it is an unpredictable, groping game of great aloneness.

I have seen many, many grown men and women burst suddenly into tears because of some unexpected gesture of utmost thoughtfulness shown by Meher Baba. I have seen many others burst into tears without that action, but rather because Baba had uncannily filled up a void in their hearts, as if through the unexpected finding of a mother or father long thought gone.

To feel complete acceptance by another being is a wonderful thing. To find that someone has absolutely no negative reaction to the wrongness or ununderstandability in one's life is worth more than all the gold in the world. It gives one courage to be one's real self and to risk whatever might come.

The matter goes still further. It is not just acceptance by another person which does the trick. It's being connected up with one's inner resources as well. The two things go closely hand in hand.

The individual is almost two persons: the outer self and the inner self, and very often they do not know how to be friendly with one another. Once another person is found who can accept one without a qualm, it is infinitely easier to accept oneself. The sting of sin and wrong-doing are removed. The black curtain is drawn aside and one may walk out as one's own friend. Only then does it become clear how badly one had been crippled by inner doubt and indecision. From there it is not as great a step as it might seem to be able to regard the oncoming lion with a smile.

On a percentage basis there is not a large proportion of people in the world who have any degree of this healing faculty—of accepting the bad as well as the good in another person. Most people at best wish to "do good" and remedy the bad.

So the individual who can *accept* is rare, and he who can accept *all* is truly the treasure of inestimable value.

It would be rash to give the impression that Meher Baba cannot be angered, or that he cannot send someone packing who has been told to do one thing, but has done something else. These situations do occur and they can be very painful. Nevertheless, while Meher Baba's left hand may be chastising severely, his right hand is holding up one's heart so that it can endure. Then, if one still cannot endure, it is not because the warm support is not there, but because humiliation has become the matter of greatest importance.

To witness Meher Baba handling the mechanics of human emotion is an awesome sight, provided one is not involved. To be embroiled in a complex emotional situation with Meher Baba at the controls is like going through a kaleidoscopic crazy house, with hands darting from walls and steam jets shooting up under foot and great magnets drawing at every bit of iron, all set loose in rapid succession.

On emerging, there is no doubt that one has really had the works, but one is sustained through it all. Even as the tremulo crescendo is at its height, there is sustainment to an exactly equivalent degree. The only things which get rattled are the loose screws which need to be rattled. They are located quite quickly.

Sustainment, then, is the second principle which draws unplumbed allegiance to Baba from his adherents.

The third is undoubtedly the most important: love, warmth, tenderness. First it comes from Meher Baba, and one is momentarily caught unawares, perhaps even embarrassed by it. Then it comes from oneself, and again there is no anticipation of the action. It springs out suddenly when least expected, and one can feel something like a sheepish puppy which has just unexpectedly wet in the middle of the living-room rug, and now wonders whether it may have done the wrong thing.

It is an odd fact of our civilization that people hunger for a lifetime for simple human warmth, and yet are afraid to show it, and suspicious when it is offered. Probably it is because there is so little of the honest variety available.

It is a rare person who blossoms in a natural plenty of warmth and affection. Most people want it, most people look for it, most people are deeply touched when they find an honest trace of it, and yet few people are capable of giving it.

The problem is confused, because the physical part of love is inextricably entangled with the purely feeling element. Many people want love, but instinctively shy away from the complex entanglements usually involved. Other people adopt the reverse principle of rebellion against inhibitions and plunge into the most compromising involvements.

Love is a very warm matter that demands some concrete means of expression. The great problem is to know where feeling and expression begin and leave off. Because people feel an inherent reaction against promiscuity, and because they sometimes cannot differentiate between warmth of feeling and intense physical involvement, they often deny the one in order to avoid the other.

This is not to be wondered at. The subject is charged with the least understood and least controllable factors in human nature. In addition to this it is beset by the greatest set of taboos in civilized existence.

Meher Baba slices perpendicularly through the tangled mass and shows a wealth of warm love, expressed in simple physical actions that melt the ice of human inhibition like a blow torch. One's first reaction is often embarrassment or awkwardness at such a simple show of human affection, and one looks instinctively for the hidden booby-trap. Certainly there must be something back of all this; or perhaps the slap in the face will come in the next moment.

Love is instinctively discounted after a few unhappy experiences. It is difficult to believe that it is true even when one experiences the real thing. After a few minutes or hours or days with Meher Baba, however, one's honest self catches onto the fact that here for the first time is spontaneous, outgoing love which demands absolutely nothing in return. It is a sheer gift of warmth, and through it one wishes in some way to be worthy of it.

How does Meher Baba express his affection for people? The first meeting may be a handshake, or a light caress of the cheek, or a warm, understanding glance. Sometimes it may be a brief embrace. However when it has become the third or the fifth or the tenth meeting, it almost inevitably becomes a seconds' long gentle embrace with cheek placed carefully to cheek, and then a slight push to indicate that the greeting is at an end. Baba rarely prolongs the physical side of salutation, but he gives it its due, and he gives it great meaning.

These are the broad bases of the attraction which Meher Baba has for people. These are the unarguing facts of the emotional needs and response of people. The individual finds an emotional satisfaction from Meher Baba which has never been matched anywhere in his previous life. It is no wonder then that this response becomes the all-important fact for him, and that usual ties begin to dim and fall by the wayside.

Much of one's involvement in business, society and even family is the result of unconscious sublimation of direct emotional needs. When someone such as Meher Baba appears who not only responds to one's deepest emotional needs, but even challenges them to deeper levels than had existed before, then there is bound to be a readjustment of the intensity of previous emotional commitments. This can be painful to other persons who have not developed a similar emotional outlet. Husbands or wives are often alarmed at the redirection of emotional drive, and bosses wonder whether their old work horses will continue to drag the load uncomplainingly.

Probably if God Himself should suddenly say in quite unmistakable tones so that the whole world could hear and know Him, "Folks, I've decided creation has fulfilled its purpose, so I'm going to abandon the project now and take you all back to Me", there would be a great shout from the souls of some billions of persons who would feel that He had made the wrong move.

CHAPTER 2

General Atmospheres

What about Meher Baba's claim to be the Avatar?

Although it may be difficult for one who has never met Baba to imagine his having a great attraction for oneself, still it may be possible from the preceding to understand the loyalty and devotion he draws. Undoubtedly these are signs of great public genius, but other persons also attract people strongly and yet lay no claim to universal spiritual importance. What source can be tapped then to judge Meher Baba's unique function?

The subjective self is peculiarly blind to comparisons. All the individual knows is that he is deeply attached, or repelled in many situations in life, and by that very reaction his ability to be objective is destroyed or at least impaired. Therefore sources of information beyond the area of impact of Meher Baba must be available to judge the probabilities of Meher Baba being the Savior of our age. Unfortunately for such an analysis, Meher Baba's immediate followers are the least fertile source of information because of the importance of the subjective element in their own relationship.

The writer is not a good source either, but perhaps he represents an acceptable over-all compromise. He is familiar with Baba and his background, and still partially able to recognize that there are definite western criteria which apply to and must be met by great spiritual genius. However he must hasten with his writing for the temptation is almost overpowering to scrap the whole thing and plunge into the fullest uncritical enjoyment of the rich relationship which is offered.

The first important atmosphere which derives from Baba is that of the miraculous. It exists, and no doubt of it. All of life around him becomes a miracle composed of the most unbelievable coincidences, astounding good fortune and split-second precipitation into acute crises. The coincidence factor (which is something like a batting average, but is inverse to pure chance) leaps to a remarkable figure.

This atmosphere of the miraculous about Baba seems to sweep everyone into its maw, whether a close associate or a casual passer-by. Often one holds one's breath in anticipation of what may happen to some complete stranger who happens to wander into Baba's neighborhood.

To people who are linked to Baba, the unexpected happens with great regularity. One is acutely aware of this extraordinary speeding up and meshing of events in life.

In previous years I have occasionally seen such an atmosphere develop to some degree around a few very remarkable people, or in certain deeply rooted religious or mystic groups. The speed, intensity and magnitude though were totally different from that generated by Meher Baba. This is the first important difference.

The second difference is that an increased coincidence factor is almost always an outgrowth of deliberate application of psychic principles. This again is not the case with Meher Baba. One cannot avoid the conclusion that these things, amazing and forceful as they are, are nevertheless by-products. They happen as they do because they must, in order to fit in with something basic which Baba is accomplishing in the individual.

In the story of Nozher that Baba tells in Part I of this volume, he points out that he does not consciously work miracles.* This to me is the most important point of all. Instinctively I know inside myself that "making miracles" would do exactly what Baba says: obscure the true relation of the individual to Baba. Instinctively I know also that it would take a being of matchless quality to have such great power in his hands that miracles occurred again and again in his shadow, and yet not use that power consciously for anything except the greatest miracle of all: the freeing of the human soul.

It does no good to document this portion of the story with incident after incident of a miraculous nature which has occurred near Baba. I could cite my own persistent sinus condition which has let up only twice in eighteen months: once while I was with Meher Baba in India, once while I was traveling with him in the United States.

Or I could tell about the doctor from New York who has had a constant skin affliction on his hands for years, and after being with

---

*On the other hand, Baba states in his "Beams" (Peter Pauper, 1955) page 39: "God does not bother about performing further minor miracles within this universe, but leaves it to the reign of laws. However, this does not

Baba for a week noted to his astonishment that the condition had improved markedly.

Baba is like an intense radiating source of sanity and health, but his greatest impact is concentrated in the ultimate: man's relation to his inner self. If he or any other great teacher once broke that cardinal principle he would undoubtedly sacrifice, partly or wholly, the ultimate for the present.

I believe with all my heart that Baba is telling the literal truth when he says that he has never had anything consciously to do with wonder-working miracles. But I also have no doubt whatsoever that many of the miracles attributed to Baba are actually due to his general influence. The world stands on its head all around him, and it would not surprise me the least bit if an entire cemetery lifted up its gravestones and walked, out of sheer interest in the man.

Whereas the *sadhu* or saint appears to produce extraordinary results through his deft ability to handle forces within the operation of universal law, Baba seems rather to sit outside the entire tangled maze and to handle the law itself. If a miracle results, it does not seem that Baba has decreed that the lame shall get up and walk, but rather that a man shall fulfill a certain life function, and if an unsound limb is healed in the process, that fact is purely coincidental.

The second general atmosphere which permeates from Meher Baba is one of quiet omniscience. I have seen him make decisions on several occasions which I felt were absolutely wrong, but after time and tide had their say I was forced to divide these situations into two categories. First, there were those in which clearly Baba had been factually correct and I had been wrong.

In the second category, a very strange thing occurs. On the surface, things seem to work out wrong, and one often has a wish that they had worked out better. Then there develops a nagging suspicion that what meets the eye is not the entire story. One is forced to stretch to a new and bigger standard, and then all at once it becomes apparent that Baba's decision was aimed at fishing for much bigger fish: the salvation of someone's soul, and the apparent values of the world could go damn if he made a dent in the real problem.

I've seen him stand up simply and unequivocally for the lowest underdog, the person everyone was running down with the most

---

apply to the God-man who may, if he deems it to be fit and necessary, perform numberless miracles in supervention of the normal routine working of the universe, without attaching any especial importance to them."

righteous indignation. I've seen him give food and diamonds and love to that person, when most of those close to Baba felt that the man had lied and cheated and already run off with a thousand times his share.

What was the answer? The man really loved Baba, and Baba knew it and stood up for him because the man needed support. And the people who were running him down needed a real crisis, and they got it.

This is an example of what goes on about Baba minute by hour by day. It takes only a few instances in which one prejudges Baba's actions, to teach one to await the outcome in neutrality in the future. In doctoring the real needs of human souls he probes quickly to the heart of the matter and decides, and I have never been able to judge him wrong. All I have been able to do is try to recognize higher and higher standards of human insight and compassion by watching the true surgeon at work.

I have even had to entertain very seriously the idea that perhaps Meher Baba gave me the responsibility of describing these *sahvas* programs primarily to keep me concentrating on him and his attributes, at the risk of having a book turned out all wrong. I know he would go to even this extremity if he felt it would help my development.

There is one additional point regarding Baba's apparent omniscience which needs examination. It can be described as Baba's "knowing and not-knowing", all at the same time. Just as a diffuse air of the miraculous surrounds him without his clear and direct involvement in miracles, so he often seems aware of all general happenings without necessarily knowing their specific details.

For instance, he will ask direct questions concerning one's actions and plans. Or he will ask what the newspaper has said about the Thailand-Red China border situation, or the nature of a train disaster in India.

The immediate question is, how can Baba be the Highest of the High if he doesn't know these things already, and if he does know them already, why does he take up time asking about them?

This is typical of the questions one constantly asks when one is near Baba. He rarely explains the conflicting facts, and one is left to try to puzzle out an answer.

In this instance I have had first to reject as erroneous the possibilities that Meher Baba does not know, or that he is engaged in some complex faking. The day-to-day facts do not support either hypothesis.

Next, it is undoubtedly true that Baba, like any astute physician of human problems, often asks a pointed question purely to crystallize the issue in the mind of the individual being queried. The question in such case is a rhetorical vehicle for the precipitation of issues rather than for the gaining of information. However, when such questions are subtracted from the total Baba asks, there remains an unexplained residue.

The best explanation for these seems to occur when one takes quite literally Baba's statement that from time to time God limits Himself in the form of a man and comes as a Christ to do a great work within the limiting conditions of the earth. If this is true, and there is certainly historical precedent for it, and if Meher Baba is that manifestation of God in limited form, then it follows at once that within him must lie all the unlimited qualities we associate with God. And yet, to do the job within the limitations of form and matter, those limitations must be literally respected.

This does not mean that the man himself is limited within himself, but that he has willingly accepted certain restrictions inherent in accomplishing the job. In brief, I believe whole-heartedly that Meher Baba is playing the game strictly according to the rules. Within himself he knows, but within that function which lives in and deals with the material world, he does not know, and so he often asks questions.

The net result, played fairly, should appear much like a highly intuitive man who lives close to the vast resources of his subconscious. There is always uncanny knowledge, but it is generally not directly available in the case of the intuitive individual, or made use of in the case of Baba.

These conclusions fit the case of Meher Baba closely. For me, it has been one of a number of factors which have caused my own reasoning to reinforce the triangulations of my heart: that there is not only a possibility, but a major probability that Meher Baba is truly what he says he is, the Avatar of this age.

A third general atmosphere which surrounds Meher Baba is that of the greatest personal power. He gives the impression of a giant electric generator, humming quietly, with its energy directed along cables which disappear through the walls of environment and out into the imponderables of creation.

Occasionally there is an opportunity to judge something of the total current that flows through this system by being linked for a few moments to one of the leads. Whether one is alone with Baba at such a time, or involved in some group project, the result is startling. Things happen with a speed and intensity nowhere matched in environment. If it be personal matters, they usually precipitate in brief moments. If they are group undertakings, they also are brought to a head as fast as hands, feet and jelling human emotions can carry them out.

I introduce the term "jelling human emotions" deliberately, for there is almost never a group project carried out for Baba which does not include this element. Human emotion is almost inevitably entangled in the matter, or else Baba deliberately prods it into entanglement. In the rapid sweep of events, group emotion is first snared and tangled in a jumble, and then unexpectedly extricated. Baba rarely allows a project with its attendant emotional schooling to go on for long. The movement is rapid and the lesson profound, and then it is all abruptly ended.

Someone may object that it would take a hard-hearted man deliberately to snarl human emotions in the physical problems of life. After all, life is difficult enough as it is, and what the individual needs is peace.

It is true that most people are emotionally exhausted by the complex entanglements of daily living, and by failure to receive compensating emotional gratification. Probably for this reason much of Baba's early contact with the individual consists in building a bridge of warmth and understanding. Over a period of time in this benevolent sunshine of sustaining feeling the raw sensitivities begin to heal and the person begins to build a plus balance of emotional energy.

Then Baba seems to start the true rebuilding job. This consists in helping the individual meet living situations that demand thought, care and energy. They occur rapidly after one has met Baba. They occur even more rapidly and more explosively in Baba's immediate presence. The astounding thing is that the tensions are no longer winding up tighter and tighter, but rather are unwinding.

With one hand Baba precipitates, with the other he sustains. Out of it the human being emerges with gained insight and emotional stamina. How could one possibly wish for more? The only other hope might be that one should learn in a rosy dream of sweet bliss. Nature, though, never produces something for nothing. The best that can be hoped for is to have the strength to meet the challenges of life as they are presented, and Baba does give that sustainment from which one's own natural resources flow readily forth.

It must seem tiresome to a reader to read constantly in terms of superlatives. Isn't there something about Baba which is imperfect, negative, downright revolting?

I have thought of this problem a good many times, for I know that I would become incredulous if someone were to describe such a paragon to me. I have even thought of deliberately playing down certain of the values one receives from Baba, for the sake of their more credible consumption. However I know as soon as I think of such a thing that, if I cannot write honestly, there is no use in writing. So I will continue to write exactly as I have experienced the thing.

The people who have been near Baba for months and years are perhaps not yet perfect. I do know though that these people have a calm and a strength of character which lifts them at the least into the rank of outstanding persons.

Baba's own physical energy and endurance in the face of strenuous activities, with little or no sleep for days and weeks at a time, is a real medical mystery.* Often he goes on long travels in India or around the world during which his schedules would be killing for even a young man. Yet he takes them in his stride and sits at attention, graciously receiving long lines of people without visible signs

---

* The question of whether Baba sleeps at all is pertinent. Baba himself gives the impression that on occasions he does sleep briefly. However, whether what he terms "sleep" for himself is identical with what constitutes "sleep" for the average person, is very doubtful. Baba has never clarified the matter.

of fatigue. Or if he does look fatigued at some point, a brief period of relaxation is ample to restore him.

The immediate *mandali* who accompany him are equally incomprehensible in their endurance. Often they too do not have an opportunity to sleep for days on end, meanwhile undergoing the most severe physical and mental strain. When asked how they hold up under it they merely shrug their shoulders and say, "Baba helps us". Then the matter is dismissed as of no importance.

It is clear that Baba emanates certain envigorating, calming, sanitizing characteristics. The effect is comparable in part to leaving an exasperating job in a dirty, noisy city and going into a range of sublime mountains where one eats, sleeps and walks in the midst of restorative nature. But whereas nature is passive, Baba is active, and so at this point the analogy breaks down.

The last diffuse atmosphere to be described is the sense of peace which steals over one in Baba's presence. A spirit of agitation is not only very much with us in the confusion of a complex civilization, but it is also very dear to us. The tempo of living picks up just to a certain degree when, instead of going into rebellion against it, the individual comes incomprehensibly to enjoy it and uses every means at his command to perpetuate or even intensify it. This is an incredible example of the self-perpetuating force of habit. A person may be crying to high heaven that he is so busy that he is about to lose his mind, and yet when the very next point of decision arises, he will deliberately choose the course involving further complexities.

This is one of the most insidious problems of our times, for it is a virtually insuperable temptation to seem simultaneously put-upon, virtuous, terribly busy, and deserving of commiseration. If recognition of one's martyrdom is not given spontaneously, it is almost impossible not to parade it before whoever will listen.

Baba again slices through the confusion with two constant injunctions: "be happy; don't worry".

It must be honestly said that this last is peculiarly difficult to accomplish when one is first around Baba. Events move with such speed, and there are so many precise things to be carried out, that one is in a constant sweat of fussing. Also it is almost impossible not to worry whether someone else will do *his* job right for Baba, because Baba is a precise taskmaster. His recognition of perfection in accomplishment is matched only by his capacity to forgive the one who was unable to achieve it.

Meanwhile, even when one is rushing about at the greatest speed with the most to accomplish, Baba is saying all the time, "don't worry, be happy". If it were anyone but Baba, one would cheerfully pick up the nearest club and whack him with it.

Strangely enough, as one rushes about, this constantly reiterated injunction begins to filter through. The tangle begins to sort into two piles. On the one hand is busyness and a host of things to be done correctly. On the other hand is calmness, peace of mind and enjoyment of the job. The two are not at war with one another. In fact, the one makes the other possible.

Like most of life, balance appears to be hooked into the appreciation of logical opposites. It seems necessary to enjoy being racingly busy, and at the same time to be completely calm in one's own heart. However, as soon as the focal point of being moves from the calmness in the heart over into the racing-to-get-the-next-thing done, then all hell breaks loose.

Baba is not training the individual to endure the unendurable, but to understand that life at its most demanding can still be lived with peace in one's soul. It takes a great teacher to show the fine line between the two, but once the demarcation has been seen it can never be forgotten.

This has been only a quick and superficial discussion of some of the most important atmospheres which Baba generates, but I too am anxious to stop this flow of words and look at what Baba himself says he is here to do.

I will not use up time apologizing for the inadequacy of my own viewpoint in trying to assess a great man. It has been offered candidly as being the thoughts, conflicts and conclusions of a man-in-the-street who has been deeply impressed by the values he has seen.

Out of it has come an experience which is best described in words of Stewart Edward White. In discussing his early reactions to much evidence of the existence of "the invisibles" who lived "on the other side", White used to say that it was possible for him to explain away each individual occurrence in completely naturalistic terms. However the total weight of complex explanations finally became so great that he was finally forced to accept the simplifying belief in the existence of the "invisibles".

My own experience concerning Meher Baba and his flat statement that he is the Avatar of the age has followed the same almost grudging assent. One day the weight of accumulating evidence becomes too great, and my own sense of honesty finally makes the decision for me.*

At best, conviction by weight of evidence is not a satisfactory substitute for direct knowledge. But as I said earlier, I am sure that I shall not have this further degree of understanding of Meher Baba's function until God grants me one day to understand that Perfection within my own.

Meanwhile, I feel as the Australian poet, Francis Brabazon, who was with me in India through the eventful *sahvas* weeks. "How does one judge whether Baba is the Avatar?" he repeated my query late one night. "I don't think you judge it. You just wake up one day with the feeling that He is."

---

* It has been ten years now since I described this frame of my own judgment of Meher Baba's avatarhood. Each one of these ten years has reinforced this conclusion through personal contact, through observation of the results of his ministry, through following the gradual unfolding of originally enigmatic statements, and most of all, through the language of the heart. It has now become established as an instinct no longer open to conjecture.

D. E. Stevens

CHAPTER 3

Baba Discusses Avatarhood

In the long run the man himself must say what he is. If he is Persian, he says so. If he is Catholic, he says so. If he is allergic to onions, he says so. At least he says so when it is important that the characteristic shall be known. If it is important that that characteristic be unknown, then he will deliberately suppress the fact.

Christ was not backward in pointing out His divine function. Mohammed and Buddha on the other hand are reported to have insisted that they were ordinary mortals. I am not qualified to argue between the two precedents from which we have to choose. I would prefer to let Baba have it his own way and not condemn or condone him on the score that "this great One did", or "that great One didn't".

The troublesome thing is that there is always a rather liberal crop of persons who proclaim with no embarrassment that they are divinely appointed to the office of Messiah. Who is right? Or are they all perhaps fakes?

Some clue to the question can be gotten sometimes by seeing a meeting between two individuals who both feel their status to be the highest. I accidentally participated in such an occasion in New York. A splendid looking man in his prime asked to see Meher Baba privately in his quarters. As he stood in the hall, his message was taken to Baba by one of the *mandali*.

The *mandali* came back to the door and said that Baba would be happy to see him, whereupon the man become perturbed and insisted that Baba himself should come to the door and invite him in. This, he stated, was no more than just in greeting someone who was One with God.

Hearing the fuss at the door, Baba stepped into the line of sight to the doorway and smilingly beckoned the man to enter. This he then did.

The temptation to assert one's divine role is almost infinite. Further, there is much evidence to indicate that it is easy for even a highly developed spiritual teacher to conclude that he has the birthright of Christhood. Even if the great teacher himself should not have these illusions, his followers often elect him to that position after his death.

The jungle is too rank for one to make a way easily through it. There appear to be only three legitimate means of concluding the matter of Christhood. The first is the way of one's own heart, through trust in the master himself. Even if one should be wrong in one's estimate, the strength of that faith in the teacher will accomplish things that will dwarf any error in one's judgment.

The second way is that of direct experience. That *per se* means perfection or at least enlightenment for oneself, and few of us may hope in this lifetime for such absolute knowledge "by being".

The third is to assess the impact of such a man on the course of civilization. This cannot be used directly at present because we still live in the man's own time. At best we can try to measure his effect on people who have been close to him. This has been essayed in previous chapters.

The best source material for further study is the man's statements about himself. These are very enlightening, for there is a splendid sense of balance in them which carries conviction in itself. This is what Meher Baba has to say on the subject of his own divine function:

"Age after age, when the wick of righteousness burns low, the Avatar comes yet once again to rekindle the torch of love and truth. Age after age, through the noise and disruption of war, fear, and chaos, the Avatar's call rings out: 'Come all unto Me'.

"Although the veil of illusion may cause this call of the Ancient One to seem as a voice in the wilderness, still its echo and re-echoes pervade through time and space, rousing at first a few, and then millions from their deep slumber of ignorance. In the midst of illusion, as the Voice behind all voices, it awakens humanity to bear witness to the manifestation of God amidst mankind.

"The time has come. I repeat the call and bid all come unto me.

"This time-honored call of mine thrills the hearts of those who have patiently endured all in their love for God, loving God *only* for love of God. There are others who fear and shudder at its reverberations and would flee or resist. And there are yet others who are baffled, failing to understand why the all-sufficient Highest of the High need give this call to humanity.

"Regardless of the doubts or convictions people may have, I continue to come as the Avatar because of the infinite love I bear for one and all. Though judged time and again by humanity in its ignorance, I come to help man distinguish the real from the false.

"The divine call is little heeded at first because it is invariably muffled in the cloak of the infinite true humility of the Ancient One. Yet in its infinite strength it grows in volume until it reverberates and continues to reverberate in countless hearts as the voice of reality.

"Strength gives rise to humility, while modesty indicates weakness. Only he who is truly great can *be* really humble.

"When a man admits his true greatness in the firm knowledge of his greatness, that is in itself an expression of humility. He accepts his greatness as completely natural, and merely expresses what he is, just as a man would not hesitate to admit that he is a man.

"If a truly great man, who knows himself to be truly great, were to deny his greatness, this would belittle what he indubitably is; for modesty is the basis of guise while true greatness is free from camouflage.

"On the other hand when a man expresses a greatness he knows he does not possess, he is the greatest of hypocrites.

"The man is honest who, knowing that he is not great, firmly and frankly states that he is not great.

"There are more than a few who are not great, yet assume an air of humility despite their belief in their own considerable worth. Through both words and actions they repeatedly express their humbleness, professing to be the servants of humanity.

"True humility is not acquired by donning a garb of humility. True humility emanates spontaneously and continually from the strength of the truly great. Voicing one's humbleness does not make one humble. Regardless of how often a parrot may say 'I am a man', it does not make him a man.

"The absence of greatness is better than the establishment of false greatness by assumed humility. These efforts at humility not only do not express strength, but on the contrary they are expressions of modesty born of a weakness which springs from a lack of knowledge of reality.

"Beware of modesty. Under the cloak of humility it invariably leads one into the clutches of self-deception. Modesty breeds egotism, and man eventually succumbs to pride through assumed humility.

"The greatest greatness and the greatest humility go hand in hand, naturally and without effort.

"When the Greatest of all says, 'I am the Greatest', it is only a spontaneous expression of an infallible truth. The strength of His greatness does not lie in the raising of the dead, but in His great humiliation when He allows Himself to be ridiculed, persecuted and crucified by those who are weak in flesh and spirit. Throughout the ages humanity has failed to gauge the true depths of humility underlying the greatness of the Avatar. They judge His divinity by their own limited standards acquired from the religions. Even real saints and sages, who have some knowledge of truth, have failed to understand the Avatar's greatness when faced with His real humility.

"History repeats itself through the ages as men and women in their ignorance, limitation and pride sit in judgment on the God-incarnated man who declares His Godhood, condemning Him for uttering the truths they cannot understand. But He is indifferent to abuse and persecution, for in His true compassion He understands; in His continual experiencing of reality He knows; and in His infinite mercy He forgives.

"God is all, God knows all, and God does all. When the Avatar proclaims that He is the Ancient One, it is God who proclaims His manifestation on earth. When man speaks for or against the Avatar, it is God who speaks through him. It is God alone who declares Himself through the Avatar and through mankind.

"I tell you all with my divine authority that you and I are not 'we', but 'One'. You unconsciously feel my Avatarhood within you. I consciously feel in you what each of you feels. Thus every one of us is the Avatar in the sense that everyone and everything is Everyone and Everything, all at the same time and for all time.

"There is nothing but God. He is the only reality and we are all one in the indivisible Oneness of this absolute reality.

"When one (man) who has realized God says, 'I am God, you are God, and we are all One', and when he also awakens this feeling of oneness in His illusion-bound selves (mankind), then questions of lowly and great, poor and rich, humble and modest, good and bad, simply vanish. It is man's false awareness of duality that misleads him into making illusory distinctions and filing the results into separate categories.

"I repeat and emphasize that in my eternal experiencing of reality, no difference exists between the rich and the poor. If however such a question of difference between affluence and poverty were ever to exist for me, I would consider the one really poor who possessed worldly riches but not the wealth of love for God. I would know that he was truly rich who owned nothing, but possessed the priceless treasure of love for God. His is the poverty that kings may envy, and that makes even the King of kings his slave.

"In the eyes of God the only difference between the rich and the poor is the intensity and sincerity of their longing for God.

"Only love for God can annihilate the falsity of the limited ego, which is the basis of life ephemeral. Only love for God can bring one to the realization of the reality of one's unlimited ego, which is the basis of eternal existence. The Divine Ego expresses Itself continually, but man, shrouded in the veil of ignorance, misconstrues this indivisible Ego, experiencing and expressing it as the limited, separate ego.

"Listen when I say with divine authority that the oneness of reality is so totally unlimited and all-pervading that not only are we all one, but even the collective term 'we' has no place in the infinite, indivisible Oneness.

"Awaken from your ignorance and try at least to understand that in this completely indivisible Oneness not only is the Avatar God, but also the ant and the sparrow and one and all of you are nothing but God. The only apparent difference is in their states of consciousness. The Avatar knows that the sparrow is not a sparrow, while the sparrow does not realize this. Being ignorant of its ignorance, it identifies itself as a sparrow.

"Do not live in ignorance. Do not waste your precious lifetime in differentiating and judging your fellow men, but learn to long for the love of God. Even in the midst of your worldly activities, live only to find and realize your true identity with your beloved God.

"Be pure and simple and love all, because all are One. Live a sincere life, be natural and be honest with yourself.

"Honesty will guard you against false modesty and will give you the strength of true humility. Spare no pains to help others. Seek no reward other than the gift of divine love. Yearn for this gift sincerely and intensely and I promise in the name of my divine honesty that I will give you much more than you yearn for."

Here we have Baba's statement on what must be said about position and abilities. He drives a hard point in differentiating between false modesty, the strength and frankness of true humility, and the blatancy of rank egotism. He then leaves out one sentence, "This is why I must tell you what I am, the Highest of the High". He does not insist that one believe him, but he states his Avatarhood as a literal fact and it is then one's own responsibility to decide whether to believe him or not.

If one rejects Baba's statement that he is the Avatar of the age, then there is a chance that one will be right, and therefore able to nod someday in agreement with millions of other people who were not taken in by the claims of another deluded messiah.

If one accepts Baba and his statement that he is the Avatar of the age, then there is a chance of having been among the relatively few who believed him and accepted him and who, as a consequence, had the incomparable privilege of his grace. One cannot help but think in retrospect of the millions who knew of Mohammed, and Jesus, and Buddha, but who failed to listen to them because the chance seemed so slight that the Avatar, or even a great spiritual teacher, was really at hand.

Meher Baba has other comments on this point. In 1953 he gave the following message to his close followers in Dehra Dun, India:

"I want you to make me your constant companion. Think of me more than you think of your own self. The more you think of me, the more you will realize my love for you. Your duty is to keep me constantly with you throughout your thoughts, speech and actions.

"They do their duty who surrender to me through their faith and love, guided by their implicit belief in my divinity. They too do their duty who speak ill of me and condemn me through their writings, prompted by their genuine conviction that Baba is a fraud. But those who constantly doubt because they do not know their own minds, are the hypocrites. Through false emotions they tend at times to believe in me, and at other times to gossip slanderously against me.

"No amount of slander can affect or change me, nor any amount of admiration or praise enhance my divinity. Baba is what he is. I was Baba, I am Baba, and I shall forever remain Baba."

In the same general period he had more to say at Dehra Dun on the subject of the coming of the Avatar, the reception He receives, and His relation to those who come to Him for guidance.

"Age after age the infinite God wills through His infinite mercy to come among mankind by descending to the human level in a human form. His physical presence among mankind is not understood and He is looked upon as an ordinary man of the world. When He asserts His divinity by proclaiming Himself the Avatar of the age, He is worshiped by some who accept Him as God, and glorified by a few who know Him as God on earth. It happens invariably though that the rest of humanity condemns Him while He is physically among them.

"Thus God as man proclaims Himself as the Avatar and allows Himself to be persecuted and tortured, humiliated and condemned by humanity, for whose sake His infinite love has made Him stoop so low. Through His very humiliation He ensures that humanity, in its very act of condemning God's manifestation as the Avatar, shall assert, however indirectly, the existence of God in His infinite, eternal state.

"The Avatar is always one and the same because God is always one and the same. This eternally one and the same Avatar repeats His manifestation from time to time in different cycles. He adopts different human forms and different names, coming to different places to reveal truth in different clothing and different languages. This He does to raise humanity from the pit of ignorance and help free it from the bondage of delusion.

"Among the best known and honored manifestations of God as the

Avatar, the earliest is Zoroaster. He came before Ram, Krishna, Buddha, Jesus and Mohammed. Thousands of years ago He gave the world the essence of truth in the form of three fundamental precepts: good thoughts, good words and good deeds.

"These precepts are constantly unfolded for humanity in one manner and another by the Avatar of the age, who leads humanity imperceptibly towards the truth. To put these precepts of good thoughts, good words and good deeds into practice is not as easy as it would seem, but yet not impossible. To live up to them though is as infinitely difficult as to practice a living death in the midst of life.

"In the world there are countless *sadhus, mahatmas, mahapurushas,* saints, yogis and *walis*. The few genuine ones of these are in a category of their own, neither on a level with the ordinary human being nor on a level with that state which is the Highest of the High.

"I am neither a *mahatma* nor a *mahapurush*, neither *sadhu* nor saint, neither yogi nor *wali*. Those who come to me to gain wealth or retain their possessions, to seek relief from suffering or help to fulfill their mundane desires, to these I declare once again that I am not *sadhu*, saint, *mahatma, mahapurush* or yogi. To seek such things through me is to court utter disappointment. However such disappointment is only apparent, for eventually it is invariably instrumental in bringing about the complete transformation of one's worldly desires.

"*Sadhus,* saints, yogis, *walis* and such others who are on the *via media,* can and do perform miracles. They satisfy the transient material needs of individuals who approach them for help.

"But if I am not a *sadhu,* saint, yogi, *mahapurush* nor *wali,* then what am I? The natural conclusion would be that either I am just an ordinary human being or I am the Highest of the High. Definitely I can never be included among those having the intermediary status of real *sadhus,* saints, yogis and such like.

"If I am just an ordinary man, my capabilities and powers are limited. I am no different from an ordinary human being. In such case people should not expect any supernatural help from me in the form of miracles or spiritual guidance. Also, to approach me to fulfill their desires would be absolutely futile.

"On the other hand, if I am beyond the level of an ordinary human being and much beyond the level of saints and yogis, then I must be the Highest of the High. In such case, to judge me with the human intellect and to approach me with worldly desires would be the height of ignorance and folly.

"If I am the Highest of the High my will is law, my wishes govern the law and my love sustains the universe. Then your apparent calamities and transient sufferings are only the outcome of my love for the ultimate good. Therefore to approach me for deliverance from predicaments and to expect me to satisfy worldly desires would be asking me to do the impossible—to undo what I have already ordained.

"If you accept Baba in all faith as the Highest of the High, it behooves you to lay down your life at his feet rather than crave fulfillment of your desires. Not this one life, but your millions of lives would only be a small sacrifice to lay at the feet of one such as Baba, who is the Highest of the High. For Baba's unbounded love is the only sure and unfailing guide which can lead you safely through the innumerable blind alleys of your transient life.

"They cannot obligate me who surrender their all—body, mind, possessions—with a motive. Nor can I be snared by those who surrender because they understand that to gain the everlasting treasure of bliss they must relinquish passing possessions. A desire for greater gain still clings to their surrenderance, and therefore the surrender cannot be complete.

"You must all know that if I am the Highest of the High my role demands that I strip you of all your possessions and wants, consume all your desires and make you desireless. This I must do rather than satisfy your desires. *Sadhus,* saints, yogis and *walis* can give you what you want, but I take away your wants, free you from attachments and liberate you from the bondage of ignorance. I am the one to *take* —not *give*—what you want.

"Intellectuals can never understand me through intellect alone. If I am the Highest of the High, it is impossible for intellect to gauge me, nor can my ways be fathomed by the limited human mind.

"I am not to be attained by those who, through love of me, stand reverentially by in rapt admiration. I am also not for those who ridicule me and point at me with contempt. Nor am I here to have tens of millions flock around me. I am for the select few who, scattered among the crowd, silently surrender to me their all—body, mind and possessions.

"Still more, I am here for those who, having surrendered all, never give another thought to their surrender. All those are mine who are prepared to renounce even the very thought of their renunciation and who, keeping constant vigil in the midst of intense activity, await their turn to lay down their lives for the cause of truth at a glance from me. Those who have indomitable courage to face cheerfully the worst calamities, who have unshakable faith in me and are eager to fulfill my slightest wish at the cost of happiness and comfort, these indeed truly love me.

"From my point of view, the atheist who honorably accepts his worldly responsibilities and discharges them conscientiously is far more blessed than the man who thinks he is a devout believer in God and yet shirks the responsibilities apportioned to him by divine law— running instead after *sadhus*, saints and yogis to seek relief from the suffering which ultimately would have effected his liberation.

"To have also one eye glued on the delightful pleasures of the flesh and to expect to see a spark of eternal bliss with the other is not only impossible but the height of hypocrisy.

"I cannot expect you to understand what I want you to know all at once. It is my charge to awaken you from time to time through the ages, sowing the seed in your limited minds which, in due course and with proper attention on your part, must germinate, flourish and bear that fruit of true knowledge which is your birthright.

"On the other hand if, led by your ignorance, you persist in going your own way, none can stop the course of progress you have chosen. That too is progress which leads you after innumerable incarnations to realize what I want you to know now.

"*Awake now* and save yourself from further entanglement in the maze of delusion and self-created suffering, which is dependent upon your ignorance of the true goal. Listen and strive for freedom by placing ignorance in its proper position. Be honest with yourself and God. It is possible to fool one's neighbors and even the whole world, but it is impossible to escape the knowledge of the Omniscient. Such is divine law.

"Seek me not to extricate yourself from predicaments, but find me in order to surrender yourself whole-heartedly to my will. Do not cling to me for worldly happiness and short-lived comforts, but adhere to me through thick and thin, sacrificing your own happiness and comforts at my feet. Let my happiness be your cheer and my comforts your rest.

"Do not ask me to bless you with a good job. Wish only to serve me more diligently and honestly, without expectation of reward.

"Never beg me to save your life or the lives of your dear ones. Only beg me to accept you and permit you to lay down your life for me.

"Never expect me to cure you of your bodily afflictions. Beseech me rather to cure you of your ignorance.

"Never stretch out your hands to receive anything from me. Hold them high in praise of me, whom you have approached as the Highest of the High.

"If I am the Highest of the High, then nothing is impossible for me. However I have often said that I do not perform miracles to satisfy individual needs, for this would only result in entangling the individual further into the net of ephemeral existence. On the other hand for the spiritual upliftment and benefit of all humanity and all creatures, at certain periods I do manifest the infinite power I possess in the form of miracles.

"However, miraculous experiences have often occurred to individuals who love and have faith in me, and these have been attributed to my *nazar* or grace. But I want everyone to know that it is not fit for those who love me to attribute such miraculous experiences to my state of the Highest of the High. If I am the Highest of the High then I am above this illusory play of *maya*.

"Therefore the miraculous experiences described by those who love me, or by those who love me unknowingly through other channels, are only the product of their own firm faith in me. That unshakable faith often supersedes the course of play of *maya* and thus produces what they describe as miracles. Such experiences derived through firm faith do not entangle those individuals into further binding in illusion, but eventually do good.

"If I am the Highest of the High, then a wish by my universal will can give God-realization to one and all in an instant, freeing every creature in creation from the shackles of ignorance. But blessed is knowledge that is gained through the experience of ignorance in accordance with the divine law. Such knowledge is attainable in the midst of ignorance through the guidance of Perfect Masters and by surrenderance to the Highest of the High."

An entire book could be written in commentary on these two important documents. However I intend to belabor only one point. If one forgets for the moment that these statements are being made by a living man and if one neglects temporarily the crisis in judgment which they pose, then one cannot but be struck by the fundamental nature of what is said.

Here without question is a man who knows to the nth degree what he is talking about and who possesses an insight into an absolute ethics which would tax the greatest hearts and minds. But the residual question which causes the reader to tend to neglect the import of what is being said, is the almost unbelievable statement by Baba that he is the "Highest of the High".

Baba says dispassionately that it is the lot of the Avatar to be accepted by only a handful in His lifetime. There would seem no need then for those who accept Baba to try to convince the rest of humanity that it is overlooking the best bet of many lifetimes. However it is important to look briefly into the meaning of rejection in general terms.

Sooner or later, each human being must be willing to annihilate for a time his own sense of self-determination in a sense of absolute trust of another.* Only in this manner can there be the opportunity to comb out the snarls of countless accumulated actions in one's nature.

Even when a person is unhappiest, he still has a persistent sense of unconscious hope that his own deliberated actions will one day lead

---

* Trust in or identification with another human being is not peculiar to the follower of the *guru*. It has its modern counterpart in the relation of patient to psychoanalyst, of friend to trusted advisor, of one who loves to the beloved. Such a relation apparently involves a very fundamental principle of nature in which the complexities of self can be attacked at their root through the loss or lessening of self in the being of another.

him to success and happiness. Usually it is only the person who has almost entirely ceased to hope who is willing to take the conscious step of annihilating his own ego in the person of another. For in annihilating his ego, he denies the very core of the "right" of free-will, of self-determination, and in that destruction there is bound to go his most stubborn, ego-centered hope for the future.

Once it is gone, he is really at sea. There is no landmark, no point of reliance or help, only that cause or person to whom he has perhaps by now given his allegiance. This is a frightening position and it is no wonder that most people would prefer to trust their own fallible but "visible" sense of self-determination, rather than surrender it to another's possible whims.

There are few people who have reached either such desperation in the successive traps of life, or enlightenment in the inner processes of the heart, to be willing to trust their fate implicitly to another being.

This is the challenge which frightens people not only with Baba, but to a degree with all religious personages, faiths and movements. Baba poses the issue indelibly, however, clearly and repeatedly. For this reason there is often little opportunity to appreciate the scope and style of his statements. The human challenge they contain is too profound.

Then one day the great teacher passes on. The words can be read with academic interest in their loftiness of precept and the beauty of their phrasing. The rugged, stripped-bare challenge of a personal and immediate surrender is no longer present. Then the great man begins to be appreciated. Or *is* he appreciated, really?

Actually, I do not think he is. The real importance of such a person is in what is done in the direct personal relationship. The important people are the ones who went through whatever hell there was in fighting the thing through in the intensity of the living challenge. What comes after may have its glory, its beauty, its mass acceptance, but these are a pale shadow to the real man and the vitality of the living relation.

This is the challenge for man, and there are always individuals on earth who will present it to him. At some time he must meet it, and finally realize that the one who poses it does not do it for himself, but for love of the people who must know themselves.

This process of finding oneself through losing the self in a Perfect Being is the essential core of Baba's technique in dealing with people. All of the puzzling and sometimes distressing admonishments he makes are aimed at this goal. It isn't that one's own self is necessarily a bad thing. It just happens to have the unfortunate property of seeming completely separate. Once having lost oneself in the Master's being—not through desire, for that again simply emphasizes the separateness, but through the welding action of a unifying love— then much or even all of the illusion of separateness is lost.

Baba's constant exhortation to give up all and come to him is first of all a dramatic but honest effort to get the individual to withdraw his attention from a multitude of distractions. This is the first essential step.

The next is to lose one's own self completely in Baba. This is the part which is resisted so mightily. Such a step has absolutely nothing to do with enhancing the prestige of Baba. If he were a sublime egotist, it could. In cold print, the repeated insistence on this point sounds as if Baba might be such a divine egotist. In the presence of Baba one understands at once that this is completely aside from the true issue.

The question of losing oneself in Baba may still be acute even after meeting Baba, but the possibility of Baba's involvement for Baba's own personal reasons falls out of the picture. The issue now is the real extent of one's trust and love, versus the persistent habit of one's sense of separateness.

In this arena the true battle is waged. It is an astonishingly passive battle on Baba's part. He is simply himself and shows constantly an unbelievable forgiveness and thoughtfulness. How can one's ego go on constantly rebelling against him? Wherever one's rebellion flares, it is met only by understanding and compassion. Finally, rebellion turns back upon itself and there is rebellion against rebellion itself.

The wall of separative egotism is breached at this point in indentification with another human being. This is the way known to lovers, to the mystics of the world religions, and to many who deal honestly and patiently with the deepest needs of modern man.

The only question is how well the person to whom one identifies, knows his own self. The positive effects resulting from the identification will depend largely on the answer. Even in the event that there is no greater depth of perception of self in the other, the fact of winning some sense of oneness is nevertheless a positive gain in the direction of reality. On the other hand, if there is greater knowledge of the self in the other being, then the possibilities of the situation are rich.

To realize those possibilities, the link between the two must be completely unobstructed, for the possibilities can be completely exhausted only if there is a complete sense of oneness born of honesty, sincerity and true depth of feeling. This means that there can be no sense of separateness or of personal interest in contrast to that of the other person. This would act only as a check-point for the free flow of self to self.

The age-old question of "desire" owes its continuing importance to its effect on this linking bridge of oneness. Desire has a simple statement to make: *I* desire *you.* It is only necessary to reflect on one's own desires to understand that they emphasize the separation of the one who desires and the unobtainable nature of the object desired. Therefore desire is a problem *not* primarily because of the physical element which is so deeply involved, but because of the emotional element of separateness which feeds it.

Love also has a very simple statement to make: *I* love *you.* One has only to reflect for a few moments to find that here the inner sense is quite different, being one of closeness, of security—in a word, of *oneness.* This is why love has always instinctively been respected, praised and sought. It feeds man and brings him far in the direction of knowing his own self through knowing another. If lust had been ordained to have this effect, lust would have been rightfully acclaimed by the poets and mystics.

Social customs and taboos are based in the long run on an almost unerring sense of what generally aids or hinders man in his constant endeavor to find his real self. Morality is not an act of piety, but of effort to lay the climate in which the seed of self-knowledge may sprout. When one is moral for the approval of society, then one is immoral and the effort is worse than worthless. When one is moral because of deep internal needs, then the sun really shines. But one should never assume that one man's morality is another's.

Social morality bears the same relationship to the love of another as religion does to the guiding of man to find his soul. It is a helpful first step, but there must be room for rapid change and progress when the real quarry comes in sight. Then morality becomes really alive, is self-generating, and often has little resemblance to the average, conventionalized version.

All morality, whether social or personal, is aimed at the eventual development of the most honest, and therefore the most complete, love of another person. The love of another person is one of the greatest goods because it strips bare the self and fuses it into the substance of another. As this happens, it is realized dimly or intensely that no fusion was necessary, the oneness was there all the time.

As the sense of oneness grows, there is the possibility of plumbing to the depths of oneself through the sense of realization of self in another. At this point enters the mystic, the great religious teacher, the saint, the *guru*, the Messiah.

It is possible to realize one's own self, one's own true nature, completely and irrevocably, through establishing a perfect sense of oneness with one who has perfectly realized himself. Such a person is called God-realized, for the theorem also states that the one who has perfectly realized himself has discovered that he and the Father are One. Therefore the immense importance of the Christ, for in Him resides the greatest opportunity to achieve perfect oneness with the Divine Being.

If one studies Meher Baba's statements in the context of this ultimate challenge to achieve the ultimate goal, then they will be seen to lead with unvarying straightness to this point. One may not be able to determine for oneself whether Baba is the perfect instrument for the achieving of this goal, but if he is not, then he has laid out the necessary course with astonishing clarity.

One final time, let us let Meher Baba speak for Himself on this point:

"I am the One so many seek and so few find. No amount of intellect can fathom me. No amount of austerity can attain me. Only when one loves me and loses one's self in me, am I found."

And again:

"All these statements and messages can lead us nowhere on the spiritual path. Reasoning and mental conviction also lead us nowhere. Even actual experience falls short of the highest state.

"The more you try to understand God, the less you understand Him. How can He, who is beyond all explaining, be described? His being infinitely easy to know has rendered Him infinitely difficult. The secret is that you have to become what you already are.

"You can know me as one of you and one in you only when the veils of separateness are lifted, and this can be done if you love me honestly and whole-heartedly.

"Lose yourself in Baba and you will find that you eternally were Baba. There can be no compromise in love. It has either to be full, or not at all.

"I say with divine authority that I am the Ancient One, and the slave of those who really love me."

Appendix I

DIRECTIONS GIVEN BY MEHER BABA
November 1955

Particularly for the participants of the *sahvas* weeks,
and in general for all connected with Baba.

I want you to read carefully and absorb these directions, as well
as the other items arranged alongside,* namely:
1. The framed gist of the Circular No. 25 of 1.5.1955.
2. The two charts on God and Love.
3. The list of donations for the *sahvas* weeks.†

No one, and that also includes those who have come for the
sahvas, should under any circumstances—either directly or indirectly
—ask me for favours, rewards, money, jobs, health or other material
things, not even for spiritual gain. The best is not to ask for anything. If anything at all is to be asked for, then first one should
ponder whether one has the required degree of determination and
courage to ask for the love of Baba. If one has that much determination and courage, one should be ready to surrender so completely
as literally to give up and let go of everything—body, mind and
heart. And the self should be able to remain alive and dead simultaneously.

To all of you who believe and feel that I am the Avatar, I say
that there is no need at all to ask me for anything, because I must
know best when and what to do for one and all, and what to give to
one and all.

Your faith and belief demand then that you should feel happy to
be resigned equally to whatever comes from me or whatever is
taken away by me. As and when I bless anyone with peace and
plenty, money and children, name and fame, etc., he and others
should not feel elated at this. Their concern should be only to keep
their minds and hearts focused on what they believe me to be, the
one reality.

If I am free to give as I wish, I must also remain free to take

---

* These "Directions", as well as the other items mentioned, were posted
on a sort of bulletin board inside the hall in which most of the *sahvas*
meetings were held.

† The donations were made by various of the Indian devotees.

239

away as and when I deem it best, in any way and at any time. That also means that as and when I take anything away from anyone, he should not raise a cry, because his concern must likewise remain focused on my reality and not on the thing I take away.

From the beginning of all beginnings I have been saying, I say it now, and to the end of ends I will say it, that *he who loves God becomes God.*

It is a fact that I have come amongst you. One of these days the whole world will come to realize how I have come, where I have come from and the purpose of my coming. I repeat once again that I have come neither to establish *panths* and *jaats* (groups and classes) nor to establish *mandirs, masjids,* churches and *ashrams* in the world. I have come to receive the beauty and give the blessings of love. All else but God—whether rites, rituals or ceremonies in the name of religion, worldly possessions, family, money or one's own physical body—all else but God is illusion.

In response to my call to one and all to leave all and come to me, some have come. A few have responded for the sake of spiritual enlightenment, others to gain peace and escape from worldly strife and entanglements, while a few have come through their love for me to find me as I am. Those who have come to me have naturally become dependent upon me, but in spite of that, I, as Baba, remain free and independent.

I have been seeing to their requirements with the money which has been coming in and going out in the spirit of love. I accept with love what is offered to me with love, and I also disburse it out of love. I neither obtain money through miracles nor am I connected with any money-making business. There are those who have offered what they can spare and there are those who have dedicated their all to me and to my cause of love, unmindful of money for the sake of money.

Under the existing conditions of no promises from me,* no bindings upon me and no undertakings by me, my dependents must also be made to feel quite free of their material dependence upon me. Thus they will be able to maintain a pure relationship of love for the sake of love.

I now wish to be outwardly what I always am inwardly: living solely in love, for love and with love. In that spirit the whole world

---

* These were the conditions laid down by Baba to his followers in Circular No. 25.

could live with me irrespective of whether or not there happened to be any provision for food and shelter for the "todays" as well as for the "tomorrows". As it is, I am free and no bindings touch me, but I should also be free of the need to bother about arrangements for others. I now want love to reign supreme outwardly as it always does inwardly in me.

How can one explain love? There are as many ways of explaining love and obedience as there are men. There can thus be no end to the understanding of them except through obedience based on love, and through love itself. All great saints, teachers and masters say the same thing in one way or another when the emphasis is laid on love for the sake of love, or failing that, on obedience in the cause of love.

For spontaneous surrender the heart must, so to speak, be worn on one's sleeve. One must be ever ready to place one's neck under the ever-sharp knife of command of the beloved, and the head should figuratively be detached in order that it might be completely surrendered at the master's feet. Obedience should be so complete that one's concern with it makes one as much awake to possibilities as it makes one deaf to impossibilities—as envisaged by the poet:

"Darmiyane qahre darya
   Takhta bandam karda-ee

Baad mi gu-ee kay
   Daaman ter makun hoshyar baash."

"I was tied to a raft and thrown in the ocean and then I was warned to be careful not to let my robe get wet."

Yet all this does not and cannot explain the required degree of continued readiness for love and obedience to love. In fact, one of the three reasons for this *sahvas* is to help you grasp what love and obedience really mean.

You must have such a clear picture in your minds of this *sahvas* as to forget completely such things as declarations, messages and discourses by me. This is not an occasion for the fulfillment or the making and breaking of past and future promises. You have got to remove from your minds any picture of me upon a dais and you sitting before me—as has been the experience of most of you present here.

I want you to be with me, near me and before me in an entirely different atmosphere, so that you can freely breathe the air of my personal presence. We must be together as intimately as if we were living under the same roof for no purpose other than that of living with each other and for each other.

Do not look forward to any functions, meetings, timetables, programs, agendas or any cut-and-dried plans. You have simply to be near me all the time that I remain with you, playing, sitting, walking, joking, discussing serious things or listening to stories. I want you to live with me the day-to-day life I normally lead.

You are not expected to read, study, meditate or pray, but to feel at home with me as naturally and unreservedly as you do at home in the midst of your own family and friends. I want you to be your natural selves, putting aside all the superficial niceties one usually assumes in social life. Being in my company, watching me and being watched by me, you will automatically learn and unlearn a lot which no amount of teaching can convey.

In short, there are three reasons for this *sahvas* program:

1. To give you my closest company in order to bring out the oneness between us.
2. To help you understand love and obedience, and to make you imbibe these twin aspects of the nectar of the infinite existence behind all life.
3. To show you how to do my work of spreading love.

However much I may explain, you cannot have a true idea of the enormous strain on my physical body in these last twelve months. To say the least, I am utterly exhausted physically, yet I intend to exert myself further for the whole *sahvas* month in order to impress thoroughly upon you certain points. There are points which I have got to drive in deeper and deeper, not only for you all who are able to be near me physically, but for all others also who love me and obey me, as well as for other reasons which are not apparent here and now. These points you will have to grasp through the three reasons of the *sahvas* as given above.

Therefore, during the seven days, above everything else forget your worries, comforts, discomforts, home and business affairs. In short, forget about everything concerning your daily life except your present life here with me. As I have stated, I have offered this *sahvas* at the cost to me of additional physical exertion, because of all who love me and obey me, including those who are physically absent.

The only explanations you should expect from me during the *sahvas* will be on:

1. Love
2. Obedience
3. Work of spreading my love
4. Freedom from the apparent binding of those dependent on me.

I want you all to take particular note that I would feel happy if each one of you not only possessed but read and digested *God Speaks* from the first to the last page, as the last book of its kind by me. I will likewise be happy if those amongst you who can possibly do so will see that this work is translated and made available in as many languages as possible for those who cannot read and understand English.

Appendix II

REMINISCENCES

Baba often reminisced during the *sahvas* month, particularly when he showed the *sahvasis* places near Ahmednagar that were associated with his early activities. The fact that a number of the *mandali* and *sahvasis* had shared in the events which rendered these spots memorable, added to the flavor of the retelling. The various reminiscences by Baba and members of the *sahvas* group have been re-grouped here for the purposes of consecutive narration, and are not therefore in the sequence in which they were originally given.

It should always be borne in mind also that Baba's gestures convey an essential idea. This in turn is clothed with words by one of the *mandali.***** Therefore the words are not always Baba's very own—unless he chooses tediously to have a word spelled out—but the sense is his.

One afternoon in commenting on a performance just given by the Telugu group of his own *Barra-Katha* (the story of Baba's life dramatically portrayed in song and dance), Baba had Eruch tell of events concerning Baba's birth which had been described to Eruch's mother by Baba's mother, Shirinmai.

Shirinmai had an unusual dream just a few days before Baba's birth (February 25, 1894). In the dream she was led to a wide, open area where she was rapidly surrounded by a sea of foreign appearing people, extending on all sides to the horizons. Shirinmai felt that all the strangers were looking steadily and expectantly towards her. She awoke in a state of alarm.

When she described this dream to relatives and friends, an elderly person told her that, rather than worry, she should feel happy, as the symbolism of the dream indicated that the child (Baba) would be awaited and esteemed by vast numbers of people.

On another occasion Ramju retold more of Shirinmai's stories:

"Merwan (Baba) † has been my problem even as a child. Some months after his birth I dreamed that I was standing in the doorway

---

* Baba gave up communication via the alphabet board in October, 1954.

† Meher Baba's name is Merwan Sheriar Irani.

244

of our house, holding Merwan in my arms. I saw that there was a well nearby in the compound (court) of the house. The figure of a striking woman, like a Hindu goddess, was rising out of the center of the well. I could clearly see the lavish green *sari* in which she was dressed, and the many green bangles with which she was adorned.

"Bright flowered designs were painted on her forehead in many colors, and in her hands she held a tray containing flowers, a lighted lamp and other articles used by Hindus in their worship. I stood motionless in fascination until the weird figure beckoned to me to hand Merwan over to her. Trying to hold him all the more tightly, I was awakened from the dream."

Shirinmai had continued her telling of her early worries about her precocious child.

"Merwan was very active and mischievous from the time he was able to toddle, and would walk out of the house when my attention was distracted. This often compelled me, when I was especially busy with housework, or had to go for my bath and there was no one in the house to look after him, to tie one end of my *sari* to his waist and the other to the bedstead. Even then I could not always keep him out of mischief. Once (about January, 1895) I had left him playing on the floor. Returning to the room some minutes later I was horrified to see him playing merrily with a big black snake. This time it wasn't a dream. With a piercing scream I rushed forward, but the snake slipped quickly out of the house and was never seen again."

Several days later Baba described the all-important occasion when the great Sufi saint, Hazrat Babajan, kissed him on the forehead, tearing away the veil which obscured his own God-realization.

"When the five Perfect Masters bring me down they draw a veil over me. Although Babajan was in the form of a woman, she was one of them (the five Perfect Masters) and she unveiled me in my present form. With just a kiss on the forehead, between the eyebrows, Babajan made me experience (May, 1913) thrills of indescribable bliss which continued for about nine months. Then one night (January, 1914) she made me realize in a flash the infinite bliss of self-realization (God-realization).

"At the time Babajan gave me the *nirvikalp* (inconceptual) experience of my own reality, the illusory physical, subtle and mental bodies—mind, worlds, and one and all created things—ceased to exist for me even as illusion. Then I began to see that only I, and nothing else, existed.

"The infinite bliss of my self-realization was, is and will remain continuous. At the moment I experience both infinite bliss as well as infinite suffering. Once I drop the body, only bliss will remain.

"But after I became self-conscious I could not have said all this. Nor could I say it even now if it had not been for the indescribable spiritual agonies which I passed through for another period of nine months (until October, 1914) in returning to normal consciousness of the suffering of others. During those nine months I remained in a state which no one else could have tolerated for even nine days.

"After physical death an ordinary man is usually dead to the world and the world is dead to him. Yet he continues to live his discarnate life beyond the sphere of gross existence. During the first three days of my superconscious state (January, 1914) I was truly dead to everybody and everything other than my own infinite reality, although my physical body continued to function more or less normally. Actually dead, though really living, I was consequently considered by others to be seriously ill. I was allowed to remain in bed, lying with wide open, vacant eyes which saw nothing.

"When man (the individualized soul) enters the seventh plane, which is the one and only plane of reality, his consciousness is fully freed once and for all from everything else. It then is wholly occupied by the reality of the real self or God. So it is said that the individual soul becomes superconscious, or God-conscious.

"To other souls who function within the illusion of duality, the God-conscious one may seem to be physically as much alive as they are. Nevertheless, regardless of the fact that the superconscious one's gross, subtle and mental bodies may remain functioning, he is dead to illusion for all time. His consciousness has transcended the illusory limitations of births and deaths that lie within the illusion of duality.

"The conscious state of God is known only to those who have achieved it. Such a state of realization of divine oneness is completely beyond the domain of mind itself. It is rare for man to become superconscious. One in millions might achieve it. It is rarer still for the God-conscious to be able to return *with* God-consciousness to normal consciousness of all the illusory existences—gross, subtle and mental—as a Perfect Master.

"Usually the gross, subtle and mental bodies of the God-conscious one automatically drop within four days if, after attaining superconsciousness, he does not begin to return to normal consciousness of the illusory world of duality.* In an unusual case all three bodies of the God-conscious one continue to function indefinitely in the relative higher and lower spheres of illusion. Then, for others, such a one is truly the ever-living dead, a real *Majzoob-e-kamil*, or conscious God in the midst of illusion-conscious humanity. To touch such a one is to touch God Himself!

"In my case, I did not drop the body on the fourth day, nor did I become established in the gross sphere as a *Majzoob*, nor did I begin to regain the normal consciousness of a Perfect Master. Only such a Perfect One is capable of knowing the state in which I had to remain for nine months.

"On the fourth day and after I was slightly conscious of my body and began to move about without any consciousness of my surroundings. I received no promptings from my mind as would an ordinary man. I had no knowledge of the things I did or did not do. I did not sleep and had no appetite. No one had any idea throughout this period that I sat, talked, walked, lay down and did everything by instinct, more like an automaton than an ordinary human being.

"My sleepless, staring, vacant eyes worried my mother most. She believed and told others that I had gone mad. In her anguish she could not refrain from going once to Babajan and demanding to know what she had done to me. Shirinmai did this because she knew that I used to go and sit near Babajan for awhile each night during the previous nine months (May, 1913–January, 1914). Babajan indicated to my mother that I was intended to shake the world into wakefulness, but that meant nothing to Shirinmai in her distress.

"For a long time I was given regular medical treatment, but no amount of drugging and injections could put me to sleep. As Shirinmai used to say, 'Having exhausted all available means', she sent me to Bombay to stay with Jamshed † for a change.

"Thinking to keep me occupied with day-to-day activities, Jamshed encouraged me to cook the food for the two of us. Sometimes I did the cooking all right, but I did it as I did other things—without knowing what I was doing. I can recall the particular bench in the Victoria Gardens on which I passed most of the time, sitting alone,

---

* For a more complete discussion see Part II, Chapter VI, The Ways to the Path and Its States and Stages.

† Baba's late elder brother.

entirely oblivious of the world and its affairs.

"Although the infinite bliss I experienced in my superconscious state remained continuous, as it is now, I suffered agonies in returning towards normal consciousness of illusion. Occasionally, to gain some sort of relief, I used to knock my head so furiously against walls and windows that some of them showed cracks.

"In reality there is no suffering as such—only infinite bliss. Although suffering is illusory, still, within the realm of illusion, it *is* suffering. In the midst of illusion, Babajan established my reality. My reality, although untouched by illusion, remained connected with illusion. That was why I suffered incalculable spiritual agonies.

"Nine months after my self-realization (November, 1914) I began to be somewhat conscious of my surroundings. Life returned to my vacant eyes. Although I would not sleep, I began regularly to eat small quantities of food.* I now knew what I was doing but I continued to do things intuitively, as if impelled to do them by inner forces. I did not do things of my own accord or when asked by others. For example, when I began to teach (December, 1915) Persian to Buasahib,† my mother tried to collect more pupils for me, thinking this would hasten my 'recovery'. But I would attend to no one else and continued to teach only Buasahib.

"Later on (April, 1915) I also began to go for long distances on foot or by vehicle. Once I left Poona by rail for Raichur (more than three hundred miles south of Poona), but after traveling for only thirty-four miles I felt the urge to leave the train at Kedgaon. There for the first time I came in physical contact with Narayan Maharaj (one of the five Perfect Masters) whose *ashram* is not far from that railway station.

"Similarly, from time to time I was also drawn to see *majzoobs* like Banemiyan Baba at Aurungabad and Tipoo Baba at Bombay. Once in the company of Behram (Buasahib) I traveled as far north as Nagpur and saw Tajuddin Baba (another of the five Perfect Masters).

"Finally (December, 1915) I felt impelled to call on Sai Baba, the Perfect Master among Masters. At that time he was returning in a procession from Lendi (in Sherdi), a place to and from which he

* It is an incredible fact that Baba did not eat for the nine months following his self-realization in January, 1914.

† The late Behram F. Irani, the first and one of the closest of Baba's disciples.

was led everyday in order to ease himself. Despite the crowds I intuitively prostrated myself before him on the road. When I arose, Sai Baba looked straight at me and exclaimed, 'Parvardigar' (God-Almighty-Sustainer).

"I then felt drawn to walk to the nearby temple of Khandoba in which Maharaj (Shri Upasni Maharaj) was staying in seclusion. He had been living on water there under Sai Baba's direct guidance for over three years. At that time Maharaj was reduced almost to a skeleton due to his fast on water. He was also naked and surrounded by filth.

"When I came near enough to him, Maharaj greeted me, so to speak, with a stone which he threw at me with great force. It struck me on my forehead exactly where Babajan had kissed me, hitting with such force that it drew blood. The mark of that injury is still on my forehead. But that blow from Maharaj was the stroke of *dnyan* (*Marefat* of *Haqiqat,* or divine knowledge).

"Figuratively, Maharaj had started to rouse me from 'sound sleep'. But in sound sleep man is unconscious, while I, being superconscious, was wide awake in sound sleep. With that stroke, Maharaj had begun to help me return to ordinary consciousness of the realm of illusion.

"That was the beginning of my present infinite suffering in illusion which I experience simultaneously with my infinite bliss in reality. But it took me seven years of acute struggle under Maharaj's active guidance to return completely to, and become established in, normal human consciousness of the illusion of duality, while yet experiencing continuously my superconsciousness.

"The more normally conscious I became, the more acute my suffering grew. For years therefore I continued to knock my head frequently on stones. That was how I eventually lost all my teeth, for through the constant knocking they became prematurely loose. This also resulted in a wound which was constantly fresh, and therefore I always used to keep a colored handkerchief tied around my forehead.

"The more I returned to worldly normality the more impatient my mother became to see me settled into the routine of life. To satisfy her I joined the Kan (Kavasji) Khatan theatrical company as its manager (1916) and traveled with the show to Lahore.

"Several years later, after becoming almost three-fourths normally conscious while retaining full superconsciousness, I went to Sakori and stayed for six months (July–December, 1921) near Maharaj. At the end of this period Maharaj made me *know* fully what I am, just as Babajan had made me *feel* in a flash what I am.

"During those six months Maharaj and I used to sit near each other in a hut behind closed doors almost every night. On one such occasion Maharaj folded his hands to me and said, 'Merwan, you are the Avatar and I salute you' ".

"For about four months after this (January–May, 1922) I stayed in a small *jhopdi* (thatched hut). It was built for me temporarily on the edge of some fields in the very thinly populated area of what is now the Shivajinagar area of Poona. In this manner I began to live independently, surrounded by men who formed the nucleus of the *mandali*. One of these was the first to start addressing me as 'Baba'.*

"Some of the men were drawn intuitively to me long before they had any clear idea of my inner state. Others were attracted to me by hints from Babajan and Maharaj. And still others I drew directly to me.

"At that time both Babajan and Maharaj began telling various people, referring to me, that 'The child is now capable of moving the whole world at a sign from his finger'. Once (May, 1922) Maharaj addressed a large gathering of the *mandali* and said, 'Listen to me most carefully. I have handed over my key (spiritual charge) now to Merwan, and henceforth you are all to stick to him and do as he instructs you. With God's grace you will soon reach the goal.' Still others, Maharaj asked individually to follow me."

In 1922 Baba established his first and ideal *ashram* in Bombay, which was called the "Manzil-e-Meem" (Abode of M). Here more than forty men of various faiths and qualifications stayed night and day with Baba for ten months, leading a routine life of rigorous discipline. In those days Baba would often become temperamentally violent, but showed no trace of malice in his actions.†

"My body," he commented, "was then very lean, but also supple, as I was constantly and energetically active. From four in the morning even in the severest cold I would move about in my thin mull *sadra* (robe). Those who did not know me well at that time might

---

* "Meher Baba" means literally "compassionate father".

† This "*jalali*" (fiery) phase is not uncommon among Perfect Masters. The recipient of the apparent anger understands it to be of spiritual benefit and a blessing to him.

well have considered me very quick-tempered, for suddenly, with or without provocation, I would beat anyone at hand.

"In those days most of the *mandali* were hefty, robust young men. Several of them were good wrestlers and some were seasoned athletes. But when I would start for a brisk walk, the majority would have to run to keep up with me. Sometimes I would ask them all to press collectively on my whole body with all the force they could exert. Within a few minutes they would be breathless and drenched with perspiration without having fully satisfied me.

"One of the group had the physique of a giant, but once in a certain mood I knocked him down with a single slap. Another had to have a doctor treat his ear because of a blow I gave him. One of the *mandali* used to go into hiding at once on such occasions and would not emerge again without asking others if my mood had changed."

On one occasion the *mandali* and Baba were sitting together in good spirits in the big upstairs hall in the Manzil-e-Meem, when Baba suddenly seized a plump fellow of about two hundred pounds, dragged him like a rag doll to the edge of the stairs and flung him down. The place rang with the crashes as the heavy man rolled and stumbled to the bottom.

Baba then struck another of the *mandali* a sharp blow on the forehead, stepping back with a smile as if nothing had happened. Both of the victims of the sudden outburst were quizzed with considerable concern by Baba as to whether they had suffered any injuries, but neither was any the worse for the squall.

Aside from these unpredictable moments of violence, Baba always appeared to be busy with various duties aimed at the physical, mental, moral and spiritual welfare of the *mandali*. In his usual candid fashion, Baba closed his own and the *mandali's* reminiscences of these early years with the unarguable statement, "When the money was finished we came over to Arangaon."

Then for more than a year and a half, to the end of 1924, Baba moved almost constantly with the *mandali* about the country, once going as far as Iran. Occasionally on arriving at some new place Baba would say that they were going to settle down there for a long time, but no sooner had the *mandali* finished the preliminary arrangements than Baba would start them on the move again. It was a period of hard labor for the *mandali*, great privation for Baba and fatiguing travel by third class rail or foot over great distances for all.

"For various spiritual reasons," Baba continued his reminiscences, "and due to the nature of the work I was then doing, I was unable to eat regularly. Practically speaking, therefore, I was fasting almost all the time. For months I would take no food or drink except at intervals of thirty-six or more hours. At times I also subsisted for a week or two at a stretch on a few sips of liquid such as tea, milk or *dal* soup. I did not fast for the sake of fasting, and I suffered and felt weak, just as any ordinary man who fasts."

"During World War I, Meherabad was a military camp divided, then as now, by the railroad to Ahmednagar, into an upper (hill) section to the west and the lower (fields) part to the east. When I arrived here with the *mandali* for the first time (April, 1923) the whole area was desolate and filled with thorns and snakes and scorpions. The military buildings were in ruins.

"In contrast to the life at Manzil-e-Meem,* the *mandali* now had to do everything without the help of hired labor. They had to draw water, cook food, wash clothes, carry loads and work all day as common laborers, as well as carry out promptly the various instructions I gave them."

Although Baba came initially to Arangaon (Meherabad) with the *mandali* ostensibly to settle there, they stayed only four days on that occasion. The second stay lasted eleven days, and the third only two. The longest stay before 1925 was the fourth, which lasted three months. This period (March–May, 1924) was known among the *mandali* as "Ghamela Yoga" (the practice of regular hard labor). This was the period when the camp was largely restored.

"By that time (May)," Baba commented, "the abandoned camp was almost shipshape again. The first new building was called the Agrakuti (also called *jhopdi,* a small square room solidly constructed of stones and mortar and made insect proof by screen placed over all openings) where I have sat in seclusion and worked on a number of occasions for various periods of time.

"Other than for one paid mason, all the construction, clearing, repairing, etc., was done by the *mandali* who worked like coolies for six hours each day. They worked so hard that most had blisters on their hands.

---

* Here the training involved rigorous mental discipline rather than actual physical hardships.

"After several months (January, 1925) we settled down and the place gradually became known as Meherabad. For almost two years (until November, 1926) it was like a small model town. In it lived about five hundred souls, working in the hospital, the dispensary and the schools. There were also *ashrams* for boys, men and women, and shelters for the poor and for lepers, all of which were established here in connection with my work.

"At that time nearly a thousand rupees a day used to be spent for the maintenance of the various services, while the *mandali* often lived on plain *dal* and rice for lunch, and milkless tea or a thin soup of *methi* (bitter spinach) leaves and coarse bread for dinner. During that period I remained generally on liquids or on limited meals taken once in a week or a fortnight.

"Weekly rations were issued to the most helpless of the Arangaon villagers. They were so needy that later, when the *ashrams* were shifted some scores of miles away to Toka, they used to travel on foot or by bullock-cart all that distance rather than miss the weekly quota of coarse grain.

"Hundreds of people from the villages near Meherabad benefited from the free hospitals, and thousands utilized the dispensary provided for out-patients. Boys of all castes and creeds including untouchables soon began to live, eat and intermingle freely.

"From dawn to dusk I would move about the place and take an active part in every phase including the cleaning of latrines. Each day I spent three to four hours bathing the school children. When the number boarding became considerable, I allowed the *mandali* to share this service with me. All the *mandali* also had to grind grain for one to three hours each day, depending upon their assigned duties. I also shared in the daily grinding for an hour or more.

"Despite my silence (starting July 10, 1925) I continued all my usual activities. At that time I communicated by writing on a slate, and also for more than a year wrote for a number of hours daily on a work which remains unseen and unpublished to this day. I did most of my writing work in my small cupboard-like room constructed underneath the big wooden table which stands near the *dhuni* (sacred fireplace). It was at this time (November, 1925) that we began to light the *dhuni* each month.

"At certain fixed hours I saw visitors freely. Hundreds came daily for my *darshan,* believing in my spiritual status, but most sought my blessing only for material benefit. On special occasions the stream of visitors would continue unbroken from morn to night and their numbers would run into the thousands." (At least twenty thousand people had Baba's blessing in 1926 on his thirty-second birthday.)

"Once an old man offered to dedicate everything he had to me, and then he would begin, he said, to lead a life of service and renunciation. However, on investigation, it was found that what would be dedicated to me was a wife and seven children to be taken care of.

"On another occasion a yogi called and sought my instructions as he said he was determined to find God at any cost. I told him to wait for my instructions under a certain tree. He remained there for seven days and walked away on the eighth, unnoticed by anyone."

One of the characteristics of Baba's activities which often puzzles people is the manner in which he will suddenly and without warning stop a project in apparent mid-career, regardless of the degree of evident success it is experiencing. In November–December, 1926 he did this to the institutions and services which were thriving at Meherabad, closing them all lock, stock and barrel.

Baba commented cryptically on this singular trait of his as follows:

"Usually a temporary scaffolding is set up around a big building which is under construction, and when the building is completed, the scaffolding is removed. Often my external activities and commitments are only the external expression of the internal work I am doing. In either case, my external activities and commitments may be continued indefinitely or I may end them promptly at the end of the inner work, depending upon the prevailing circumstances."

While showing the *sahvasis* about Meherabad Hill, Baba often told stories of the Meher Ashram and the Prem Ashram days (1927–1929).*

"At that time, in addition to continuing my silence, I also gave up writing (January, 1927). Shortly thereafter I started to communicate by spelling out words on an English alphabet board, which I discarded recently (October, 1954).

"The school known as Meher Ashram was started as a small day

---

* A detailed account is given in *Sobs and Throbs*, Ramju Abdulla, now unfortunately out of print.

school for the boys of the adjoining village of Arangaon. After some time it was turned into a regular boarding school (May, 1927) that housed more than a hundred boys. Efforts were made to collect them from various cities and different countries. One of the *mandali* was sent to England for that purpose. None came from the West, but a number of boys from Iran did join the Meher Ashram.

"My first aim was to arrange for teaching the boys English through their various vernaculars, by standards set up in the University of Bombay. Having accomplished this, I began to spend all of my time, day and night, on the general welfare and spiritual upliftment of the boys. Even though I had entrusted several *mandali* with the job of keeping watch over the boys round the clock, still I would frequently appear in the dormitory in the dead of night to see if they were well wrapped and sleeping all right.

"This was also the period when I carried out one of my longest continuous fasts, which lasted five and one-half months (November, 1927–April, 1928). Once during this period I took nothing but a few sips of water for more than twenty-eight days. The remainder of the time I lived on cocoa in milk taken once in twenty-four hours.

"Even this was in scant supply as it happened. Lahu (Baba's favorite among the untouchable boys) used to carry my supply to me every day, and on the way he would drink half of it and then pass on the other half to me. I found out about this at the end of my seclusion when the women *mandali* assured me that they had sent Lahu regularly, as I had originally instructed them, with the thermos bottle full of cocoa. When I questioned Lahu about this, he readily confessed pilfering half my cocoa every day. I pardoned the little fellow as readily as he had acknowledged the guilt.

"During part of this period I remained continuously indoors for more than three months (November, 1927–February, 1928) at the spot where my future tomb is located. I did not step out of the crypt (the underground part of Baba's future tomb) and the temporary small structure placed over it. The temporary hut has now been replaced by the present domed building.

"In the daytime I spent most of the time in the upper room, which had two windows level with the floor, and at night I would retire into the crypt. One of the two windows in the upper room faced the Meher Ashram on the east and was in line with a raised platform before the *ashram*. The boys and the *mandali* would sit on this, near me but outside my room, and I would give them discourses and carry on discussions with them with the help of my alphabet board.

"Through the west window I could see the *sadhak-ashram* (hermitage), which consisted of a string of small rooms standing at that time near my place of seclusion. Some of the *mandali* were also in seclusion in these small rooms, fasting under my directions on a small quantity of milk taken once or twice a day."

The following account of one of the incidents which occurred during that period is adapted from *Sobs and Throbs:*

On January 1, 1928, the fifty-second day of Baba's fasting and the twelfth of his self-imposed confinement, a majority of the boys began to break into tears at different times throughout the day. In the evening matters came to a climax. Each boy in the *ashram* burst into tears and began to sob as if all his dear ones had suddenly been reported dead.

For about one hour, between seven and eight in the evening, this awesome phenomenon held the onlookers spellbound. The tumult could be heard a quarter of a mile away from the *ashram*.

Attempts were made by those in charge to quiet the boys and to find out the cause of the outburst. But it was all to no avail. All seemed to be engrossed in crying, and deaf to all else. "Baba, Baba," were the only words which could be heard distinctly in all this tumult. Finally the boys were brought close to Baba's presence, and with magical swiftness they became silent again.

Continuing his reminiscences to the *sahvasis*, Baba said, "At a later stage (March, 1928) Meher Ashram was divided into two sections. The new portion was called 'Prem Ashram' (Shelter of Love). In it were housed the boys most awakened to love. They were given some freedom from the daily school routine to allow for their preoccupation with meditation and the spiritual experiences that most of them periodically had.

"One of the boys from Iran, of about eighteen years, lost consciousness of his body and surroundings for four days. Had an enema not been given to him then at my orders he would have died. Thereupon the boy regained ordinary normal consciousness, but not the consciousness which is regained after union with God, as that is an entirely different and unique achievement. For a long time afterwards he would weep and complain bitterly about my having dragged him down from the blissful state in which he said he had seen nothing but Baba.

"When some of my (internal) work had to be done afresh (June, 1928), both the *ashrams* were shifted root and branch to Toka (about forty-five miles north of Ahmednagar). There the area of my seclusion included the whole of the Prem Ashram. It was a picturesque spot at the junction of the rivers Godavery and Paravra. Swimming was added to the daily recreation of the boys.

"Here again I fasted on a few sips of water and milkless tea for a number of days (forty-two days, September–October, 1928). The boys were overjoyed when I ended my fasting by drinking some orange juice. As it happened to be the birthday of Krishna, they insisted on carrying me in a *palanquin* around the new colony of 'Meherabad', dressed as Krishna.

"Singing and dancing, they tossed my *palanquin* back and forth. Due to the fast I had just ended this jerky ride was excruciatingly painful for my abdomen. Out of my love for the boys and their love for me I managed to remain cheerful at the time, but I suffered the physical consequences for two months afterwards."

Often during the course of the *sahvas* weeks Baba would discuss the need to keep fit and avoid colds. Some of his most enlightening comments concerning his own physical susceptibilities were embodied in his reminiscences of his first trip to England in September, 1931, not long after the closing of the Prem Ashram.

"Some of you might ask why, being the Avatar, I could feel or catch cold. You might as well ask also why I should feel hungry or need rest! We have bodies and they are naturally subject to all sorts of ailments, and as a consequence we must suffer. Therefore one should take all practical precautions to avoid, and take proper treatment to recover from, the bodily ailments.

"The God-realized ones who do not return to ordinary normal consciousness and yet happen to retain their bodies (*Majzoobs*), have no body-consciousness: just as they have literally no consciousness of anything other than their own Self. Their own bodies also remain to them as 'nothing', and therefore nothing can affect 'nothing'. As long as it is necessary, their infinitely conscious divinity *directly* supports their bodies within illusion as 'supports' for the maintenance of the whole illusion of creation.

"*Masts*, who are mad and absorbed in God-love, also remain immune as a rule to bodily ailments. The intensity of their 'smokeless' fire of love neutralizes all bodily reactions, and thus they continue freely living their life of love for God.

"Once the God-realized soul comes down with his God-conscious-ness to normal consciousness of the illusion of duality, then the physical body of even such a God-realized Perfect Master is subject to ordinary contagion and disease. Simultaneously I exist at every level, and as I am therefore on a level with your consciousness, then I suffer, experience and enjoy just as you all do.

"On our first visit to England I had not anticipated having to experience the bitter London cold without proper clothing. This came about due to the fact that the English *mandali* were eager to perpetuate their remembrances of their first direct contact with me by taking pictures of me in garments such as I had worn in India.

"The warmth of their love and devotion compelled me to take off all my warm clothes. Then, for more than an hour, I allowed them to make me sit, and stand in various poses, remaining cheerfully in the open air with only my cotton *sadra* on. They were very happy to get the pictures they wished, and I was no less happy to see them happy. However I alone know how the cold bit to the very bone.

"The westerners did not love me any less then, but they under-stand me more deeply now. In the automobile accident (Oklahoma, June, 1952) several of us suffered very painful injuries, and a num-ber of my bones were broken. However, the love all bore for me was quickened rather than shaken. In the distant past, as Krishna, I died physically when I was accidentally shot with an arrow."

In his reminiscing Baba also spoke often of the *ashrams* for the mad and the *masts* which he conducted in his next period of external public activities (1936–1947). Most of the inmates of the Mad Ashram (August, 1936–September, 1940) were gathered from among the ordinarily insane men who had no one to love or care for them. They were brought from near and far, regardless of caste or creed. No medical efforts were expended on treating their mental infirmities, but they were physically well attended and they were indulged in any innocent idiosyncracies.

Baba planned and supervised the Mad Ashram, and he also served and nursed its inmates with patience, tolerance and love.

Aside from its humanitarian and spiritual aspects, the Mad Ash-ram also prepared the *mandali* for the subsequent running of the Mast Ashrams. The seven principal ones of these were maintained at different remote places such as Ajmer, Jabalpur, Bangalore,

Meherabad, Ranchi, Mahabaleshwar and Satara (1939–1947). The nature of the external routine was common to both mad and *mast ashrams*, just as there was considerable similarity between the externally alike but internally dissimilar inmates.

Baba clarified the dissimilarity as follows: "Ordinarily it is very difficult, and cursorily it is impossible, to distinguish between a madman and a *mast*. One is actually mad and the other appears to be mad. Internally the two are poles apart. The mad has lost the power of correct reasoning. The *mast* has transcended the limitations of intellect. A madman is mentally infirm, a *mast* is spiritually enlightened. The mad have distorted ideas about their bodies and surroundings. The *masts* have an utter disregard for theirs because their hearts directly experience inner truths beyond the gross sphere, and they are more or less imbued with God-love.

"Even in the Mad Ashram there were a few *masts*, but most were more or less ordinary madmen. One of the latter, Fakir Bua, assumed the airs of a sage. He would nod his head and utter monosyllables mechanically without any meaning, but his movements and utterances gave the appearance of his agreeing or disagreeing with what he heard. He also made frequent gestures with his fingers. However this was only habit, as there was no sense or significance to the gestures, although the contrary is true in the case of a *mast*.

"When the Mad Ashram was closed (September, 1944), Fakir Bua, along with the rest of the insane, was sent back to the place from which he had come (Poona). Through a misunderstanding, a rumor spread through the grain market in Poona that Fakir Bua had returned from my *ashram* as a saint.

"This error was discovered some months later when one of the *mandali*, who was searching for *masts* and saints for my work, heard that there was one in the Poona area whom hundreds of people worshiped. When the *mandali* had managed to jostle through the crowds he found none other than poor old Fakir Bua sitting on cushions placed on a coarsely decorated platform, happily nodding his head to the crowds around him.

"There are undoubtedly many in India who are genuinely engaged in the search for truth, but the masses are more eager to win cheap material benefits through rare spiritual blessings. Equipped with long hair and an ochre colored robe (the garb of the wandering holy man), an unscrupulous man can easily dupe hundreds among the masses here. If one person worships some individual, hundreds will quickly follow suit, hoping thereby to rid themselves of their immediate problems for the asking.

"Years ago among the growing number of new *mandali* there was one individual who followed carefully my directions to observe silence, keep fasts and do *japs* (repeating the name of God). After leaving the *mandali* however he began to pose as a saint and induced people to worship him. I sent him a word of warning against his pretentiousness, but he did not heed it.

"After some time he became involved in an affair with a woman and ultimately returned to me suffering with leprosy. I pardoned him, embraced him and advised him to go humbly about the country giving my message of love and truth to the people. He is now no longer a leper and remains steadfast in his love and service for me.

"Although most of the *mandali* know of only three or four cases of such fraudulence, there have been seven pretenders who have claimed falsely that they had been spiritually enlightened by me and were my spiritual successors.

"*Masts* are those who become permanently unconscious in part or whole of their physical bodies, actions and surroundings, due to their absorption in their intense love and longing for God. My love for the *masts* is similar in many ways to that shown by a mother who continues to look lovingly after her children regardless of their behavior. To make her child clean a mother does not even mind soiling her hands with the child's excrement.

"I am the mother of the *masts*. If God were not there, there would be no *masts*. They also are like parts of my body. Some are like my right and some are like my left limbs and fingers. Some are nose, ears and eyes for me. I am helpful to them and they are helpful to me. The *masts* alone know how they love me and I alone know how I love them. I work for the *masts*, and knowingly or unknowingly they work for me."

Discovering and collecting the mad had been child's play compared to the task the *mandali* were now assigned: to trace, contact and induce the *masts* to come into the Mast Ashrams.

Although Baba had started contacting the God-mad in 1915, his regular *mast* trips did not start until 1938. They remain to this day (1957) one of the most active external manifestations of his internal work. A splendid account of seventy-five thousand miles of Baba's *mast* trips in which he contacted twenty thousand *masts*, as well as a description of Baba's Mad and Mast Ashram activities, has been given by one of the resident *mandali,* Dr. William Donkin, in his unique work, *The Wayfarers* (1948, Meher Publications).

Baba once pointed out seven mango trees to a group of *sahvasis* visiting Meherazad. "These are the offshoot of one of my cherished *mast* contacts. This *mast* had presented me with seven mangoes. As I promised the *mast,* I ate them all completely and the seven seeds I planted here where you now see them grown into trees.

"As the *mandali* well know, I soon give away whatever I have chosen to receive, except what I receive from the *masts.* Even if they give me pieces of rags or wastepaper I treasure them."

And later, "I and those who accompany me on a *mast* trip keep moving night and day for weeks at a time without regular or adequate meals, and only rarely do we rest for a night.

"On one such exceptional occasion we were sleeping on a railway platform for the night. At daybreak someone was found sharing my blanket with me. The stranger admitted on questioning that he was a petty thief known to the police. However he insisted that he had not been trying to rob us, but to seek shelter for the night. The *mandali* were inclined to hand him over to the police but I let him get away."

From mid-October, 1949 to the end of January, 1952 Baba lived what he called his life of complete external renunciation. So far, no complete account has been written of it. The full story of the hardships and crises incident to this life of self-created helplessness remains known only to the companions Baba took with him in his New Life adventure. These were the handful of men and women who had chosen and were allowed to participate in the venture. They traveled with him from place to place in distant parts of India, mostly on foot, and under the most trying conditions, having no ready shelters, no money and no day-to-day provisions to draw upon.

Once referring to the "caravan" (built of an old motor van) which is also preserved at Meherazad, Baba said, "At a later stage of the New Life, this was used as a ready shelter for the night for the women among my new life companions. The caravan was drawn by a pair of bullocks, which were the charge of the men. The men also had to take care of a camel, a horse, two donkeys and two cows, which we took with us for a period.

"My companions suffered unimaginable hardships. At times we used to beg for food and for other day-to-day requirements.

"The last period of over two months of the New Life was spent at Meherazad. During most of that time I did my *man-o-nash* (annihilation of the mind) work in seculsion, and it was then that the two cabins were removed from the (Seclusion) hill and added to the seclusion area adjoining the garden.

"You who are here for my *sahvas* are indeed fortunate that I am with you at these various spots at Meherabad and Meherazad where I have done many of my internal and external works. Sixty years from now they will become world centers to which thousands will make pilgrimages, vying with each other to sacrifice their very lives in my name."

At the completion of the *man-o-nash* period Baba traveled to Europe and the United States where the auto accident referred to above occurred. Arriving back in India in September, 1952, he again plunged into his *mast* work as well as into his "Fiery Life." * Numerous mass *darshan* programs were held in many villages, towns and cities in different parts of India, drawing five to fifty thousand people at a time.

In one of the large *darshan* programs held at Ahmednagar in September, 1954, several score from Europe, America and Australia also participated.

Following the *sahvas* programs in November, 1955, Baba immediately began plans for a year's seclusion starting February 15, 1956, broken only by his *mast* work and a one month's flying trip around the world in the early fall of 1956 to greet his devoted followers on four continents.

---

* See *The Awakener,* Vol. I, No. 1 and following.

Major Meher Baba Centers

Avatar Meher Baba Trust
King's Road, Post Bag 31
Ahmednagar
Maharashtra State 414001
India

Meher Spiritual Center Inc.
10200 Highway 17 North
Myrtle Beach, SC 29572
Telephone 803-272-5777

Avatar's Abode
Meher Road
Woombye Qld. 4559
Australia

There are Meher Baba groups in most major cities in the West.

Sources of Books by and about Meher Baba

Sheriar Press Book Division
3005 Highway 17 North Bypass
Myrtle Beach, SC 29577
Telephone: 803-448-1107
Fax: 803-626-2390
Email: SheriarBks@aol.com

The Love Street Bookstore
Avatar Meher Baba Center of Southern California
1214 S. Van Ness Avenue
Los Angeles, CA 90019-3520
Telephone: 310-837-6419
Fax: 310-839-2222
Email: Bababooks@aol.com

Meher Baba Association
228 Hammersmith Grove
London W6 7HG, England

Avatar's Abode
Meher Road
Woombye Qld. 4559
Australia

Electronic Book Stores
http://www.amazon.com
http://www.barnesandnoble.com
http://www.eastwest.com
http://www.slbooks.com

Website
http://davey.sunyerie.edu/mb/html/mb.html

Please note: There are connections to many Meher Baba home pages around the globe through this website.